Lesbian Stages

Plays by Sarah Dreher

New Victoria Publishers Inc.
A Feminist Literary and Cultural Organization

Published by New Victoria Publishers, Inc.
P.O. Box 27 Norwich, Vermont 05055

Library of Congress Cataloging-in-Publication Data
Dreher, Sarah

Lesbian Stages.

1. Lesbianism--Drama. I. Title.

PS3554 . R485L4 1988 812 ' .54 88-61508
ISBN 0-934678-15-4 (pbk.)

TABLE OF CONTENTS

Introduction

I grew up in a world without television. For entertainment, we read or listened to the radio—which, in those days, was pretty much like today's television programming, except that you listened instead of watching. I think that was important, as it taught us how to turn spoken words into pictures in our heads. We went to movies, of course (though not on Sundays in my small, church-dominated home town). But, most of all, we had Theater.

My mother was crazy about theater. At least once a year we took the train to New York to gorge ourselves on plays. Any plays. Musicals (*South Pacific, The Pajama Game* with Shirley MacLaine dancing in the chorus), mysteries (*Witness for the Prosecution, Dial M for Murder*), drama (*The Deep Blue Sea* with Margaret Sullavan), comedy (*Inside U.S.A.* with outrageous Beatrice Lillie). We would stay two nights and see three shows. In summer, we were within driving distance of two summer theaters, and we never missed a play. Maybe it was this shared experience, or my Welsh genes (also from my mother), but I was in love with words. The right words, put together in just the right way can stop me in my tracks. Spoken well, they are like crystals. I've been behind the scenes in theater for more than ten years now, and it's still a miracle. Lighting technicians, set builders, costumers are magicians. Scripts are made up of lines, each of which is only the iceberg's tip, a suggestion of whole paragraphs of feeling and experience. Actors and directors take those tiny hints and, with their bodies and minds and voices, bring forth the hidden worlds. It isn't always perfect, but how amazing that they can do it at all.

The first production of one of my plays happened when I was in 10th grade. It was a silly play, I guess: awkwardly written, sentimental, performed with great verve and little restraint by my classmates. It was then that I experienced for the first time a skein of emotions which has become so familiar to me: pride, embarrassment, wonder, and a barely-controlled desire to run away and hide. Now, when I see performances of my work, I do a pretty good job of appearing cool and worldly—but inside I'm still in 10th grade.

When I got to college, I let go of theater for a while. I guess I was intimidated by other students who seemed much more skilled and self-assured than I. Besides, I was busy preparing myself to go to graduate school in clinical psychology, and trying to come to grips with being a lesbian in a homophobic world. Deep in my heart, I still wanted to be a writer, but that seemed like a pipe dream. Once I left college, I put writing aside to concentrate on more "practical" activities. That hiatus lasted 16 years.

In 1974, a friend talked me into performing in a revue sponsored by our local Women's Center, to celebrate International Women's Week. My performance was far from memorable (at least in any positive sense), but it launched my involvement in women's theater.

Girl of Our Dreams was a unique experience for both cast and community. For many of us, it was our first experience with non-traditional theater. For many, it was a way to recapture our 'stage struck' high school years. And for all of us, it marked the first time we had seen a stage show with an all-female cast, crew, and writers, in celebration of woman-identified women.

After the show closed, several of us decided to stick together and continue to produce theater by, for, and about women. It is this group, currently incarnated as Theater, Too, for which I've been writing ever since. First came a collaborative effort, a musical, on which I co-authored the book and wrote the lyrics. Then another musical. I began to realize that co-authorship wasn't working out for me (I am, after all, an Aries), so I tried my first solo venture, *Special Cases,* a musical about a mythical Women's Army, for which I also wrote the lyrics.

My writing was beginning to take a more serious turn about this time. I had handled rape and homophobia in *Special Cases*, but those issues were imbedded in a more light-hearted, up-beat context. My first 'serious' play was a one-act called *Ten Years After*, which ten years later came full circle to become the full-length *Alumnae News: The Doris Day Years*.

Most of my work is autobiographical, more or less. I believe all writing is, at least to the extent that we write from emotions which are familiar to us, though we might change the settings, characters, conflicts, and even the outcomes. By the time I've finished with them, the characters may bear little resemblance to the people who inspired them. I've written about people I've loved, and people I've hated. It's more pleasant to write about people I've loved, but we take inspiration where we can. The themes, too, come out of personal experience. It may be a sense of frustration, or nostalgia, or a conviction of something being wrong, or a desire to honor a cherished friend.

As a writer, I've learned that honesty is the best policy. If I write about what I sincerely feel, it works. If I write out of pretense, or in an attempt to force a piece of work into a shape I think it "ought" to have, I fall flat on my face. I used to be afraid, if I put my deepest feelings and experiences "out there" for all the world to see, everyone's eyes would glass over and no one would understand what I was talking about, and then I'd be truly and forever alone. It hasn't happened.

I've learned that the first rendering of a manuscript is only the beginning of a long process. Rewriting, polishing, reworking until you get it right are as important as inspiration. In fact, I suspect it is the willingness to do the "dirty work" that separates people who want to write from those who want only to have written.

As a playwright, I've learned that the best way to learn to write plays is to work as part of a theater group. There are many things peculiar to playwriting, not the least of which is that what you write has to be humanly possible to perform. I have written lines of dialogue that sound lovely in my head, but are physically impossible to say—much less project.I have written impossible set changes, driven props persons to the brink of insanity, and once wrote a scene in which I allowed an actor 15 seconds to change from her civilian clothes into a full-dress uniform—and we didn't realize it until dress rehearsal.

I've learned to let go. No cast ever looks the same as the imaginary people in my head, and no director ever stages a play the way I see it. I write for proscenium staging (raised stage, audience in front), probably because that was how plays were staged during my 'formative' years. My plays usually end up staged in the round, three-quarter thrust, or any of a number of bizarre and creative ways.

Working in theater sends you to the heights of elation and the depths of despair. Invariably, there comes a point during the rehearsal process when the sad moments don't seem touching and all the jokes are falling flat, and nobody is getting along with anyone, and the Goddess of Anxiety reigns supreme. And we stop and ask ourselves why we're doing this: are we crazy? Masochistic? Should we pack it in? But we go on, and the lights dim, and the audience grows silent ... and the magic begins all over again.

* * *

These plays are about being a lesbian. Sometimes well-meaning souls suggest that I "widen" my viewpoint, write for "a larger audience", or other variations on the old "pretend to be like the rest of us" theme. I can't do that, and I won't. I am a lesbian, and I see the world through lesbian eyes. The loneliest years of my life were those in which I couldn't accept myself as a lesbian. I didn't like myself, and I didn't like my life, and I couldn't write. When I came out, I began writing. How can we be creative if we can't be proud of who we are?

* * *

So here, for your entertainment, are some of my plays. I hope you'll find yourself in them. Because that, to me, is the point of writing—to help us all feel a little less lonely.

(If you would like to produce any of these plays, please contact me, to discuss royalties and for the latest script up-date and just so we can meet, at 21 Valley View Dr., Amherst, MA 01002.)

Alumnae News: The Doris Day Years

Introduction

Alumnae News and I have been together for a long time. Back in 1956, when I was a Freshman at Wellesley College, a jealous student went to the Dean of Students with the rumor that a close friend and I were lovers. We weren't. The Dean called us into her office and threatened to expel us.

I didn't know much about being a lesbian then, but I knew I had feelings for some of my friends which seemed to be very different from the feelings they had for one another. And I knew there was something about it that was definitely not all right.

Alumnae News draws its inspiration from that incident (though Real Life didn't have such a happy ending). The feelings and reactions of the characters are as true to life as I can make them. But the play itself has gone through many different forms throughout the thirty-plus years we've been together, and as I look back at it, I can see how the development of the play parallels the unfolding of my life.

In its first version, it was a short story called *Ten Years After*, Karen comes to visit Stacey unexpectedly after an absence/silence of ten years. Karen confesses her unhappiness to Stacey, and then leaves. The love between them remains unspoken and one-sided, and Stacey is left trying to learn once more how to live without feeling.

Next it became a one-act play. This time Karen and Stacey declare their love, but Karen cannot sacrifice the security of a conventional "straight" life. Again, she leaves.

Finally, the version you have here. The characters have gone through many changes. Stacey is no longer the passive victim of a homophobic world. She has to be closeted (it is, after all, only 1966), but she is strong and able to be herself within the constrictions the world places on her. Karen, too, is stronger. She has lived the conventional life, and she is confused, but once she faces her real feelings she has the courage to act on them.

A world of difference in half a lifetime. When I was working on the play, I often went back and relived those early years. For me, to be a lesbian in the '50's meant learning to live—once I had decided to live at all—as a heterosexual woman. Or learning to live without love. I forged a career for myself (thereby obeying my mother's warning to "never be financially dependent on a man"). I learned to live alone. I learned to travel alone. I learned to avoid the people I was most attracted to. I learned not to reveal personal information, for fear someone would "guess." It wasn't a happy life, but it was one I could settle for, as least for the time being.

But then the Women's Movement happened, and the Gay Rights Movement. And suddenly everything was different. It took a while for my inner feelings to catch up with the changes in the outside world, just as it took *Ten Years After* a while to become *Alumnae News*. Stacey and Karen were with me through it all.

Terry's appearance on the scene created a challenge. I'm not comfortable writing about villains. To do it well, you have to understand them—or the process of writing about them makes you understand them—and I didn't want to understand Terry. You let yourself understand someone, the next thing you know you're forgiving her. Terry didn't deserve to be forgiven. And you have to connect with qualities, tendencies, emotions in yourself that you might not be particularly proud of. After all, there's a little bit of Terry in us all, but we try not to let it out in polite company. To play Terry creates the same challenge/danger for the actor. Just as playing Stacey or Karen forces an actor to draw up those pockets of hurt and fear. But we managed it.

When I see *Alumnae News* on stage, it gives me the strange feeling that I have one foot in the '50's and the other in the '80's. In many ways, it's an exhilarating experience. But at those moments when I get stuck in the time warp, and think it's 1956 all over again, are devastating.

My greatest concern about productions of *Alumnae News* is that the actors and director won't understand what the homophobia of those times meant. (It has happened, but not as often as I had feared.) We didn't touch. Not only didn't we touch, we didn't <u>think</u> about touching. And it wasn't just about sex. We were afraid to touch in any way, through affection, or comfort, or joy. When Karen and Stacey touch, they're throwing caution to the winds. Karen can touch Stacey before she becomes aware of her attraction to Stacey, but not after. Stacey can touch Karen to comfort her, but she has to overcome tremendous resistance and fear to do so; it's a true measure of her love for Karen.

Finishing *Alumnae News* (to the extent that any play is ever 'finished') has been a bittersweet experience for me. On the one hand, I'm pleased that it's finally taken shape, that it can be shared with my lesbian sisters, that so many women have been entertained and moved by it. But there's a sadness, too. Stacey and Karen were a tender part of my life for a more than half my lifetime—and now they don't belong to me alone anymore. Now they belong to everyone. There's a line from a Wellesley Step-singing song, "Where, oh where are the staid alumnae? Lost, lost in the wide, wide world."

I hope the world will treat them kindly.

CAST OF CHARACTERS.

STACEY HOLCOMB is 31, a lesbian, and an assistant professor of college English. She appears to be in control of her life, and gives the impression of openness. She is probably liked and respected by her peers for her intelligent humor and her courage in standing up for her beliefs. But there is always a little something held back with Stacey, places no one is invited to visit, pain no one is allowed to see. Instead, like many romantics, she covers her vulnerability with a veneer of cynicism.

KAREN MARTIN is also 31, divorced, and dependently wealthy although she doesn't really like relying on her family for financial support. She is charming—it isn't her fault, she was born and raised that way. People are drawn to her because of her attractive personality. She's not particularly proud of this, and in fact sees her ability to get along as a weakness, which it sometimes is. She has a real need to be accepted, and this has led her to make some unfortunate choices. Her motives are not always clear to her. In coming to see Stacey, she is acting on impulse. The class reunion has brought up old feelings— feelings of guilt and longing and regret.

TERRY BECK, Stacey and Karen's classmate, is one of those people who appear foolish and innocuous, but are really very dangerous. She is possessive and ruthless, particularly where Karen is concerned. Her "antennae" are out almost from the moment she meets Stacey, and she recognizes—not necessarily consciously—that Stacey can upset the established order of things. What she doesn't recognize about herself (which makes her all the more dangerous) is that she and Stacey are rivals for Karen's affection.

All three women were classmates at Wellesley College—Class of '56.

PLACE: The porch and front yard of Stacey's home, in the country near a small college town, somewhere in New England.

TIME: A June afternoon, 1966. The play takes place in two acts, with a brief intermission.

ACT ONE

SCENE: The front porch and yard of Stacey's home.The house is old, a little run-down, But comfortable.The yard is over grown, but not uncontrolled.

Stacey enters, dressed in bluejeans and a casual shirt. She carries a stack of college exam blue books. She sits on the porch step, takes out a red pencil, and begins to grade exams.

Karen enters hestitantly, unseen by Stacey. She has just driven over from their college reuion, and is dressed accordingly. She carries a sweater, and a large tote bag containing a change of clothes.

KAREN: *(After a moment)* Hi.

STACEY: *(Startled, looks up)* Karen?

KAREN: Have I changed that much?

STACEY: *(Flustered)* No, I ....

KAREN: I should have called.

STACEY: No, it' s fine.

KAREN: If you' d like me to go ....

STACEY: I was <u>concentrating</u>. Slow down, will you?

KAREN:You weren' t at the reunion, so I thought I' d drop over.

STACEY: Forty miles is a long "drop."

KAREN: Ten years is a long silence. *(Waits for response. Gets none)* What are you up to these days?

STACEY: Teaching.

KAREN: Do you like it?

STACEY: Yes. What are <u>you</u> up to?

KAREN: Not much.

STACEY: Do you like it?

KAREN: *(Starts to go)* This was a mistake.

STACEY: How did you find me?

KAREN: Alumnae office.

STACEY: That figures. They tracked me across three states during the last fund-raising drive. Collecting?

KAREN: Hardly.

STACEY: Good.

KAREN: I wanted to see you.

STACEY: Why?

KAREN: We used to be friends.

STACEY: Theoretically.

KAREN: Stacey....

STACEY: I'm sorry. You caught me off guard. *(Tries to be polite)* Make yourself at home.

KAREN:*(Indicating the blue books)* Grading finals? *(Picks one up. Glances through it.)* American Lit.

STACEY: I <u>teach</u> American Lit. What's in <u>there</u> is anybody's guess.

KAREN: Melville. You were the only English major in the class of '56 to graduate without reading *Moby Dick*.

STACEY: Now I have to read it every year. Must be Divine Retribution. *(An awkward silence)* Last fall I got to do Kerouac. Half the class dropped out and went On the Road.

KAREN: *(Indicating)* Not <u>that</u> road.

STACEY: Even the kids next door take it at a crawl.

KAREN: I can see why.

STACEY: Still, anything that inspires two adolescent boys in a beat-up Studebaker to observe the speed limit can't be all bad.

KAREN: Stay, I'm sorry. About how things turned out between us.

STACEY: We were friends, and then we weren't friends. It happens.

KAREN: It was my fault. I shouldn't have ....

STACEY: It's water over the dam, or under the bridge, or whatever.

KAREN: I mean it.

STACEY: Look if we can have a pleasant visit, great. But if you're here to rummage through old garbage ....

KAREN: Okay, forget it.

STACEY: I had.

KAREN: Do you want me to leave.

STACEY: I don't know. *(Pause)* What's new with the class of '56?

KAREN: Babies, husbands, husbands' promotions, the usual talk.

STACEY: My God. In the past ten years we've had an uprising in Hungary, race riots, Sputnik, the Peace Corps, the Cuban Missile Crisis, Vietnam, and Kennedy's assassination. And they're talking about babies and their husbands' promotions?

KAREN: They're only people, Stay. Wellesley didn't make them bigger than life.

STACEY: *(With a laugh)* Don't get me started on <u>that</u>.

KAREN: To tell you the truth, I'm a little horrified, myself. *(Pause)* Do you know Terry's been to every reunion? She flies all the way back here from San Francisco.

STACEY: *(With an edge)* Gosh, all that way, just for that?

KAREN: Did I miss something?

STACEY: She just flies and reunes? No little side trips to Greenwich?

KAREN: We usually meet for lunch, okay?

STACEY: None of my business.

KAREN: She's moving to Europe.

STACEY: Alas, poor Europe.

KAREN: *(Laughs, then hesitatingly)* I've missed you.

STACEY: I really doubt that, Karen. It's been a two-way silence

KAREN: *(Starts to go)* I shouldn't have come here.

STACEY: Didn't you get Terry's permission?

KAREN: What does that mean?

STACEY: Unless my memory deceives me, you couldn't even go to the bathroom without her back at Wellesley. I'm surprised people didn't talk. But they already had plenty to talk about, didn't they?

KAREN: You think I <u>liked</u> having her for a shadow?

STACEY: There were more than four hundred women in our class. You could have done better.

KAREN: I tried.

STACEY: Not very hard.

KAREN: It's been a long time, Stacey. Let's not fight.

STACEY: Sorry.

KAREN: Mind if I sit down?

STACEY: Be my guest.

KAREN: Thank you.

STACEY: *(With a shrug)* We used to be friends. Where's your car?

KAREN: I left it by the mailbox.

STACEY: Want to pull into the driveway? It looks worse than it is. I hope.

KAREN: It'll keep *(Pause)* How have you been?

STACEY: Fine. You?

KAREN: That's not what I mean. I mean, that's not the way I meant it. Stacey, did I do the wrong thing?

STACEY: When?

KAREN: Coming here.

STACEY: It's a free country. If you want to take a nostalgia tour, far be it from me to stop you.

KAREN: I <u>wanted</u> to see <u>you</u>.

STACEY: Why?

KAREN: I <u>liked</u> you. *(Stacey laughs)* Well, up until a few minutes ago, I liked you. *(No response)* I wouldn't risk life, limb, and brand new sixty-dollar shock absorbers to lurch down that cow-path of a road to see you if I didn't like you, would I, for crying out loud?

STACEY: Did you say all that in one breath?

KAREN: What.

STACEY: That's the longest sentence I've heard in my life. Faulkner aside.

KAREN: Stacey ....

STACEY: But I suspect Faulkner wrote to be read, not spoken. Karen, what do you want from me?

KAREN: Nothing.

STACEY: At least <u>that</u> hasn't changed.

KAREN: We were <u>friends</u> ten years ago.

STACEY: Eleven.

KAREN: You meant a lot to me, Stay.

STACEY: The hell I did. It was Stand Up and Be Counted Time. You didn't stand up.

KAREN: You could have come to me.

STACEY: Could I really?

KAREN: But you shut yourself up in your room like a ... like a troll with a grudge.

STACEY: A what?

KAREN: If we met in the hall, you cut me off.

STACEY: A troll with a grudge?

KAREN: Well, that's the best I can do.

STACEY: A troll with a grudge.

KAREN: I didn't major in English. *(Starts to leave)*

STACEY: That's right, leave. You can walk out any time. I can't.

KAREN: Why not?

STACEY: I live here.

KAREN: Oh.

STACEY: Oh? That was the funniest thing I've said since 1956. Maybe the only funny thing I've said since 1956, and what do I get from you? Oh??!

KAREN: Oh, Stacey.

Touched and a little frightened, Karen turns aside, walks away.

MEMORY SHIFT

To the day they first met on the steps of Tower Court dorm, overlooking the lake. Karen is coming up from the lake, Stacey on the steps, Karen drops her sweater, Stacey picks it up.

STACEY: Excuse me. You dropped this.

KAREN: Thanks. I don't think we've met.

STACEY: Stacey Holcomb.

KAREN: Karen Martin. You're the new transfer? I live down the hall, on the end.

STACEY: I covet your view.

KAREN: Come use it any time. Are you settling in okay?

STACEY: I guess so. I found the lake. *(Karen laughes)* I mean it. I saw this campus two years ago, and I've been obsessed with it ever since.

KAREN: You came to Wellesley for the scenery?

STACEY: Why else?

KAREN: The education? Faculty? Reputation? Twelve miles from Harvard?

STACEY: Come on, we're talking Gothic here. The ivy-covered Groves of Academe. The quintessential intellectual experience. Reputation? Who cares about reputation? I spit upon Reputation.

KAREN: I can't tell if you're serious.

STACEY: Neither can I. It's irrelevant. I'm in love.

KAREN: You are?

STACEY: Absolutely. With the lake, the oaks, the hemlocks. With the names of things. Green Hall, Tupelo Point, Alumnae Hall, Hunnewell Arboretum, Fiske House. These are noble names.

KAREN: I don't want to appear rude, but I think you might be crazy.

STACEY: Of course I'm crazy. Love is crazy. Haven't you ever been in love?

KAREN: Not with buildings.

STACEY: Ah, but the lake. Admit it, you're a little bit in love with the lake.

KAREN: Well, a little bit, but I wouldn't want it to get around.

STACEY: Late in February, when winter's breaking up, does it crack?

KAREN: Like rifle shot.

STACEY: I've died and gone to Heaven.

KAREN: Lucky you. I had to take College Boards to get in. You're from the University of Delaware, aren't you?

STACEY: Does it show?

KAREN: Mrs. Reed, the Head of House, wrote us about you over the summer.

STACEY: Why?

KAREN: So we could make you feel welcome.

STACEY: Welcome! It makes me feel paranoid. What did she say?

KAREN: That you're from Delaware, majoring in English, and living in Tower Court West, third floor ....

STACEY: I don't believe it! All those people know about me.

KAREN: And you're an Honors student.

STACEY: Oh, great. Wonderful. Do you know what they do to Honors students? They lurk outside your door muttering imprecations and incantations, epithets and epitaphs. Once, it is rumored, an Honors student was spirited out of Columbia University under cover of darkness, and has never been heard from again.

KAREN: Stacey ....

STACEY: Think of it, Karen. Never Heard From Again. Those are terrible words, Never Heard From Again.

KAREN: Well, don't worry. I've never had any trouble.

STACEY: You're in the Honors Program? Oh, thank God. What field?

KAREN: Political science. Or, as the in-group says, "poly sci".

STACEY: Pre-law "poly sci"?

KAREN: Pre-M.R.S. "poly sci".

STACEY: Engaged?

KAREN: Shopping. Being shopped, I guess.

STACEY: Then why not graduate school?

KAREN: Men don't like brainy women.

STACEY: Don't get married.

KAREN: Oh, fine. We already have enough trouble with the lurkers and mutterers, not to mention Never Heard From Again, and now you want me to think about not getting married? Did someone send you here to make trouble for me?

STACEY: My lips are sealed.

KAREN: Want me to introduce you around?

STACEY: *(Hanging back.)* I guess so.

KAREN: What's the matter?

STACEY: I'm a little intimidated.Everybody's known each other for about a million years. I mean, they'll carry on complicated, convoluted conversations in perfectly understandable English, and I won't have the vaguest idea what they're talking about.

KAREN: "Complicated, convoluted conversations?" I'm not sure **I** know what **you're** talking about.

STACEY: I have a sneaking suspicion I'm trying to impress you.

KAREN: Why?

STACEY: Insecurity, maybe.

KAREN: I'm harmless.

TERRY: *(Offstage)* Karen!

KAREN: Oh, God. *(Calls)* Down here.

TERRY: It's almost time for **dinner**.

KAREN: I'll be along.

TERRY: We have to **dress**.

KAREN: I **am** dressed.

TERRY: What are you doing?

KAREN: Don't shout out the window, Terry. It's rude. *(To Stacey)* My roommate. She speaks in italics.

STACEY: Do you always dress for dinner?

KAREN: Only the nights before and after vacations.

STACEY: I'm in trouble. My luggage is at the railroad station. Is it a rule?

KAREN: More like a tradition.

STACEY: So much for first impressions.

KAREN: I'll change into jeans. We'll start a new tradition.

STACEY: Do you think dinner really cares what we wear? Is it going to take offense and walk out in a huff?

KAREN: If it's anything like our usual lunches, it might.

STACEY: Today's was peeled off the highway. I kid you not. I saw it, squashed by a laundry truck out by the main gate. Was there anything on the road when you came in?

KAREN: No.

STACEY: I rest my case.

KAREN: I'm going to enjoy you. We don't get many psychotics on Three West.

STACEY: I still can't believe I'm here.

KAREN: You're here.

STACEY: Have you ever wanted something so much it made your stomach hurt?

KAREN: Why, Stacey? What's the appeal?

STACEY: I don't know. There's something about the atmosphere. It feels ... outside the world of pettiness and ugliness and mundane things. It feels ... honorable.

KAREN: Wellesley has a lot to live up to.

STACEY: I have a lot to live up to. I probably shouldn't talk like this, should I? It's probably not cool.

KAREN: Don't worry about what I think. I'm caught between Sophomore Slump and Senioritis, and looking for a life preserver. You might be it.

STACEY: Thank you.

They look at each other, a little startled to find they like each other so much so soon.

Terry enters in a rush.

TERRY: Karen, it's late.

KAREN: *(To Stacey)* This is Terry Beck. Stacey Holcomb.

TERRY: *(To Karen, ignoring Stacey)* Where's your blue sweater?

KAREN: Say hello to Stacey, Terry.

TERRY: Yeah-hi-how-are-you-you're-going-to-love-Wellesley-it's-the-greatest. *(To Karen)* So where is it?

KAREN: Probably in the brown suitcase.

TERRY: You're not unpacked?

KAREN: Not entirely. I just got ....

TERRY: God, Karen, you've been here forever.

KAREN: I didn't feel like it, okay? Where is it written I have to unpack the minute I hit campus?

TERRY: We have dinner and then Step-singing and chapel ....

KAREN: I know the routine, Terry.

STACEY: Chapel? Is that a rule?

TERRY: It's a tradition.

KAREN: You can break the rules, but not the traditions. Wellesley's very big on tradition.

TERRY: You'll never get unpacked.

KAREN: It'll get done.

TERRY: You want our room to look like puke?

KAREN: It'll get done.

TERRY: When?

KAREN: When I get around to it.

TERRY: Sometime next semester?

STACEY: Look, if it's a problem, put your stuff in my room.

TERRY: That isn't the point.

STACEY: I'm a little dense. What is the point?

TERRY: Karen procrastinates.

STACEY: *(Mock shock)* Oh, my God!

KAREN: I don't procrastinate, Terry. I just don't do things the way you do them.

TERRY: It would make life a lot easier if you did. I need your blue sweater.

KAREN: What for? *(As Terry starts to answer)* I forgot. *(To Stacey)* Wellesley colors.

STACEY: Rule? Tradition.

TERRY: For Step-singing. *(Urgently)* Karen.

KAREN: If you have to go to the bathroom, say so. Don't bob about.

TERRY: We'll be late.

KAREN: I won't be late.

TERRY: I'll get your blazer from the storage room.

KAREN: I don't want my blazer. It's too hot.

TERRY: You're not wearing that? God, Karen, you look cruddy.

KAREN: Thank you.

TERRY: I better get your blazer. *(Exits)*

STACEY: Fun meeting you.

TERRY: *(Offstage)* Get with it, Karen.

KAREN: I'm so embarrassed.

STACEY: She's amazing.

KAREN: Gung ho.

STACEY: With her around, I'll bet you don't miss your mother.

KAREN: Stepmother. Now that you mention it, there is a resemblance.

STACEY: How long have you roomed with her?

KAREN: This will be our third year. She has her good points. Last year she joined the Civil Air Patrol. For ten hours every week, she stands on top of Sage Hall and watches for enemy bombers.

STACEY: I feel a whole lot safer knowing that.

KAREN: Terry's our secret weapon. If the Communists ever attack, we're going to drop her on the Kremlin. Am I being catty?

STACEY: I think so.

KAREN: "Wellesley girls don't talk about other Wellesley girls behind their backs." Or anything else the Deans think up.

STACEY: Including not unpacking?

KAREN: I'm humiliated you heard that.

STACEY:You didn't do anything, except not unpack.Of course, we all know not unpacking is a sign of low moral character.

KAREN: Okay, Stacey.

TERRY: *(Offstage)* Karen!

KAREN: All right. *(To Stacey)* Coming?

STACEY: I don't know.

KAREN: What's wrong?

STACEY: I don't think I want to be seen with someone who procrastinates.

KAREN: You really are afraid, aren't you?

STACEY: I don't like strangers. The day I was born, the first thing I saw when I opened my eyes was strangers.

KAREN: You've met the worst, honest.

STACEY: I feel so ... out of it.

KAREN: You have to face it sooner or later.

STACEY: Later?

KAREN: Stacey.

STACEY: Nobody knows me. Who'd miss me?

KAREN: I would. *(Pulls her up)* I promise I won't let you out of my sight.

SHIFT TO PRESENT

STACEY: Heavy irony.

KAREN: Excuse me?

STACEY: Memories.That's the trouble with reunions.They get you whether you go or not.

KAREN: Do you think about those times much?

STACEY: Not if I can help it. They remind me of wet wool, slush, and codfish balls for Friday dinner. Among other things.

KAREN: I have no control over my memories. My mind's like one of those kitchen drawers full of buttons and thumb tacks and small metal objects you find on the floor that don't look like anything you ever saw before but must be an important part of something.

STACEY: And if you throw them out, the refrigerator dies.

KAREN: The vacuum cleaner blows up.

STACEY: The car won't start.

KAREN: And the Post Office loses your change-of-address card.

STACEY: But not the Alumnae Office.

KAREN: Never the Alumnae Office. Stay, about our Senior year ....

STACEY: I told you I didn't want to talk about that.

KAREN: We have to talk about it.

STACEY: We don't <u>have</u> to talk about <u>anything</u>.

KAREN: Yes, we do. We were friends. Good friends. You at least owe me ....

STACEY: I owe you nothing.

KAREN: Damn it, I didn't start the rumors.

STACEY: You believed them.

KAREN: Sort of. A little.

STACEY: And acted accordingly.

KAREN: I didn't know what to do. It made me ... feel funny.

STACEY: Yeah? Well, it made me "feel funny" too. It certainly did make me "feel funny."

KAREN: Not the way you think.

STACEY: How, then?

KAREN: How what?

STACEY: How did it make you "feel funny"?

KAREN: Strange. Confused. How should I know what I mean by "funny"?

STACEY: You seem to know what I <u>think</u>. You should know how you <u>feel</u>.

KAREN: I can't talk to you if you're going to be like this.

STACEY: Then don't talk to me. *(Karen looks at her helplessly)* Let me give you what you came for: the rumors were true. I'm the queer of the class of '56. Go back to your reunion and spread the news.

KAREN: <u>It isn't news</u>. Stacey, how are you, really?

STACEY: Great.

KAREN: Are you sure?

STACEY: I said so, didn't I?

KAREN: I don't know ... there's something about you ....

STACEY: I have a Ph.D. in English and a dissertation published in an obscure but respectable journal. I'm a pretty good teacher. In a few years, I'll be a very good teacher. Eventually, I might be a spectacular teacher. I have a dog, and a home I love. Which may not look like the Taj Mahal to you, Miss Westchester County, but it expresses me.

KAREN: I'm glad. I do care about you, you know.

STACEY: Damn it, don't condescend to me. *(Karen makes a gesture of frustration)* You're not being held here against your will.

KAREN: *(Blowing up)* I'm not leaving. You can call the police, they might make it out here in about two hours. Or the adolescents in their beat-up Studebaker. Or anyone else you have lurking in the woods. But I'm staying. I'm going to go inside and change my clothes. You can storm around all you like, and call me names, and take offense at my mere existence. But I'm not going until I've said what I came to say.

Karen exits the house

STACEY: *(Shouts)* Screw you, Karen.

KAREN: *(Offstage)* Screw you, too.

Stacey storms around impatiently until she feels foolish, sits and tries to get back to grading exams.

<u>MEMORY SHIFT</u>

Stacey is in the dorm room lounge studying.

KAREN: Stay! Is it safe?

STACEY: *(Looks around)* All clear.

KAREN: Thank God you were down here.

STACEY: Don't thank God. Thank your roommate.

KAREN: Now what's she up to?

STACEY: I'm not sure, but it involves loud music and peals of girlish glee.

KAREN: I can't face it.

STACEY: Stay here a while. They'll run down soon.

KAREN: I don't want to disturb you.

STACEY: I need a break. With the Romantic poets, a little goes a long way.

KAREN: With romance a little goes a long way.

STACEY: Rough night?

KAREN: Jim Henley's the Continental type—Russian hands and Roman fingers. If he were going to med school, he'd specialize in gynecology. I think I'm a little tight.

STACEY: *(Amused)* I think you are.

KAREN: His friends call him "Chick." You know—Henley, Hen, Chick?

STACEY: That must be the famous Harvard wit.

KAREN: Darn. Forgot to sign in. *(Starts to get up)*

STACEY: I took care of it. The minute the clock strikes 11:30, Mrs. Reed heads for the sign-in book like Pavlov's dog. Why didn't you take a one o'clock?

KAREN: Wishful thinking. *(Goes to pull of her earrings. finds she is missing one.)* I lost an earring. Probably in the back seat of Henley's roommate's car.

STACEY: Was that tonight's battlefield?

KAREN: That and his room, and the balcony of the Shubert. I've been fondled so much, I feel like a Rosary. If he met me on the street, he wouldn't recognize me until he closed his eyes and felt me up.

STACEY: Sounds grim.

KAREN: I hate it. Stay, do you think there's something wrong with me?

STACEY: Because you don't like being manhandled? Who does?

KAREN: Apparently, most girls. If you don't believe me, take a stroll out there some balmy evening. It looks like a snake pit. Sometimes I think life would be simpler if I didn't date.

STACEY: It might.

KAREN: You don't date. Do you know something I don't know?

STACEY: Such as?

KAREN: Boys are creeps.

STACEY: You don't have to go out with him, Karen. It's not a graduation requirement.

KAREN: Tell that to my stepmother. Her greatest fear is that I won't be engaged by Spring Vacation of my Senior year.

STACEY: Seems to be everybody's greatest fear. Have you taken a good look at the Senior class lately? Diamonds are popping up like sow beetles in a woodpile.

KAREN: Honestly, sometimes you have the most unfortunate way of putting things. How come your parents don't pressure you to date?

STACEY: They do. I lie a lot. *(Karen laughs)* Really. I have an amazing social life. It's a miracle I'm still a virgin.

KAREN: I envy you. I could never pull it off.

STACEY: Anyone our age who can't lie to her parents is seriously lacking in survival skills.

KAREN: My parents have spies everywhere. The Henleys are Country Club buddies of theirs.

STACEY: Is this one of those Medieval, pre-arranged, "combine the family fortunes" relationships?

KAREN: Just a "wouldn't it be nice?"

STACEY: Well, if you don't like the way he treats you, dump him.

KAREN: Dump him? Dump the best catch in the Harvard Business School?

STACEY: There must be other fish in the Country Club pool.

KAREN: *(With a laugh)* I don't believe you said that.

STACEY: Neither do I.

KAREN: How would I explain it?

STACEY: Don't explain. If anyone asks, just look away and say, "I ... sharp intake of breath ... can't talk about it."

KAREN: I ....

STACEY: Sharp intake of breath.

KAREN: ... can't talk about it.

STACEY: Now, work up a tear. Nothing copious, just enough to tremble beautifully on the brink of the eyelid. Then pull yourself together and smile sadly, but bravely.

KAREN: I ... *(Giggles)* ... can't.

STACEY: The trick is to get exactly the right tone. Makes them feel guilty even when they haven't the vaguest idea what you're talking about.

KAREN: I wish I could. I wish I could lie and pretend. I feel like a complete and total jerk.

STACEY: Well, I can't do it either.

KAREN: What?

STACEY: I lied. I can't do it.

KAREN: You dog.

STACEY: It'd be fun, though, wouldn't it? Just once?

KAREN: Heaven. His family's spending the summer in Bar Harbor. So is mine. Do you know what that means? Moonlight sails, picnics on the beach ....

STACEY: And good old Chickie's Continental hands. I thought you were going to France with Terry and her Merry Band.

KAREN: Only until mid-July. First Nice, then Bar Harbor.

STACEY: They say Nice is nice.

KAREN: *(Gives her a look)* I hate Bar Harbor. Everyone's up-beat.

STACEY: Everyone's up-beat here.

KAREN: Not you.

STACEY:Oh, great. I'll go down in history as the girl who brought angst to Wellesley.

KAREN: You're the only one in this place who doesn't make my face hurt.

STACEY: Thank you. I think.

KAREN: I'll bet they have angst at Phantom Ranch.

STACEY: Believe it. The only way to descend the Grand Canyon is on foot or muleback. Middle-aged ladies and portly gentlemen have been known to fling themselves into the Colorado River rather than face the trip back up.

KAREN: I wish I were going with you.

STACEY: Do it.

KAREN: My father'd have apoplexy, to say nothing of my stepmother. And what would I say to people here?

STACEY: Tell them your family's prone to apoplexy.

KAREN: *(Laughs then serious)* Stay, do you ever feel ... well, like an outsider?

STACEY: Constantly. Probably because I am. Do you?

KAREN: Yes.

STACEY: You're kidding.

KAREN: No.

STACEY: You're one of the most popular ....

KAREN: *(Cuts her off angrily)* Don't.

STACEY: I'm sorry.

KAREN: It's all a game. Sometimes I think, what if one morning we all woke up wearing our real faces? Not the ones we put on because it's the thing to do, our deep-down-inside real faces?

STACEY: Now there's a horrible thought.

KAREN: I'll bet you wouldn't change.

STACEY: Would you?

KAREN: Probably. I've spent so much of my life trying to please people, I don't even recognize myself most of the time.

STACEY: Are you having a bad night?

KAREN: Probably That Time of Month.

STACEY: Is it?

KAREN: No. I want something and I don't know what it is. Do you know what you want?

STACEY: "The Mysteries of Life in an Orderly Manner."

KAREN: I like that.

STACEY: So do I. Jessamyn West, *Love, Death, and the Ladies' Drill Team.*

KAREN: I adore English majors. They footnote everything.

STACEY: *(Thoughtfully)* What I really want, all kidding aside, is to find some place I'm comfortable.

KAREN: Where would that be?

STACEY: Somewhere I don't have to dress for dinner. No, somewhere that whether or not you dress for dinner doesn't have anything to do with anything.

KAREN: That eliminates Bar Harbor.

STACEY: If you hate it there, don't go. It's your life. You can mess it up any way you like.

KAREN: Not me.

STACEY: Keep thinking that way, and one of these days you'll wake up and find yourself married to that guy.

KAREN: It wouldn't surprise me.

STACEY: Karen.

KAREN: I'm just confused. We're supposed to be confused at our age, aren't we?

STACEY: No, our generation's supposed to be alienated.

KAREN: Stay, how am I going to make it through the summer without you?

Terry enters in little girl nightie and fuzzie slippers.

TERRY: Karen, do you know what time it is?

KAREN: And a gracious good evening to you, Miss Beck. I see we're doing cute.

TERRY: I knew I'd find you here. Where Holcomb goes, Martin follows.

STACEY: And, sooner or later, Beck shows up.

KAREN: I was out. On a date. Remember?

TERRY: Right. Who with?

KAREN: Henley.

TERRY: Neat-O! He's a fab make-out.

STACEY: *(To Karen)* Translation?

KAREN: She admires his technique.*(To Terry)* I didn't know you'd made out with him.

TERRY: I haven't. I saw you at the Dunster House Formal.

Embarassed Karen covers her head.

STACEY: Gosh, Beck, I'd never suspect you of voyeurism. *(Quickly)* I take that back.

TERRY: I didn't sit and stare the way some people would.

STACEY: Not me. I'm afraid of sex. Nasty stuff.

TERRY: So it seems. I'm going to bed.

STACEY: Should I call the newspapers now, or will it keep for the Sunday edition?

TERRY: *(To Karen.Ignoring Stacey)* Are you coming?

KAREN: In a while.

TERRY: But I want to go to bed.

KAREN: Fine. Go.

TERRY: You'll wake me up.

KAREN: I'll be quiet.

TERRY: You always wake me up.

KAREN: Stacey and I are talking. When we finish, I'll be up.

TERRY: You can talk tomorrow.

KAREN: We're talking now.

TERRY: It's the middle of the night.

KAREN: I won't be long.

TERRY: I have a bio quiz tomorrow. If I'm awake all night ....

KAREN: All right, I'll sleep in Stacey's room.

TERRY: I'll bet she'd love that. *(To Stacey)* Wouldn't you?

STACEY: Suits me.

TERRY: See?

KAREN: Terry, what are you getting at?

TERRY: She knows. *(To Stacey)* Don't you?

STACEY: Do I?

KAREN: Knows what?

TERRY: Nothing.

KAREN: If you have something to say, spit it out.

TERRY: Don't get mad at me. I'm not the one who's talking.

KAREN: About what?

TERRY: Nothing.

KAREN: Am I drunk, or is everyone crazy?

STACEY: Everyone's crazy. And you're drunk.

TERRY: *(Scandalized)* Drunk!?

KAREN: This is too much. *(Gets up to leave. To Terry, who follows)* Stay here. I'm not that drunk.

TERRY: What do you mean?

KAREN: If you watch me make out, I'm sure as hell not about to undress in front of you. See you tomorrow, Stay.

Karen exits. Stacey goes back to work. Terry fiddles and diddles for a few seconds.

TERRY: You don't like me, do you?

STACEY: What?

TERRY: Why don't you like me?

STACEY: *(Pretends to give it some thought.)* I don't know.

TERRY: Because I room with Karen, and you wish you did.

STACEY: I like rooming alone.

TERRY: Naturally, you wouldn't admit it.

STACEY: *(Trying to get back to work)* I probably wouldn't.

TERRY: I know how you feel about her.

STACEY: Good.

TERRY: I think it's pretty interesting. We all think it's pretty interesting.

STACEY: *(Deliberately misunderstanding)* Byron? Not as interesting as Shelley.

TERRY: You and Karen.

STACEY: Karen and I what?

TERRY: You know.

STACEY: Look, Terry, it's been swell chatting with you, but I really have to ....

TERRY: You're angry because I broke up your little *tete-a-tete*.

STACEY: For God's sake, Beck.

TERRY: Odd, isn't it? Every time she goes out on a date, you happen to study down here.

STACEY: I study down here every night because you and your cronies turn Three West into a barnyard.

TERRY: At least I'm not a grind.

STACEY: I'll grant you that.

TERRY: You're supposed to have a good time in college, not be a grind.

STACEY: You're not going to believe this, but I actually like to study.

TERRY: Be real.

STACEY: Terry, why did you come to Wellesley?

TERRY: It's closer to Harvard than Vassar.

STACEY: No other reason?

TERRY: My mother went here.

STACEY: You must have had decent grades, to get in.

TERRY: They were okay. They take almost everyone from my prep school, anyway.

STACEY: What made you decide to major in Sociology?

TERRY: It's a gut.

STACEY: I envy you, you know. Four years of this.

TERRY: Yeah, it's the greatest.

STACEY: We won't ever have a chance like this again.

TERRY: Like what?

STACEY: To be here. To study, and learn, and think. With nothing else to worry about. We don't even have to cook for ourselves.

TERRY: I never cooked for myself.

STACEY: Since Monday I've changed the way I look at the world at least five times. Everything gets turned upside down from one day to the next. And when I realize I only have one more year ... God, you don't know what you've had here.

TERRY: You know, Holcomb, you'd probably get along better if you weren't so self-righteous.

STACEY: *(Realizes she's wasting her time.)* I probably would.

TERRY: You've only been here six months, and you act like you own the place.

STACEY: You're absolutely right.

TERRY: You think you own Three West.

STACEY: You're absolutely right.

TERRY: You think you own Karen.

STACEY: You're absolutely wrong.

TERRY: She can't go out without you sitting up waiting for her, for God's sake. How do you think that looks? When we play bridge, you're always her partner ....

STACEY: Because we always win, Sweets. And I love the look on your face when you lose.

TERRY: She used to do everything with us. But you're always dragging her off ....

STACEY: *(Angrily)* Look, Beck, Karen and I happen to like each other. I didn't plan that. I didn't plan to live in this dorm. And, God knows, I didn't plan to room down the hall from you. It's all existential. *(Turns back to her work)*

TERRY: *(After a while)* What were you talking about?

STACEY: Nothing much.

TERRY: Excuse me. I didn't know it was personal.

STACEY: We were discussing our summer plans.

TERRY: She's going to France with us.

STACEY: Was that the collective "us" or the Imperial "us"?

TERRY: We go every summer.

STACEY: *(Turning back to work)* I'm very happy for you.

TERRY: *(Just a Stacey begins to concentrate.)* Where are you going?

STACEY: What?

TERRY: Where are you going this summer?

STACEY: To the Grand Canyon. Where, in addition to my usual job, I will spend every free minute making up the work I'm not doing tonight.

TERRY: It's not my fault you can't tear yourself away from my roommate.

STACEY: *(Losing it)* From seven-thirty until a quarter of nine, I tried to study in my room. Your outbursts of mirth—resembling, as they do, the ravings of a psychotic chicken—made that impossible. From a quarter of nine until nine, I indulged in fantasies of revenge, which I won't tell you about since I might want to carry them out one day. At nine, I gave up and came down here, where I studied in relative peace until Karen came in at eleven-fifty ....

TERRY: She was supposed to be in at eleven-thirty.

STACEY: Obviously, she'll never amount to anything.

TERRY: She'll have to go before House Council.

STACEY: It's okay, I signed in for ...*(Realizes she's just made a big mistake)*

TERRY: You signed in? We're on the Honor System.

STACEY: I realize that, Terry. But it seemed like such a minor ....

TERRY: You can't make the rules.

STACEY: All right. Turn me in. Turn Karen in. Let them shoot us at sunrise, just leave me alone.

TERRY: You're the one who signed her in.

STACEY: Let her report me.

TERRY: She won't do that. Don't think you're special or anything. Karen's just like that.

STACEY: Clearly a born psychopath.

TERRY: Now I don't know what to do.

STACEY: About what?

TERRY: You signing her in.

STACEY: Forget it. It's not your problem.

TERRY: I'm responsible for what I know. We're on the Honor ....

STACEY: Honor System. Well, why don't you scamper off and search your conscience?

TERRY: Why do you always make trouble?

STACEY: I was born that way.

TERRY: You don't even take it seriously.

STACEY: Terry, years from now we'll look back on this and laugh.

TERRY: I won't.

STACEY: Okay. I'll talk it over with Karen. Maybe we'll confess and fling ourselves on the mercy of the House Council. With luck, they won't expel her for coming in 20 minutes late.

TERRY: You don't care about Wellesley, do you?

STACEY: What?

TERRY: If you cared about Wellesley, you'd care about standards.

STACEY: Terry, I ... Never mind.

TERRY: I don't know what to do.

STACEY: Sweets, if you don't get out of here and let me study, I won't get into graduate school. My mother will die of a broken heart, my father will sue you, and my brother will use his Mafia connections to put out a contract on you. What to do about this will be the least of your ....

TERRY: If I don't report you, they could take away my one o'clocks for a month.

STACEY: Then report us! Please! I beg you—report us!

TERRY: If I lose my one o'clocks, I'll miss the M.I.T. mixer.

STACEY: God forbid.

TERRY: You don't even care about boys. All you care about is Karen.

STACEY: Wrong. All I care about is GETTING BACK TO WORK.

TERRY: Spare me. You're not the first person in history to go to graduate school.

STACEY: I may be the first person in history to do it from Death Row.

TERRY: You don't have to be <u>rude</u>.

STACEY: Yes, I do.

TERRY: I'm not trying to make you flunk out. I'm not trying to ruin your <u>life</u>. I'm only trying to be <u>friendly</u>. *(No response)* It wouldn't hurt you to be friendly. *(No response)* It wouldn't <u>kill</u> you.

STACEY: I was friendly Monday night. I was friendly Tuesday night. I was friendly Wednesday night, and part of Wednesday afternoon. Thursday is my night to be unfriendly.

TERRY: You're never unfriendly to Karen.

STACEY: Go away, Terry.

TERRY: It's not good for you to be so dependent on her.

STACEY: I'll take it under advisement.

TERRY: *(Gives up)* Last year, up in the Quad, they caught two Sophomores in bed together. Naked. They were kicked out. Goodnight.

Terry exits.

<u>SHIFT TO PRESENT</u>

Karen enters from house. She has changed into jeans and an old sweatshirt and carries paper plates with sandwiches.

KAREN: Recognize this?

STACEY: What?

KAREN: The sweatshirt. I wore it to every final for four years. It brought me luck. *(Offer Stacey a plate)* Lunch.

Stacey refuses to take it. Karen puts it down beside her goes to opposite side and sits with her sandwich.

Eat.

STACEY: I'm not hungry.

KAREN: Eat, anyway. It's the polite thing to do.

STACEY: *(Fingering her sandwich)* How do you know I don't hate this stuff?

KAREN: It was in your kitchen. *(Pause)* Stop pouting.

STACEY: I'm not pouting.

KAREN: I know pouting. You're pouting. *(Stacey takes a bite from her sandwich)* That's better. *(Stacey puts her sandwich down)* Well, this is interesting. Sort of like being married. *(Pause)* Karen, old girl, you may not be good for much, but you're one heck of a cook.

STACEY: You are not.

KAREN: A voice! Did you hear a voice? *(Stacey is trying not to smile)* I thought I heard a voice. It must have been God. *(Stacey laughs)* Goodness, what was that?

STACEY: I laughed.

KAREN: She laughed. It's a miracle! You're not angry any more?

STACEY: I laughed, but I'm still angry.

KAREN: That must be confusing.

STACEY: Yes, it's confusing.

KAREN: I didn't mean to hurt you back then, Stay.

STACEY: This has to be the dryest sandwich I've ever eaten. Reminds me of dorm cooking.

KAREN: All your food's sitting on the kitchen table, and there's nothing in the refrigerator.

STACEY: I'm defrosting.

KAREN: Great way to get botulism.

STACEY: Don't nag. Care for coffee?

KAREN: No, thanks. I don't drink coffee.

STACEY: You're an intelligent, educated woman. How can you not drink coffee?

KAREN: Maybe I have a chromosome missing.

STACEY: You can't have something missing. Either you have it, or it's missing.

KAREN: For this you got a Ph.D.?

STACEY: I got a Ph.D. to read *Moby Dick*. Coke?

KAREN: I'd rather talk.

STACEY: The choice is not between having a Coke, and talking about the past. The choice is between having a Coke, and not having a Coke.

KAREN: You know, you're a little touchier than you used to be.

STACEY: What do you expect, for God's sake? You come sashaying in here, unannounced, after ten years of silence....

KAREN: "Sashaying"?

STACEY: I don't even know what you're doing h....

KAREN: "Sashaying"?

STACEY: I went to graduate school in Iowa. Do you want a Coke, or don't you?

KAREN: If you're all out of "sasparelly "

STACEY: All right, Karen *(Takes a coke from the cooler)*

KAREN:I snooped around inside.*(Stacey looks at her)* It's done, even in polite society. No evidence of a roommate.

STACEY: No roommate, just me and Carson McCullers.

KAREN: Carson McCullers? The writer?

STACEY: Carson McCullers the Dog.

KAREN: What kind of dog?

STACEY: Even her mother doesn't know. Or won't tell.

KAREN: Where is she?

STACEY: In the swamp.

KAREN: The swamp.

STACEY: It's a truly disgusting swamp. One of the all-time Truly

Disgusting Swamps.

KAREN: I know I'll be sorry I asked, but why is Carson McCullers in the Truly Disgusting Swamp?

STACEY: She got skunked last night and I wouldn't let her sleep on the bed. As soon as she thinks I'm not watching, she'll come back and roll on the couch. *(Offers her the coke)* Glass?

KAREN: I'll rough it.

Karen reaches for the coke. Their hands touch. Stacey quickly goes back to her seat and picks up the sandwich.

You really don't have to eat that.

STACEY: You went to a lot of trouble to poison me. The least I can do is meet you half-way.

KAREN: I wish you'd meet me half-way about ....

STACEY: Karen, it takes a lot to make me angry. But once I'm angry, I stay that way for a very long time.

KAREN: Ten years? That's not a long time, it's a world record.

Stacey pointedly turns her back. Karen shrugs—no luck this time, try again later. Watches Stacey.

<u>MEMORY SHIFT</u>

Stacey is in her room alone. Karen enters.

Stay, are you busy?

STACEY: Reading. *(Tosses her book aside)* Trash. Something wrong?

KAREN: Not really.

STACEY: You and Beck have a fight?

KAREN: I leave that to you. I missed you at dinner.

STACEY: A bunch of us from the writing seminar went over to Framingham for pizza.

KAREN: Have a nice time?

STACEY: Sure. We're human when we're not being intense and artistic.

KAREN: *(Wandering to the window)* Full moon. The next time I see a full moon, I'll be in France.

STACEY: I'll be at the bottom of the Grand Canyon.

KAREN: Will you write to me?

STACEY: Of course. Will you?

KAREN: I don't write very good letters.

STACEY: If I want Literature, I can read Gertrude Stein. Excuse me, Hemingway. <u>Men</u> write Literature. <u>Women</u> write fiction. Are you sure you're all right?

KAREN: A little blue, I guess.

STACEY: Spring does that. It's so <u>GREEN</u>.

KAREN: Today's my birthday.

STACEY: You're kidding. Why didn't you tell me? We could have celebrated.

KAREN: *(Quickly)* I don't celebrate my birthday.

STACEY: Why not?

KAREN: It's only another day.

STACEY: But it gives the people who love you a chance to show it.

KAREN: When I was nine, my father took me to F.A.O. Schwartz in New York for my birthday. I could have anything I wanted, he said. I fell in love with a life-sized plush Dumbo. Well, it wasn't life-size life-size, but I wasn't life-size, either, so it seemed life-size. I lugged that silly animal all over Central Park.When we got home for cake-and-ice-cream time, my mother had cleared out.

STACEY: Cleared out?

KAREN: Bag, baggage, and midnight blue Cadillac sedan. My father dragged me through the house, looking for her, one room after another, over and over, and I dragged Dumbo. Then he stood there, in the middle of the room, in the middle of the silence, and said, "Happy Birthday, Karen." So much for people who love you.

STACEY: *(Touches her)* I'm sorry. Why did she leave?

KAREN: I don't know. I didn't even know they were divorced until he married Helen. When I'd ask him about it, he'd say, "You don't have a mother." That's it. "You don't have a mother." *(Pause)* I keep thinking it was something I did.

STACEY: *(Holds her)* Karen, that's crazy.

KAREN: Why didn't she take me with her?

STACEY: I don't know. People are hard to figure.

KAREN: If I did something wrong, would you tell me?

STACEY: Karen ...

KAREN: You wouldn't go away, would you? You'd give me a chance to fix it?

STACEY: You're not going to do anything wrong.

KAREN: I wouldn't do it on purpose.

STACEY: Karen, you're not going to do anything wrong.

KAREN: I'm sorry. I don't know why that all came out.

STACEY: It's okay.

KAREN: It was twelve years ago, for crying out loud.

STACEY: It's <u>okay</u>.

KAREN: You won't mention this to Terry, will you?

STACEY: Give me a little credit.

KAREN: I can just hear her. "Twelve years. Be <u>real</u>." God, she's so ...I don't know, smug. Sometimes I want to....

STACEY: Kill her?

KAREN: Do something to wake her up. There are <u>real</u> <u>people</u> in the world. With <u>real</u> <u>feelings</u>. And terrible things happen. But she can't see beyond her own nose.

STACEY: She's getting on your nerves tonight, isn't she?

KAREN: She gets on my nerves <u>every</u> night. It's funny, until this year I didn't care that much. I mean, I wasn't <u>happy</u> playing Good Time College Girl, but I wasn't <u>unhappy</u>. It was just kind of ... what it was. I'm either growing up or going sour.

STACEY: I know what you mean.

KAREN: I can't put up with the babble any more. Who's going to what dance? What are they wearing? Who'd you make out with last night, and how far did you go? I feel so raw. Sometimes I want to scream at them, "There are worse things in life than not having a date for Saturday night." And sometimes I just want to come in here and ....

STACEY: What?

KAREN: Cry. For you, for me, for the whole world.

STACEY: For me?

KAREN: Especially for you. Because things matter to you, and sooner or later you're going to be hurt.

STACEY: *(Self-conscious)* I'll survive.

KAREN: If I hadn't promised her, back in September, I'd room with her next year ....

STACEY: I know. Well, as you once said, she has her good points. She's out of the room a lot.

KAREN: Right.

STACEY: I wish you were coming to Arizona with me this summer.

KAREN: So do I. Next year.

STACEY: Do you mean that?

KAREN: Of course I do.

STACEY: What about Nice?

KAREN: I'll bet Phantom Ranch is nicer.

STACEY: Especially under a full moon. Want to take a walk?

KAREN: I'd love it. *(As Stacey turn to put her book away)* Stay?

STACEY: Yeah?

KAREN: *(Hugs her impulsively)* Thank you.

SHIFT TO PRESENT

KAREN: Damn it, Stacey, this isn't right. We cared about each other back then. Maybe you can't trust me, but at least we can be civil. I mean, my God, I can't hurt you any more, can I?

STACEY: No.

KAREN: We thought it was simple. You felt betrayed, I felt betrayed....

STACEY: You?

KAREN: You promised you'd never go away without giving me a chance.

STACEY: You're right. I did. I'm sorry, Karen.

KAREN: I don't want an apology. I want you to understand, it worked both ways.

STACEY: I understand.

KAREN: I don't believe it. I actually got the upper hand.

STACEY: Well, as they used to say back then, don't abuse the privilege.

KAREN: Now will you eat that sandwich?

STACEY: Karen, it's ...

KAREN: It's a perfectly respectable sandwich.

STACEY: But it's so ... domestic.

KAREN: A cheese sandwich is domestic?

STACEY: When it's made for you, in your own home, by someone you ... yeah, it is.

KAREN: So what?

STACEY: I'm not used to it.

KAREN: Do you mean to tell me no one's ever made you a sandwich in your own house? Even men do that. What kind of lovers have you had?

STACEY: Not the domestic kind. Not many at all. It's too casual. And too desperate.

KAREN: Have you been in love?

STACEY: Love's complicated. I like things simple. How about you?

KAREN: I had an affair, briefly. It didn't mean anything. I guess I wanted to give Henley a reason to divorce me.

STACEY: Did it work?

KAREN: Certainly did. There's one thing I'll say for Jim Henley. He was one righteous son-of-a-bitch.

STACEY: Why did you marry him? You didn't even like him.

KAREN: Three guesses.

STACEY: You're kidding.

KAREN: Don't I wish?

STACEY: You didn't have to marry him.

KAREN: What was I supposed to do? Breeze into the living room and say, "Hey, Dad, Helen, and assorted half-siblings, if you haven't picked out my graduation present yet, I'd really love an abortion "?

STACEY: It might have been the lesser of two evils.

KAREN: You don't know my family.

STACEY: Couldn't you do it without them?

KAREN: A back-alley job? I was afraid to go it alone, and there wasn't anyone ....

STACEY: What about me?

KAREN: But you were barricaded behind locked doors, nursing your vow of silence. Anyway, old Chick was so hot to marry, he jumped at the chance. To tell you the truth, I've always suspected he set me up. Remember how they used to say a gentleman never took advantage of a girl who'd had too much to drink? Either Jim Henley was no gentleman, or that was the biggest myth since they called the Korean War a Police Action.

STACEY: Jesus.

KAREN: I didn't give in without a fight, though. Knitting needles—size 8, I think, or was it a 5? Messy work. If you ever decide to do that, do it in the bathtub.

STACEY: Karen, you could have died.

KAREN: The thought crossed my mind. Modern doctors work miracles, you know. They saved me, and they saved the baby, not necessarily in that order. The cat was out of the bag, of course, even if the baby wasn't. Dear Helen arranged a quick but terribly festive wedding. Terry was ravishing in apricot organza. Everyone blew kisses and the happy couple sailed off for Jamaica to wallow in connubial bliss. Three weeks later, I went into labor. Must have been the tropical sun.

STACEY: The baby?

KAREN: Little devil was stillborn. I couldn't blame it. Four months premature and it had already been through a lifetime of horrors. I should have put that in the Alumnae News I wonder if they'd have listed it under Births or Deaths. Maybe I'd have gotten double billing. For a generation raised on June Allyson and Doris Day, we're not doing very well, are we?

STACEY: Do you live with your family?

KAREN: I have a tasteful little bachelor-girl apartment, subsidized by Daddy. And a superfluous fund-raising job at the local Art Museum. Also, I suspect, subsidized by Daddy.

STACEY: Do you think you'll marry again?

KAREN: Maybe. I'm going with a man, Grant Evans. Lawyer, considerate, in love, and not subsidized by Daddy.

STACEY: Grant Evans? Sounds like a line of expensive clothes. "For her going-away ensemble, the bride wore a simple Grant Evans original." Do you love him?

KAREN: I don't think so.

STACEY: For God's sake, Karen, get a grip on your life.

KAREN: How do you make it all come together? What you want, what you're supposed to want, what other people ...?

STACEY: What do you want?

KAREN: *(Starts to answer. Changes her mind)* Potato chips.

STACEY: Excuse me?

KAREN: You don't have potato chips. You're an intelligent, educated woman. How can you not have potato ... *(Her voice breaks. Bursts out)* Damn it, Stacey, why did you close me out?

STACEY: Karen ....

KAREN: Maybe you couldn't come to my room, because of Terry. But there were other ways.

STACEY: I couldn't do it.

KAREN: We used to go out to Tupelo Point during Step-singing, remember? We'd look out at the lake and listen to the music and talk. Every Step-singing, all through that fall, I went out there and waited for you.

STACEY: I couldn't do it, Karen.

KAREN: Your friendship meant more to me than anything in my life, and you threw it away over ....

STACEY: <u>I was in love with you</u>. *(Pause)* Shocked? *(No response)* If you'd known that, I wonder if you'd have waited on Tupelo Point. *(No response)* Don't worry, I got over it. I don't fall in love any more.

KAREN: There was nothing like that between us.

STACEY: Not on your part. But I thought about you every day and every night. I fell asleep thinking of you. I woke up thinking of you. I wanted to be near you, to touch you, to hold you. I loved you, and loved you, and the more I loved you, the more I hated myself. Even when you stayed away, I kept on loving you. I was hurt, and I loved you. I was angry, and I loved you. I was ashamed, and I still loved you.

KAREN: I don't want to hear this.

STACEY: You wanted to talk, you're going to hear it. After a while I began to think Terry was right. It wasn't friendship, or—God forbid—affection that was behind your kindness to me. I wasn't special.

KAREN: You <u>believed</u> her?

STACEY: <u>You</u> believed her. All she had to do was whisper that little word in your ear, and it was ,"So long, it's been good to know you."

KAREN: It wasn't that simple.

STACEY: It's the simplest thing in the world. I'm diseased. Unnatural. I didn't belong at Wellesley. I don't belong anywhere.

KAREN: Stop it.

STACEY: I teach at the University, but I don't belong there. Every day's a test: can I get through it without anyone finding out? Am I dressed all right? Did I say anything, do anything to give myself away? Was that gesture <u>feminine</u> enough? Is it time to make up another boyfriend? Because if anyone guesses, or even wonders, it won't be just my job at stake. All the things I am, all the years I've lived, all the complexities that make up <u>me</u> will be lost behind one word: LESBIAN.

KAREN: Stacey ....

STACEY: I never would have hurt you. I only wanted to be with you. To sit with you by the lake and watch the seasons change. To talk with you about things that mattered. To show you the desert under a full moon. To celebrate your birthday.

KAREN: Please, don't.

STACEY: But I wasn't allowed to do that. Not that, or any of the other things friends do. I'm not allowed to do normal things because I'm not normal.

KAREN: I'm telling you, <u>stop it</u>.

STACEY: Everything has a different meaning when you're not like other people. You can't touch, because your touch is dirty. You can't care, because caring might hold the black little seeds of something ugly. You can't love. Whatever you do, you mustn't love.

Karen pulls Stacey to her and kisses her hard. Shocked and frightened at what she's done she quickly pulls back.

KAREN: I ... I'm sorry.

STACEY: Karen?

KAREN: I wanted to stop you. It didn't ....

STACEY: *(Reaches out to reassure her)* It's all right.

KAREN: *(In a panic)* Don't touch me!

STACEY: <u>Karen</u>.

KAREN: I'm not queer! Do you hear me? I'm not queer!

Stacey bolts, exits. Karen realizes what she's done.

Oh, God, Stacey, I ... Stacey!

END OF ACT I

ACT TWO

A little later. Karen is alone, waiting for Stacey to come back.

MEMORY SHIFT

Karen waits for Stacey on Tupelo point. It is the first day of their senior year, the last time they will be together.

Stacey enters. Karen looks up eagerly.

KAREN: Happy Senior Year, Miss Holcomb. *(Wants to embrace her , but has turned shy over the summer.)* I was afraid you'd stood me up.

STACEY: *(Keeping her distance)* I had to see ....

KAREN: How was your summer?

STACEY: All right. Karen, I ....

KAREN: *(Bubbling over with excitment)* Your letters were wonderful. I'm sorry mine were such a drag, but it really was a wretched time, and I figured you wouldn't mind. After all, you were the girl who brought *angst* to Wellesley.

STACEY: It was okay.

KAREN: Know what got me through it? Every time I couldn't take it any more—the endless parties, night after night, the constant forced gaiety—I mean, come on, nobody's that happy—the nightly make-outs on the beach—believe me, there's nothing romantic about sandy hands ....

STACEY: Look, I need to ....

KAREN: *(Running on)* Every time I couldn't take it any more, I'd go off and hide and pretend to talk to you. Really. And you always found something to say to make it bearable.

STACEY: I'm glad. Look ....

KAREN: But that was it, Stay. The end. No more Henley, no more Daddy and Helen, no more Karen Goody-Two-Shoes. As soon as I have that diploma in my hot little hand ... Next summer it's the Grand Canyon with you. I'll bet I can wait tables with the best of them.

STACEY: Karen, this is hard ....

KAREN: God, listen to me, babbling like a waterfall.

STACEY: I have to talk to you.

KAREN: I have Helen's car until the weekend, bless her little pointed head, and tonight I'm taking you out for a lobster dinner like you never imagined in your wildest dreams.

STACEY: *(Firmly)* I can't do that.

KAREN: What?

STACEY: I can't go to dinner with you.

KAREN: Oh. Well, we can make it tomorrow.

STACEY: Not then, either. I can't ....

KAREN: Did I do something wrong?

STACEY: Of course not. It's just ....

KAREN: What's going on?

STACEY: Nothing. I mean... Oh, God, I can't do this. *(Starts to leave)*

KAREN: Can't do what? Stacey. Can't do what?

STACEY: Look, I ... I have to cool it a little.

KAREN: Cool what?

STACEY: Us. I mean ... I can't goof off so much this year, okay?

KAREN: Okay.

STACEY: So I'll see you around. *(Starts to leave)*

KAREN: I did something, didn't I?

STACEY: No.

KAREN: Tell me what I did.

STACEY: Nothing.

KAREN: *(Panic rising)* I don't believe you. Tell me what I did.

STACEY: *(Reaches out to touch her, Pulls back)* It's all right, Karen.

KAREN: It's not all right. Something terrible is happening. You have to tell me ....

STACEY Please, this is hard enough.

KAREN: What's hard enough? What the hell is going on?

STACEY: I have to study, okay? I'm not as smart as you, okay?

KAREN: I could help ....

STACEY: *(Sharply)* Leave it alone.

KAREN: All right. I won't ask questions. Just tell me when we can have dinner.

STACEY: I don't know.

KAREN: Next week? Next month?

STACEY: I don't know. Please ....

KAREN: I'm sorry. Whatever it was, I'm sorry, all right?

STACEY: There's nothing for you to be sorry for.

KAREN: There has to be. You wouldn't ....

STACEY: It doesn't have anything to do with you. It's ... graduate school.

KAREN: Right.

STACEY: So as soon as I can see my way clear, I'll let you know, okay?

KAREN: Right.

STACEY: Good-bye, Karen.

KAREN: *(As Stacey leaves)* Know what, Holcomb? I've been dumped by creeps who did it better than you.

Stacey exits.

RETURN TO PRESENT

Karen decides to give up and go. Retrieves her tote bag from the house, is about to leave when she decides to give it one last try.

(Calls) Stacey! *(No answer)* God damn it, get back here!

STACEY: *(Enters muddy and disheveled. Spots the tote bag.)* Leaving? Have a nice life.

KAREN: You're a mess. What have you been up to?

STACEY: Hosing down Carson McCullers.

KAREN *(Reaches out to wipe the dirt from Stacey's face with her sleeve.)* Did you get in the swamp to do it?

STACEY: *(Brushes her off. Glacial)* Better not. You might have to explain it to the laundry.

KAREN: I'll tell them I was mugged. Stacey, I ... I'm sorry.

STACEY: Everybody's sorry. It's a sorry world.

KAREN: That was the worst thing I've ever done in my life.

STACEY: Lucky you. Lucky me.

KAREN: Do you want me to go?

STACEY: Would it make any difference?

KAREN: If you'd let me explain ....

STACEY: We were doing all right before you came, me and the field mice and C. Mc. C. I had bad moments, but at least they weren't vibrant. Well, thanks for bringing it all back in living color.

KAREN: Stacey, after what we meant to each other, there must be something we can salvage.

STACEY: You want us to be friends.

KAREN: If we can.

STACEY: So you can drop in once a year, or once every ten years, for a little chat? Maybe you'll bring Grant Evans along. Or your children, when you have them. No, you wouldn't bring your children. I might touch them.

KAREN: That was unnecessarily nasty.

STACEY: Ten years ago my world turned to ice. I didn't think I'd make it, but I did. And now you want to finish the job.

KAREN: That's not ....

STACEY: Maybe I'll always be alone, and maybe I'll never be loved, and maybe I'll never open my heart to anyone the way I opened my heart to you. But I'll survive, Karen. Write it in your notebook: I will survive.

KAREN: You have to know I cared. Back then, whatever I did or didn't do, I cared.

STACEY:Your caring is duly noted. Good-bye. *(Turns away)*

KAREN: *(Tries to make a connection)* I've been dumped by creeps who did it better than you.

STACEY: *(Stops, brought up short for a moment, turns angrily.)* Listen to me. What Terry and her cronies did was lousy. They took away my self-respect. They took Wellesley and everything it stood for. But what you did was a thousand times worse.

KAREN: Stacey ....

STACEY: I loved you. I trusted you And when I needed you, you went over to the other side.

KAREN: You threw me out of your life.

STACEY: Because I couldn't bear to say good-bye. What I don't understand is why you had to come here and do it again. I'll say one thing for Terry. With bigots, you always know where you stand.

KAREN: Will you let me explain...

STACEY: You pull me toward you with one hand, and push me away with the other.You kiss me—kiss me, for God's sake—and tell me not to touch you. Maybe Grant Evans gets his jollies out of that little game, but I don't.

KAREN: *(Explodes)* God damn it, you are so self-righteous! Since when does being queer make you morally superior?

STACEY: *(Stunned)* What?

KAREN: Your motives are so bloody pure, aren't they? Instant insight and crystal clarity. I'm not allowed to be confused. When you want to divide the world into the good guys and the bad guys, there's no room for someone who doesn't fit.

STACEY: Look, I ....

KAREN: Did you spend one minute walking in my footprints? Did you ask yourself why I stayed away? Did it ever, for one spilt second, occur to you to wonder what was happening to me? Or did you only want to lick your wounds and count up your grievances against life?

STACEY: No. I'm sorry ....

KAREN: You were the one person in that college, the one person in my life I was close to. You knew things about me no one has ever known, and no one ever will again. And suddenly, for no apparent reason, without a word of explanation, you were gone. And it was "Happy Birthday, Karen", all over again.

STACEY: I couldn't do anything else.

KAREN: I came here to try to make up for what I'd done. Okay, maybe it's too late, but at least I tried. Which is more than you've done in ten years. And all I've gotten from you is hostility and abuse. So if I'm not handling it perfectly, you'll have to excuse me. I'm doing the best I can.

STACEY: You don't know what they did.

KAREN: I know I made a mistake back then. I was a coward, I was wrong. But I don't need you to punish me for it. I've been doing that very nicely for the past ten years. I go along from day to day, filling the minutes of my busy, empty life—and suddenly I remember. The times I stood outside your door, wanting to knock but afraid. Watching you sit alone in the dining room. The day I saw you in the hall and ducked out of sight before you could see me. The nights I lay awake, waiting for Terry to fall asleep so I could cry without her hearing.

STACEY: Look, it's ....

KAREN: I wanted to reach out to you, but I was confused and

frightened. So I ran. I ran to Terry. I ran to Jim Henley. I drank too much, and partied too much. Anything not to be alone. Anything not to think.

STACEY: Karen, it's okay.

KAREN: Don't close me out again, Stacey. I'm not the villain.

STACEY: They went to the Dean about me.

KAREN: They what?

STACEY: Went to the Dean. She gave me a choice. It was you or Wellesley.

KAREN: They went to the Dean?

STACEY: She agreed to let me stay, to keep the whole thing out of my record, if I agreed not to see or talk to you again. If I'd been thrown out of Wellesley for this—no graduate school, no job, no life.

KAREN: I swear, Stay, I didn't know anything about it.

STACEY: Maybe I was wrong to go along with it, but we didn't have a future. A summer, maybe. A year or two after that. Then you'd have gotten married. There's no way you were going to spend the rest of your life with me.

KAREN: My God, what did we let them do to us?

STACEY: When I first began to love you, I told myself it wasn't... that. I knew how wrong it was, even though no one had ever said it. But the words were always there, unspoken. And when she spoke them, it wasn't gently. It's never gently. I wonder what they'd sound like, spoken .... *(Can't go on)*

KAREN: Just now, when I kissed you, I thought I heard them laugh. Have you ever heard that laugh.

STACEY: Plenty of times, outside my door at Wellesley.

KAREN: Oh, Stacey.

STACEY: I wish I could hate you, but I understand. God damn it, I understand.

KAREN: I am sorry.

STACEY: So am I. The Dean said everyone was talking about me. Was it true?

KAREN: I never heard it, except from Terry and her bunch.

STACEY: You might not have heard.

KAREN: I was on House Council our Senior year, remember? They talked about everyone and everything. Penny James cheated on tests. Mona Lawrence filched sweaters from the laundry room. Sue Cox picked her nose. If people were talking, I'd have heard it.

STACEY: And I wasn't ... before that, I wasn't bothering you?

KAREN: Bothering me?

STACEY: Well, she said ... I didn't believe it at first. Later ... well, you know.

KAREN: She never asked me if it were true.

STACEY: Who?

KAREN: Madame Dean. If I was the injured party, why didn't she ask me?

STACEY: I guess Terry was convincing.

KAREN: She didn't care about the truth. Terry brought her that story, and she lapped it up like a cat with a saucer of cream. The woman ought to be locked away. She's a danger to the civilized world.

STACEY: I'm afraid that's a minority opinion. She was revered around there.

KAREN: She played God with your life, and the minute you left her office, I'll bet she never gave you another thought. Or, if she did, you were "that little unpleasantness in Tower Court."

STACEY: I wish I'd been a big unpleasantness. I wish I'd picked up her damned Italian glass paperweight and smashed her face in.You might want to remember that. It's a good thing to focus on while you're begging for your life.

KAREN: Do your parents ....

STACEY: I told them. In a moment of weakness ... or desperation.

KAREN: What did they say?

STACEY: My mother's first reaction was "how could you do this to me?" Then she set out to make me "normal." If you ever need something truly feminine, I have a closet-full of dresses that could get you arrested for prostitution.

KAREN: Do you see them?

STACEY: At the required holiday get-togethers. It's ... difficult.*(A touch of bitter humour)* They don't make Christmas like they used to.

KAREN: Oh, God, Stay, it's all so horrible. Isn't there anything we can <u>do</u> to them?

STACEY: Not that I know of.

KAREN: The whole thing makes me feel so <u>helpless</u>.

STACEY: Yeah. Hey, here we are, ten years later. Maybe that's the best revenge. How about another of these swell sandwiches?

KAREN: You expect me to <u>eat</u>?

STACEY: It's my way of making up.

KAREN: Forcing me to choke down a dried-up bread and salmonella-infested mayonnaise and cheese sandwich which I probably have to make myself?

STACEY: We could share a joint.

KAREN: You have marijuana? Here?

STACEY: In the house.

KAREN: My God, you could be arrested.

STACEY: Busted. Popular usage is 'busted'.

KAREN: Where did you get it?

STACEY: Appreciative student. I gave him a passing grade he didn't deserve to keep him out of Vietnam for one more year.

KAREN: In <u>our</u> day, we showed our appreciation by inviting the faculty to Wednesday afternoon tea. You really smoke that?

STACEY: Once in a while I get wrecked and discover Great Truths, which I promptly forget.

KAREN: What's it like?

STACEY: Your mind goes kind of slippery, like Mazola oil. Then it narrows down to a pin-point of concentration. You sort of become whatever you're focusing on.

KAREN: With my luck, I'd be contemplating a flu germ.

STACEY: Well, it's not the same for everyone.I wonder how it'd be to go to a reunion stoned.

KAREN: Let's do it. I mean it. Let's.

STACEY: I don't know. Dope makes me mellow.

KAREN: Forget that. Have you ever been back? Stoned or sober?

STACEY: Popular usage is "straight."

KAREN: Have you?

STACEY: Once, in the summer, when everyone was gone.I guess it was kind of like slipping a Band-Aid off a sore to see if it had healed.

KAREN: Had it?

STACEY: I walked from Tower up through the Arboretum ... remember that little waterfall in the Arboretum? The one we used to have picnics beside? Did you know you can turn it off with a valve at the top, just over the hill? Do you think there's a message in that?

KAREN: I'm sure of it, and I don't want to know what it is.

STACEY: I went down to Tupelo Point, along the path by the lake, and up the steps to our courtyard. I pretended it was 1954 again, and none of it had happened, and I was meeting you by the sundial ....

KAREN: Meeting me?

STACEY: *(Quickly)* Then it all came back ... wondering who knows, what they think, feeling invisible and conspicuous at the same time. And all the while there was the lake, and the carillon tower against the sky, all of it looking so calm and honorable .... People ruin everything, don't they? Well, *(Indicates her home)* they can't ruin this.

KAREN: How could they? They can't get down the driveway. So, this is your life, Stacey Holcomb.

STACEY: This is my life. I teach, I come home. Except for demonstrations. I'm very big on demonstrations. Something make you angry? Call me. I can have 700 rugged, ragged undergraduates there in half an hour.

KAREN: We should have done more of that at Wellesley.

STACEY: We should have done any of it. Our idea of Social Action was one afternoon a month, volunteering at a Roxbury settlement house.

KAREN: I'm ashamed to say that's more than I do now.

STACEY: That doesn't sound like you.

KAREN: Well, the people I know think there's something quaint and amusing about "bleeding hearts," as they call them. I guess I got tired of jokes about "Karen's latest craze."

STACEY: I thought the Suburban Set had better manners.

KAREN: It's money they have, not manners.

STACEY: What do they do with their time?

KAREN: Meet for lunch, dress for dinner, and update the living room drapes.

STACEY: How about you?

KAREN: I do my share. I don't like it, but I do it.

STACEY: And for the rest of your life?

KAREN: Marry Grant Evans, I guess.

STACEY:That'll take up a good hour. More, if you have an elaborate reception. Then what?

KAREN *(A little defensive)* I don't know "then what."

STACEY: I want you to be happy, that's all.

KAREN: Well, I'm not happy, and I probably won't be happy, so what do you suggest I do about it?

STACEY: Find something to feel passionate about, I guess.

KAREN: And how does one do that? Whip over to Bloomingdale's?

STACEY: Cut it out, Karen. I'm on your side.

KAREN: I'm sorry. I ...*(Spots something offstage.)* I could feel passionate about that. What is it?

STACEY: *(Looking)* Carson McCullers. For God's sake, she swamped again. I'm going to kill you, McCullers. I mean it. I'm going to flush your head down the toilet.

KAREN: That's the biggest dog I ever saw. It looks like a cross between a Great Dane and a Wooly Mammoth.

STACEY: *(Proudly)* Salt of the earth.

KAREN: She's not of the earth. She is the earth. Is she dangerous?

STACEY: Only if you make a threatening move.

KAREN: Who, me? I love her. She's so ugly.

STACEY: That dog is a work of art.

KAREN: Picasso. Want to take her to the reunion?

STACEY: Want her in your car? Karen, what are you going to do about your life? *(No response)* You can't marry that man if you don't love him. *(No response)* For crying out loud, it'll be Henley all over again.You can't go around marrying people just to please them.

KAREN: Why not? Women have been doing that for thousands of years.

STACEY: Karen.

KAREN: I don't know what else to do, Stay.

STACEY: Change your name and disappear. Join the Army. Go to San Francisco and become a Flower Child. Get a law degree. Run for President. Claim you talked to God and start a new religion. Anything.

KAREN:I hope your teaching duties don't include vocational counseling.

STACEY: I mean it. Don't throw yourself away.

KAREN: Marriage is throwing yourself away?

STACEY: It is if you don't love ....

KAREN: *(Dryly)* Love. Which you don't do any more.

STACEY: Which I don't.

KAREN: And that's that.

STACEY: That's that.

KAREN: No more love.

STACEY: No more. All gone.

KAREN: It's such a waste.

STACEY: And now the world is diminished. Poor world. Well, that's what happens when you don't take care of your toys.

KAREN: Stop it.

STACEY: What do you want me to do, walk around with my wrists bleeding?

KAREN: You used to be so gentle.

STACEY: And look where that got me.

KAREN: It got you me.

STACEY: Temporarily.

KAREN: Talking to you was always safe. It made other things possible. I always knew who I was around you. Even when I was confused, I knew it was real, and it was all right.

STACEY: Of course it was all right. But don't you see, Karen, what happened to us—and what we did with it—says a lot about the world we live in.

KAREN: I don't want to believe that.

STACEY: Believe it. Last spring I went down to Selma, to the Civil Rights March. There were eight of us, camped out in an old barn. The night before the march, we sat around in the half-dark, talking and singing to keep up our nerve. I told them. I don't know why. There was a silence. A long silence. I looked at them, one after another. Looked into their eyes. And every one of those brave, young, ready-to-die-for-justice liberals looked away. Every one. Like locks closing. Click, click, click, click.... In the morning, when they left for Selma, I left for home.

KAREN: Stacey.

STACEY: I stopped at the kennel to pick up Carson. The minute she saw me, she bounded across the room, her silly tail going in circles. She jumped up and put her paws on my shoulders. And she looked right into my eyes. *(Begins to cry.)*

KAREN: *(Reaches out to touch her tentitively)* Please forgive me.

STACEY: I didn't want to love you. I couldn't help it.

KAREN: Neither could I. Take my hand, Stay.

Stacey does. Karen embraces her.

(After a while) Why couldn't you fall in love with someone who deserves you? I love you, Stacey.

STACEY: *(Forces herself to pull away.)* If you ever write your memoirs, today should merit an entire chapter. *(To cover her shakiness)* Sure I can't get you something? Beer? Another Coke?

KAREN: No, thanks.

STACEY: I apologize for breaking down like that. It really isn't like me to be maudlin. Actually, it's exactly like me, but I try not to do it in public. Of course, you're not exactly public ....

KAREN: Are you nervous?

STACEY: Nervous? Yes, I'm nervous. As a matter of fact, I've reached a whole new level of nervous.

KAREN: Well, I get nervous, too. But where I come from we're not supposed to show it.

STACEY: Do people <u>live</u> in Greenwich, or do they only stop by to mow the lawn?

KAREN: They live there. And <u>they</u> don't mow the lawn. They hire the less fortunate to do that. The meaning of life among the upper classes is to maintain the fiction that wealth and beauty are synonymous. Therefore, one is not allowed to sweat, sneeze, grieve, have problems, gain weight, grow old—except gracefully—be in a bad mood, or succumb to debilitating illness.

STACEY: Now I know why I don't live there.

KAREN: You don't live there because you're queer.

STACEY: They wouldn't let me join the Country Club?

KAREN: Child, they wouldn't let you join the Public Library.

STACEY: Do you enjoy living like that?

KAREN I was born to it. It's easy for me.

STACEY: Is that an answer?

KAREN: Not really. No, I don't like it I'm used to it. But sometimes I feel as if I'm on a collision course with disaster.

STACEY: You are. You're about to marry Grant Evans.

KAREN: Stay, may I tell you something?

STACEY: Sure.

KAREN: Some mornings, when I wake up, I wish I were....

STACEY: This isn't Westchester County. It's all right to say dead.

KAREN: Do you ever feel that way?

STACEY: Old friend, there have been periods of my life when I've dealt with suicide on a day-to-day basis.

KAREN: Because you're a lesbian?

STACEY: Because I'm lonely.

KAREN: What do you do about it?

STACEY: Paint the woodwork. A totally mindless activity requiring complete concentration.

KAREN: Does it work?

STACEY: It passes the time. Rather like the living room drapes, I suspect.

KAREN: The living room drapes are an end in themselves.

STACEY: You know, for all its drawbacks, I think I prefer my life to yours.

KAREN: Well, it expresses you.

STACEY: And you?

KAREN: I told you, I don't know. Believe me, I'd give everything I ever had, have now, or stand to inherit in the future for one minute of crystal clarity.

STACEY: A momentary lifting of the veil of ambiguity, as it were.

KAREN: *(Laughs)* "As it were." Lord, I haven't heard that in ten years.

STACEY: Now I see your problem. Your world lacks intellectual pretension.

KAREN: Who used to say "as if were?" Strong in Sociology? Havens in Economics?

STACEY Something we both took. It was ... it was ....

BOTH: Vining! Modern European History!

STACEY: My God, that woman was a terror. I must have repressed her.

KAREN: Every time she called on me, I'd be so panic-stricken my stomach would cramp up to the size and texture of a walnut.

STACEY: You always seemed perfectly composed.

KAREN: I'm a phoney.

STACEY:*(Starting for the house)* Well, my hunger's real enough.

KAREN: You wouldn't be hungry if you'd eaten lunch. Let me do it. If you don't get at least one exam graded, I'll never forgive myself.

STACEY: You'll think I only invited you here to do the cooking.

KAREN: Stacey, you didn't invite me.

STACEY: Right, you barged in. In that case ....

KAREN: On the other hand, you're not too crazy about my cooking.

STACEY: I am so. I was being a brat.

KAREN: Any requests? Or should I whip up some good old Wellesley barf-on-a-bun?

STACEY: *(Holds up old sandwich)* Let's try whatever this was before it died.

Karen goes into the house. Stacey picks up a blue book and makes a stab at working, but is all to aware of Karen's presence and her own pleasure at having her there.

KAREN: *(Offstage)* Cheese and mustard?

STACEY: Mayo.

KAREN: Not this Mayo. It's gone off.

STACEY: It was all right an hour ago.

KAREN: *(Entering with jar)* Well, it went off in the meantime. You can see through it.

STACEY: All right, mustard.

Karen goes back inside. Stacey goes back to work.

KAREN: *(Offstage)* Plain or spicy-brown.

STACEY: Spicy-brown.

KAREN: Swiss or munster?

STACEY: I thought the point of this was to let me work.

KAREN: You want me to decide, then?

STACEY: I want you to decide.

KAREN: *(After a moment)* Stacey?

STACEY: Yes, Karen?

KAREN: This is fun, isn't it?

STACEY: Yes, Karen. *(Looking at blue book)* How do you spell acquiesce?

KAREN: A-c-q-u-i-e-s-c-e.

STACEY: *(Corrects blue book)* Functional illiterate.

KAREN: Should I feed Carson McCullers?

STACEY: Sure. It's too early for dinner, but there's a knuckle bone in a paper bag.

KAREN: *(After a moment)* I can't find it.

STACEY: Oh, it's on the porch.

KAREN: *(Enters, finding bag on porch looks in, recoils in horror.)* My God, that's revolting. It smells like an open grave. It looks like an open grave. Are you trying to kill that beautiful dog?

STACEY: Rancid meat's good for them. Keeps their intestinal bacteria alive.

KAREN: I don't want to know about that.

STACEY: You have them, too.

KAREN: There are no living things in my intestines.

STACEY: Suit yourself. You don't have to touch that. *(Bone)* Just dump it in her dish by the back door.

KAREN: *(As she exits, holding the bag delicatley by two fingers.) Godzilla Meets Carson McCullers*. I think I'm going to be sick.

STACEY: Country living takes some getting used to.

Stacey goes back to work. in a few seconds, Karen enters with a joint.

KAREN: Stacey, is this what I think it is?

STACEY: Depends on what you think it is.

KAREN: A marijuana cigarette.

STACEY: Popular usage is "joint."

KAREN: That bloody thing out there is a joint.

STACEY: This is also a joint. Where'd you find it?

KAREN: In the cupboard over the sink, in an olive jar. That's a very strange place to keep something like this.

STACEY: It's illegal. I can't leave it in the middle of the coffee table.

KAREN: Popular usage is "cocktail table." *(Starts to unwrap it)* How do you work it?

STACEY: For God's sake, don't destroy it!

KAREN: Smells funny.

STACEY: Not to the cops. Listen, are you in a hurry to get back?

KAREN: Not particularly.

STACEY: Want to get wrecked and discover Great Truths which

we'll promptly forget?

KAREN: Shouldn't we eat first?

STACEY: Take a good drag on that, and you'll fight McCullers for the bone.

KAREN: We'll eat first.

Karen exits. Stacey goes back to work. Terry enters decked out in her reunion best.

STACEY: *(Looks up)* Holy shit.

TERRY: Is Karen around?

STACEY: Making lunch. Excuse me, but what the hell are you doing here?

TERRY: You should have come to the reunion. <u>Everyone's</u> there.

STACEY: If this keeps up, everyone'll be <u>here</u>.

TERRY: *(Starts for the house calling)* Karen!

STACEY: I wouldn't disturb her if I were you. She's a bear when she's cooking.

TERRY: You know this from experience, of course.

STACEY: Think this is the first time she's cooked for me? Silly girl.

TERRY: In this house?

STACEY: In that very kitchen.

TERRY: I see. *(Starts for the house)*

STACEY: *(Casually blocks her way)* So, how's every little thing, Beck?

TERRY: Fabuloso. *(Starts for the house again)*

STACEY: I hear you're moving to Europe.

TERRY: Yes, we are.

STACEY: France?

TERRY: Belgium. God, I hope it's <u>clean</u>.

STACEY: And for the moment you reside in ....

TERRY: San Francisco.

STACEY: That's nice. Good climate and all. Bet you'll be sorry to go.

TERRY: Hardly. Between the Hippies and the homosexuals, it's not safe to go out on the street.

STACEY: Yeah, homosexuals can get pretty nasty. Your husband's in what, banking?

TERRY: International finance.

STACEY: International finance. I'm impressed. By the by, old sport, I have something that belongs to you. *(Brings out a knife)* You left this in my back.

TERRY: *(Barely glances at it. Heads for the house.)* What's she doing in there?

STACEY: Hard telling. Hope she hasn't decided to do the laundry.

TERRY: We don't have all day. *(Calls)* Karen!

Karen enters with sandwiches.

KAREN: I don't believe this.

STACEY: Believe it.

KAREN: *(To Terry)* You followed me.

TERRY: Why did you leave the reunion?

KAREN: Get out of here, Terry.

TERRY: Right in the middle of everything. God, that's rude.

KAREN: Rude.

TERRY: Everybody was asking where you went.

KAREN: So you came trotting on out here like a good little Girl Scout? Well, you can turn right around and trot on back.

TERRY: Are you coming with me?

KAREN: What?!

TERRY: Are you ....

KAREN: I heard you the first time.

TERRY: Then come on.

KAREN: *(Blowing up)* Damn it, Terry. You weren't invited here. You don't belong here. Get out.

TERRY: Karen ....

KAREN: Get out !!

STACEY: *(To Terry)* Do you see this lady? She is a very angry lady. She is angry at you. She doesn't want you here. She wants you to go away. Can you say that? "Go away?'

TERRY: Very funny. Karen, are we going to the reunion or ....

KAREN: FUCK YOURSELF !!

STACEY: The angry lady wants you to fuck yourself. Do you know what those words mean? Do you know how to do that?

TERRY: *(To Karen)* I'm worried about you.

KAREN: *(To Stacey, handing her the sandwich)* We were out of spicy-brown.

TERRY: Karen.

KAREN: *(To Stacey)* Want a Coke with that?

STACEY: Long as you're up. Ever tried Karen's cooking, Beck? Fabuloso.

TERRY: *(To Karen)* We really should get back.

KAREN: Go.

TERRY: I'm not going without you.

KAREN: *(Calls)* McCullers! Kill!

TERRY: It's our tenth reunion.

STACEY: Can't argue with logic like that.

KAREN: Screw our tenth reunion.

TERRY: You don't mean that.

KAREN: GET OUT OF HERE!!

TERRY: *(Trying to draw Karen aside)* Karen, this doesn't look good.

KAREN: What?

TERRY: You know what they used to say about her ....

KAREN: Who used to say?

TERRY: You know.

KAREN: No, I don't know. Who used to say what?

TERRY: About her. And other girls.

KAREN:*(Deadly)* Her and what other girls, Terry? Other girls like me?

TERRY: I don't know what you're upset about.

KAREN: Don't you?

TERRY: Come on, Karen. We don't have time to play games.

KAREN: Weren't you satisfied throwing dirt? Or was it your way of kissing up to the Dean?

TERRY: *(Turns on Stacey)* Did you tell her about that?

STACEY: *(Taken aback)* What?

TERRY: That was none of Karen's business.

KAREN: Let me get this straight. You're angry with Stacey because she told me you screwed her to the wall?

TERRY: It didn't have anything to do with you.

KAREN: It had everything to do with me.

TERRY: Because she involved you.

KAREN: I don't have a mind of my own?

TERRY: Typical. You spend five minutes with her, and suddenly everything's my fault.

KAREN: Do you know what you did to her?

TERRY: Every time you get around her, it makes you strange.

KAREN: Do you know what you did?

STACEY: Of course she knows.

KAREN: I'll never forgive you for that.

TERRY: See? All she has to do is look pathetic.

KAREN: Get out of my life, Terry.

TERRY: She never liked me. Right from the start, she thought she was better than me.

KAREN: She is better than you.

TERRY: There's no point in talking to you if you're just going to be defensive.

KAREN: What gives you the right to sit in judgment?

TERRY: Come on, Karen. You know she wasn't good for you. Everybody knew....

KAREN: And you decided to do something about that, is that right?

TERRY: Roughly.

KAREN: But you didn't bother to tell me.

TERRY: I didn't want to upset you.

KAREN: You self-righteous ....

TERRY: You know how you are when you're upset.

KAREN: ... self-serving PRIG.

TERRY: Be real.

KAREN: Real? You want real?

STACEY: *(As Karen is about to go at Terry)* Easy. She's not worth that.

TERRY: *(To Karen)* For God's sake, you know what she is.

KAREN: Yes, I know.

TERRY: Did you want them to say the same things about you? That could follow you around for the rest of your life.

KAREN: It's my life!

TERRY: You didn't know what you were doing. People like her suck you in before you know it. You should be grateful to me.

KAREN: Grateful?

TERRY: And what about Wellesley? You don't want people to call it a Queer College, do you?

KAREN: Stacey loved Wellesley. She worked harder to get there, and stay there, than you or I ever worked for anything. Wellesley stood for something for her. A way of being that was above pettiness. Above nastiness, and meanness. But you brought it down into the dirt.

TERRY: Well, excuse me for living in the real world.

KAREN: You live in the mud, Terry. Like a worm.You and your precious Dean.

STACEY: Karen, you don't have to fight this battle for me.

KAREN: Yes, I do.

TERRY: It's not my fault if Wellesley didn't live up to her expectations. She wanted too much.

KAREN: She wanted to believe in Honor. That isn't very much.

STACEY: Listen, this is kind of embarrassing.

KAREN: Eat your lunch.

TERRY: It's really nauseating, the way you protect her.

KAREN: What you see here is love.

TERRY: Oh, right. Know what I think? I think what I see here is something very familiar.

KAREN: Terry, you are so slimey.

STACEY: Please, not while I'm eating.

TERRY: I'm not ashamed of what I did. Somebody had to stop her.

KAREN: Why?

TERRY: She's queer.

KAREN: Is that a crime?

STACEY: As a matter of fact, it is.

KAREN: Grade your papers.

STACEY: "Eat your lunch. Grade your papers." Jeez.

TERRY: Look, are we going to the reunion, or ....

KAREN: NO, I AM NOT GOING TO THE REUNION!!

TERRY: People will wonder.

KAREN: *(Beginning to get hysterical)* Then let them wonder. My God, let them wonder ....

TERRY: All right, Karen, calm down. We'll discuss this rationally.

KAREN: I don't want to discuss it rationally. I want you to go. I want you to leave me alone.

STACEY: *(Goes to Karen)* Hey, kid, take it easy.

KAREN: *(To Terry)* I loved her.

STACEY: Don't.

KAREN: *(Ignores Stacey)* She was everything safe and honest in my life. And you ruined it. You put your dirty hands on it, and broke it into little pieces, and I'm trying to put it back together, and I almost had it ... I almost had it and you had to come here and ....

TERRY: She's queer, Karen.

KAREN Look at her. She's a human being. She has a dog. She teaches. She laughs, and bleeds, and cries. But the only thing you care about is whether she lives up to your standards.Well, maybe some other people don't live up to your standards, either.

STACEY: *(To Karen)* Stop it.

TERRY: *(To Stacey)* This is between me and Karen.

KAREN: *(To Terry)* Get out of here before you ruin it again.

TERRY: Ruin what? *(Silence)* Ruin what, Holcomb?

STACEY: Nothing.

TERRY: Picking up where you left off?

KAREN: That's right.

STACEY: *(To Karen)* You don't know what you're saying.

KAREN: I know exactly what I'm saying.

STACEY: You're overwrought.

KAREN: I want it out in the open.

TERRY: How'd you get her here, Holcomb? Did you tape a note to her door, the way you used to back at Wellesley? "Karen, meet you at the Well at four. Going to the Libe. See you there. One of the kids from Modern Drama's cooking Southern at Tizzie tonight. Want to join me?"

STACEY: The woman has a photographic memory.

TERRY: Or was it a long, sensitive letter like you wrote her in France?

KAREN: You read my mail?

TERRY: *(Ignoring Karen, to Stacey)* She always showed up, didn't she? All you had to do was name the time and place.

KAREN: I wanted to be with her.

TERRY: *(Still at Stacey)* People of your persuasion are good at getting someone all to yourself, aren't you?

KAREN: I loved her.

STACEY: Karen, this is serious ....

KAREN: I love you.

TERRY: *(To Karen)* She's turning you against me again.

KAREN: You managed that on your own. Any time you don't get your way you whine, and complain, and manipulate. I roomed with you for four years because it was easier than listening to you whine.

TERRY: That's a lie.

KAREN: Want to bet?

TERRY: We had a good time together, before she came along.

KAREN: You had a good time.

TERRY: I did a lot for you back at Wellesley. I didn't turn you in that night you came in late and let her sign in for you. I could have gotten in a lot of trouble for that.

KAREN: For God's sake.

TERRY: When I went to the Dean about her, I kept you out of it. Doesn't that count for anything?

KAREN: No.

TERRY: Whatever I did, I did for you. If she hadn't changed you....

KAREN: She didn't change me. I changed. I got sick of you and your happy band of argyle knitters.

TERRY: When you married Henley, you asked me to be your Maid of Honor.

KAREN: *(Laughs a little hysterically)* Honor!

TERRY: I supported you through your divorce, remember? We talked on the phone almost every day.

KAREN: You called me.

TERRY: You didn't hang up. You were glad enough to talk.

KAREN: Who was I supposed to talk to? Stacey? I couldn't talk to Stacey, could I? You made sure of that.

TERRY: You were my friend first. You belonged to me.

KAREN: I don't belong to anyone.

STACEY: There's nothing nastier than a lovers' quarrel.

KAREN: *(What Stacey said hits home)* That's it, isn't it? That's been it all along.

TERRY: What?

KAREN: Stacey was your rival.

TERRY: Don't make me sick.

KAREN: From the minute you met her, you hunched over me and growled like a German Shepherd with a bone.

TERRY: Don't put me in the same class with her.

KAREN: Don't worry. You'll never be in the same class.

TERRY: I can still make trouble for you, Karen.

KAREN: Go ahead.

STACEY: *(To Karen)* You don't mean that. You're out of control.

KAREN: I mean it.

TERRY: I wonder what Grant would say if he knew you and Holcomb ....

KAREN: Tell him.

STACEY: Karen ....

KAREN: And while you're at it, remind him that you and I roomed together for four years. Let's see what he makes of that.

TERRY: Let's. *(Starts to leave)*

KAREN: Tell him! Tell the entire class of '56. Take out an ad in the God damn New York Times.

STACEY: *(Reaches for her)* Take it easy.

KAREN: KAREN MARTIN IS QUEER!!! Am I getting through to you, Beck?

TERRY: *(Exiting)* Loud. And. Clear.

Karen starts after her.

STACEY: Stop it, now. Calm down.

KAREN: *(Still shouting)* I loved Stacey Holcomb. I still love Stacey Holcomb. I'm queer, Beck. Eat it raw!

STACEY: *(Gently, holding on to Karen)* You really did it this time, pal. Didn't your stepmother ever tell you to count to ten before you pop off? *(No response as Karen begins to realize what she did)* Hey, it's okay. Kind of a mess right now, but we'll think of something.

KAREN: Oh, God.

STACEY: What say we hop into my old Ford V-8 and run her off the road? We'll take McCullers along. Think of it, the last thing she sees before the lights go out is Carson's drooling jowls. There's an image to carry into eternity. I wonder what Doris Day would do in a situation like this. Well, que será será.

KAREN: I'm sorry I got you involved.

STACEY: Hell, the woods are full of people like Terry. Turn over a rotten log and out they come. I can't spend the rest of my life being careful. If she tells, she tells.

KAREN: It could mean your job.

STACEY: I've always wanted to see California. Any place Beck's moving to Europe to get away from can't be all bad. I could like Hippies and homosexuals. What are you going to do?

KAREN: I don't know.

STACEY: Even as we speak, Terry is speeding toward our Alma Mater, gossip burning a hole in her tongue. This is not the moment to be obsessive.

KAREN: I mean, it depends on you.

STACEY: What?

KAREN: Is "no more love" a permanent condition? Or just a phase you're going through?

STACEY: What?

KAREN: I love you, Stacey.

STACEY: What?

KAREN: Will you stop with the "what-what-what"? You sound like a percolator.

STACEY: I thought you only said that to annoy Terry.

KAREN: No one ever takes me seriously. No one ever did. Not you, not my family, not even Terry. Do you know how crazy that makes me? Do you know what it's like when no one takes you seriously?

STACEY: I'm sorry.

KAREN: If you need time to think it over, I'll just go out back and smoke this swell marijuana cigarette.

STACEY: You ... uh ... love me.

KAREN: Right.

STACEY: You're considering ... a future with me?

KAREN: Right again.

STACEY: You're not afraid?

KAREN: Terrified. But the bridges are crossed and burned, it's a brand new day, so why not reach for the moon?

STACEY: Mixed metaphor.

KAREN: Dear God, in a world full of dime store clerks and car hops, why did you make me fall in love with a knee-jerk English teacher?

STACEY: Karen, I ....

KAREN: Look, I don't mean to back you into a corner, but I'd sincerely like to be out of Daddy's subsidized apartment before Terry drops her bomb. Daddy Dear hates bad news, and he's been known to turn foul when things don't go his way. Life in Greenwich isn't all white duck pants and Sperry Top-Siders. Anyway, at the risk of appearing cowardly, I'd prefer to handle the fall-out from a nice, safe distance. So wherever I'm going, I'd better get there in one speedy-quick damn hurry.

STACEY: Do you want to stay here?

KAREN: Well, that depends, you see. It could be the Best of All Possible Worlds. On the other hand, I'm going to have enough problems. I don't need to spend every day eating my heart out from unrequited love. I'd want to <u>see</u> you no matter what, in a friendly sort of way, but on a daily, mundane, domestic basis—I think not, thanks.

STACEY: I'd ....

KAREN: Money's going to be a problem. Wouldn't you know it, when the sky falls in, it happens on a Saturday. I have my own account, but Daddy plays golf with the bank president on alternate Sundays, and men do have a way of sticking together, don't they?

STACEY: I can help with money.

KAREN: Then there's the future to think about. I didn't know being queer meant making so many decisions. Must be why it's so unpopular. Okay, start slow. Graduate courses in summer school, think about law school for the fall.Is your program any good?

STACEY: Good enough, I th ....

KAREN: Scholarship. <u>That'll</u> be a new experience. It's <u>all</u> going to be new, isn't it? Today is the first day of the rest of my life, or whatever they say. *(A nervous laugh)* Little Karen Martin from Greenwich. Oh, my God.

STACEY: I'll bet you're not the first.

KAREN: Well, I hate to run this into the ground, but could you give me some idea of how things stand with us? Keeping in mind, of course, that I'm totally naive about these things, and not much of a bargain, and would probably be a bit of a burden until I get the hang of it, but I am a fast learner, I think. Did I mess it up for good back at old W.C.? I mean, what are the chances that "no love, no nothing" was just a lot of face-saving bullshit?

STACEY: Yes. No....

KAREN: Yes-no what?

STACEY: Yes, it wasn't ... you didn't ....

KAREN: *(Jumps to conclusion)* Hey, it's my own fault. I had my chance.

STACEY: Will you let me get a word in edgewise? You didn't mess it up.

KAREN: Meaning?

STACEY: Meaning I ... I ....

KAREN: You can't even say it, for crying out loud. No wonder we screwed up back at Wellesley.

STACEY: What do you expect? I've spent the last ten years try ing not to say it.

KAREN: Big deal. I've spent the last ten years trying not to know it. Okay, you have ten seconds to say it or not, or I'm leaving.

STACEY:*(After a long pause, as Karen turns to go)* I-love-you.

KAREN: That's a start. Now do it right.

STACEY: *(Embracing her)* I love you, Karen. I love you, I love you, I love you.

KAREN: Twenty-five corny responses just ran through my head.

STACEY: See? You should have majored in English.

KAREN: Stay? It'll be all right, won't it?

STACEY: It'll be all right.It might even be fun.

KAREN: You don't mind that I've ... been around?

STACEY: You're the most bizarre woman I've ever met.

KAREN: There's just one thing—how many beds do you have?

STACEY: One.

KAREN: From now on, Carson McCullers sleeps on the floor.

THE END

Base Camp

Introduction

This is one of several plays about being afraid to love and to be loved, a theme which manages to creep into most of my plays. It's one of my earlier plays, and has been rewritten several times. It's also the play in which I found my "voice."

I don't want to say I was "experimenting with language" in this play. That's altogether too high-falutin' for what I was actually doing. I was playing with language, enjoying the sounds of words and the challenge of putting words to thoughts and impressions. You'll see Meredith do this several times. When I had finished it, I realized that I finally felt in command of my language, comfortable, as if I had worked out with it and worked it out.

I faced two major challenges while writing this play. The first was to make it very clear that Meredith was not just hiding away on a mountaintop to lick her wounds. I had to show that—if anything—the devastating break-up with Claire only served as a catalyst to her actually making the move. I tried to show this in two ways: directly though her speeches relating how she feels about her life, and indirectly through more subtle devices such as Claire "knowing" Meredith would be at Rockchuck Lodge.

The second problem was Claire herself. If Meredith was to be a strong person (and I think she is), how could Claire bruise her so badly that she would be afraid to let herself love or be loved? One way, of course, would be to undermine her faith in herself. The best way to undermine someone's belief in herself is to make her think she's crazy, and one of the best ways to do that is by constantly changing her reality—to put it bluntly, "mindrape." Well, we've all had more than enough experience with that kind of thing, so it was relatively simple from then on.

Not so simple for the actor playing Claire, though. Because Claire—and by extension the actor playing her—has to believe in herself. She can spin her web consciously, taking some perverse pleasure in hanging Meredith's sanity out to dry. Or it can be unconscious, a reaction to the loneliness of her life and her hurt and anger at Meredith's rejection of her advances. Or she might be operating out of some motive I haven't even thought of. The choice is up to the actor and the director.

There are some technical inconveniences in this play which point up how much one takes for granted while sailing along in one's head, writing away, not asking oneself "can this be done?" Which is why, if you're going to write plays, going through the actual process of putting on your play will teach you more than all the graduate writing courses you can find.

The two problems here are: set—a Dreaded Kitchen Play—and props. Not just props, but <u>food</u>. Food is a terribly tricky thing on stage. If it's there and no one eats it, it stands out. I don't know of any other prop that attracts attention by <u>not</u> being used, the way food does. (Except maybe guns, and I haven't written a play with guns.) Then, if you <u>do</u> use it, all sorts of terrible things can happen. An actor takes a bite of sandwich, then realizes she has the next line. Does she spit it out? Smile bravely and try to speak around it? Or sit there in silence—a silence like the silence that will follow Armageddon—and chew?

And what kind of food? Actors, being as neurotic, persnickety, and pedantic as the rest of us, can display an amazing array of allergies, dislikes, and disapproval where food is concerned. To say nothing of the practical problems. There are foods which turn into disgusting things when left exposed to air and stage lights. Foods which render the lips dry and the tongue immobile. Foods which cause fits of coughing. Foods which stick to the teeth. Foods which fling themselves from forks with wild abandon. Foods which stick to serving spoons with the tenacity of Super Glue. Breakfast is the worst. In the two productions of *Base Camp* which I've seen, cottage cheese with yellow food coloring, and Rice-A-Roni were used as substitutes for eggs. Neither was exactly fun for the cast.

Don't get me wrong. These aren't insurmountable problems. Actually they can be a challenge—part of the frustration which is part of the fun of theater. If we didn't have these minor frustrations, what would we reminisce about?

CAST OF CHARACTERS

MEREDITH BRYANT, owner of Rockchuck Lodge, an ex-teacher in her late 20's.

LIZ RAYMO, mountain climbing guide and Meredith's friend.

NATALIE WENNIGER, recently divorced.

CLAIRE STODDARD, Meredith's ex-lover, now married to the president of Stoddard Industries.

PAULA PRYOR, married to a junior executive at Stoddard Industries.

PLACE: In the living room and kitchen of Rockchuck Lodge, in the Bitterroot Mountains near Anaconda, Montana. It is a typical tourist lodge, knotty pine and Indian rug motif. The living room contains comfortable chairs, book shelves, a fireplace, desk, and typewriter. Exits lead to the outside, to Meredith's room, and to the kitchen. The kitchen contains tables and chairs, a wood-burning stove for cooking and heat, cupboards, sink, and counter space. Exits lead to the living room and staff quarters. An off-stage exit leads from the staff dormitory to the outside.

TIME: The present, during a three-day blizzard in mid-October.

ACT ONE

SCENE 1: Late afternoon **SCENE 2:** The next morning

SCENE 3: After dinner that night.

ACT TWO

SCENE 1: The next morning **SCENE 2:** That night

SCENE 3: Early next morning. **SCENE 4:** Later that morning

ACT ONE

SCENE 1: It is late afternoon at Rockchuck Lodge. The lodge is closed for the season. The bright, angled sun of late afternoon pours through the windows. Meredith is alone in the kitchen. She pours herself a cup of coffee, carries it into the living room, adds a log to the fire and sits behind her typewriter to work.

Liz enters.

LIZ: Busy?

MEREDITH: (*Surprised*) Not really.

LIZ: (*Realizes she just barged in*) I'm sorry. I get so used to walking in....

MEREDITH: (*Indicates it's okay*) I thought you were through for the season.

LIZ: Please! It hurts when I laugh!

MEREDITH: Uh-oh. You're not having a good time.

LIZ: I'm having a <u>terrific</u> time. I love post-season trips. The gentle patter of sleet on tent canvas. The thrill of bathing in an icy stream. The soft murmur of tourists griping around the campfire. I wish I'd known, when I married Tony, I was marrying Rockchuck Mountain, too.

MEREDITH: Coffee?

LIZ: (*Flings herself into a chair*) No, thanks.

MEREDITH: It'll settle your nerves.

LIZ: The only thing your coffee would settle is an argument.

MEREDITH: Don't be abusive.

LIZ: (*Takes Meredith's cup, tries it*) Not bad. (*Keeps it*)

MEREDITH: You're working?

LIZ: You guessed 'er, Chester. Haulin' a party up this here good ole mountain.

MEREDITH: What kind of a party?

LIZ: A Bar Mitzvah. Jesus, Meredith.

MEREDITH: That's what I love about you. Your irrepressible good humor.

LIZ: Tony was learning to use a razor again. I was about to take a course in remedial reading. It's been so long since I've read a book I've deteriorated to third-grade level. The phone rang. It's safe to answer the phone after October first, right? Wrong. Good news, kids. Got a job for you.

MEREDITH: You could have refused.

LIZ: They made us an offer we couldn't pass up.

MEREDITH: Such as?

LIZ: Do it, or take up sheep-herding.

MEREDITH: Come on.

LIZ: Those Anaconda outfitters stick together like sand in cement. We'd be blackballed in the Bitterroot Range. Probably in the whole Rocky Mountains. Probably in the entire damned continental United States.

MEREDITH: If you made this your base camp, you could make your own decisions. And save three days' travel time.

LIZ: Let's not go around on that again.

MEREDITH: I've been asking you for years.

LIZ: We have no stock, and no equipment. Are we supposed to ask Santa Claus ....

MEREDITH: I can help.

LIZ: Damn it, Meredith! You know Tony.

MEREDITH: I know Tony. How long will it be?

LIZ: Another winter of teaching. Another summer of climbing. Maybe.

MEREDITH: We're certainly scaling the heights of testiness today.

What's eating you, Liz?

LIZ: This trip. I didn't want to do it. Tony did. We had a difference of opinion. An argument. A fight. A knock-down, drag-out, plate-smashing bilingual donneybrook. Tony won. His Spanish is better than mine. This really is good coffee.

MEREDITH: I'll alert the media.

LIZ: I'm tired of being dirty. I'm tired of ripped fingernails. I don't care if I never smell another horse. I'm tired of being told when to climb, and where. I'm tired of risking our asses, year after year, for people who think climbing a mountain's as simple as leafing through *National Geographic*.

MEREDITH: You're tired.

LIZ: I'm beginning to hate that mountain.

MEREDITH: So do I, sometimes. But what can we do? We love it, and we hate it, but that mountain's got us.

LIZ: I don't think fatalism's what I need right now.

MEREDITH: More coffee?

LIZ: No, thanks.

MEREDITH: Sandwich?

LIZ: I'm not hungry. Don't <u>hover</u>, Meredith.

MEREDITH: You're not climbing on up, are you?

LIZ: Not if the storm breaks. How does it look to you?

MEREDITH: Air's as hard as a diamond. I'd say it's on the way. Shouldn't you head back to civilization?

LIZ: If this were a sane world.

MEREDITH: You're not sitting it out over at the camp?

LIZ: That's how the current thinking is running.

MEREDITH: That's ridiculous.

LIZ: It isn't dangerous.

MEREDITH: But masochistic.

LIZ: It wasn't <u>my</u> idea. Don't get on <u>me</u>. We were all ready to break camp, when Ralph has a flash of brilliance. Winter camping. Perfect! We have the tents, and God knows we're about to have the winter.

MEREDITH: Ralph?

LIZ: Mr. Ralph Stoddard master-minded this little expedition. And, as he has reminded us a dozen times a day, he's paying for it.

MEREDITH: What about Tony?

LIZ: He loves it. The harder, the messier, the colder the better for good old Tony. I'd leave him in a minute if he didn't have such a cute ass.

MEREDITH: You're worn out, aren't you?

LIZ: All the way up here I've felt that mountain push against me. I haven't slept in three nights, since we left Anaconda. I lie there in that sleeping bag and feel the cold creep into my joints. I think about the morning, making the fire in that cold, taking down the tents, loading the horses. Riding all day, unloading the horses, putting up the tents. Every time I dismount, I feel as if someone threw me down an elevator shaft.

MEREDITH: Are you okay?

LIZ: Just feeling my age.

MEREDITH: Pushing thirty?

LIZ: After twenty-five, it's all downhill.

MEREDITH: Want to stay here until the storm's over? Tony can handle the camp.

LIZ: There are five people in that party. Most of them don't know a ridge pole from a guy line.

MEREDITH: Liz.....

LIZ: *(Quickly)* How's your writing going?

MEREDITH: Liz.....

LIZ: Change of subject.

MEREDITH: I spent the first week plotting revenge against tourists. Maybe I should try mysteries. I have ideas that would put Agatha Christie to shame.

mitory) Are we really supposed to sleep on those beds, or are we doing penance for past sins?

PAULA: I'm tired enough to sleep on the floor.

NATALIE: How did you get past Tony?

CLAIRE: He went out to check the horses.

NATALIE: *(A little frantic)* But you don't even know what to bring!

CLAIRE: Relax. I'm sure Merry has whatever we need.

NATALIE: Claire....

CLAIRE: The cupboards are bursting already, Lord knows with what. *(Browsing)* Bisquick! I've never seen so much Bisquick.

PAULA: Well, if she stays here all winter....

CLAIRE: I hope she doesn't go on over the joys of solitude. Styrofoam is bad enough. I thought I'd lose my mind on the way up.

NATALIE: It keeps you in crystal and flatware, doesn't it? *(To Paula)* Let me take that stuff. At least we can get it out of the way. *(Natalie starts to the dormitory, bumps into Liz.)*

LIZ: What is this?

NATALIE: Don't look at me.

PAULA: *(Holds up a foil-wrapped package)* Liz, how are we ever going to put this together with that *(stove)* and come up with something we can eat?

LIZ: I hope you don't. That's the toilet paper.

PAULA: Pack me in snow and roll me down the mountain. I can't cope.

LIZ: Claire, dear heart, how about a little activity?

CLAIRE: I don't know what to do.

LIZ: Cook, clean-up, chop wood, latrine duty ....

CLAIRE: Latrine duty! What's wrong with the bathroom?

LIZ: According to my calculations, the pipes are about to freeze.

CLAIRE: Really, this is too primitive.

LIZ: You're welcome to start hiking.

Claire gets up with great reluctance. Meredith enters with blankets.

Ah, our genial hostess, Meredith Bryant. Paula Pryor, Claire Stoddard. You've met Sister Natalie.

PAULA: Hello.

MEREDITH: Stoddard?

CLAIRE: Long time no see, Merry.

LIZ: You've met?

CLAIRE: We went to high school together.

A silence. Liz looks from one to the other.

LIZ: Well, I hope you don't keep us up all night giggling about the good old days down at the soda shop.

MEREDITH: What?

LIZ: Try to contain your enthusiasm, girls. Those raucous squeals might bring down an avalanche.

MEREDITH: Blankets.

Meredith shoves her blankets at Liz and makes a bee-line through the living room, headed for the front door. Liz shoves the blankets at Claire and heads after her. Claire exits to dormitory.

LIZ: Hold it. Where are you going?

MEREDITH: Outside.

LIZ: *(Takes her coat)* I don't think so. What's up. You look as if someone just told.

MEREDITH: A blast from the past.

LIZ: You're not pleased to see her.

MEREDITH: We didn't get along. I never expected ... *(Trails off helplessly)*

LIZ: Is this going to be difficult for you?

MEREDITH: It's just a shock.

NATALIE: *(To Liz)* Please don't.

LIZ: Sorry.

CLAIRE: *(To Natalie)* Liz can't help herself. She's a snob. *(To Liz)* Aren't you?

LIZ: Sure am.

CLAIRE: *(Phoney cowpoke accent)* And danged proud of it, I'll wager.

LIZ: Danged proud.

NATALIE: Look, we have to get through the next three days. Can we call a truce?

CLAIRE: <u>I'm</u> going to call it a day. I'm exhausted. *(Exits to dorm)*

LIZ: I'm sorry, Paula.

PAULA: She does that any time she can find a partner. Most of us have learned how to stay out of the way. We call it the Stoddard Two-step. Now that I've made coffee, I don't want it. Anyone else?

NATALIE: I'll clean up first.

LIZ: Leave the dishes in the sink. We can do them in the morning.

PAULA: I think I'll pull the covers over my head and pretend I'm a mole. Goodnight, sleep tight, don't let the bedbugs bite. *(Exits to dorm)*

LIZ: Made an ass of myself, didn't I?

NATALIE: If you hadn't, I probably would have. Three days, huh? This could be more fun than <u>Macbeth</u>.

LIZ: Should I apologize to Claire?

NATALIE: And ruin her evening?

LIZ: Well, something tells me I have some fences to mend in there *(Living room)*. One of the problems with having a temper like mine is I spend half my life saying I'm sorry.

NATALIE: Don't worry about it.

LIZ: And ruin <u>my</u> evening? *(Enters living room)* There's coffee. Want some?

MEREDITH: Not right now.

LIZ: You doing okay?

MEREDITH: How about you?

LIZ: Trying. Very trying.

MEREDITH: You don't have to fight any battles for me, you know.

LIZ: If Claire Stoddard were your dearest, long-lost bosom friend, I'd try real hard to like her. Since she isn't, I'm not about to risk a psychic hernia. But I <u>will</u> try to be more polite.

MEREDITH: Be careful of Claire.

LIZ: She's just having a little fun.

MEREDITH: You don't know her.

LIZ: You do?

MEREDITH: She was a mean adolescent. She's probably a malicious adult. I was afraid you were angry with me, earlier.

LIZ: I can't get angry at you. Well, I can't <u>stay</u> angry at you. But you know, pal, your silences can hang pretty heavy.

MEREDITH: I'm sorry.

LIZ: Forget it. Between that mess out there *(Outdoors)* and that mess out <u>there</u> *(Dorm/kitchen)* I could work up a terrific grouch. Guess I'll curl up with a good dirty book.

MEREDITH: I didn't know there <u>were</u> any good dirty books.

LIZ: My standards are lower than yours. Sweet dreams, dear heart. *(Exits to kitchen. To Natalie)* Coming to bed?

NATALIE: In a while.

Liz exits to dorm. Natalie pours herself some coffee, tastes it, shudders, and pours it out. Sits at the table to think. Claire enters.

I thought you were turning in.

CLAIRE: Need a book. *(Goes to living room, pretends to scan book shelves.)*

MEREDITH: The John D. MacDonalds are on the third shelf.

CLAIRE: You remembered.

MEREDITH: They're the most popular.

CLAIRE: So this is your famous Rockchuck Lodge.

MEREDITH: Claire, what the hell are you doing here?

CLAIRE: Ralph wanted to go mountain climbing ....

MEREDITH: Why this mountain?

CLAIRE: We thought it would be amusing.

MEREDITH: The Rockies are full of amusing mountains. There are some in Wyoming that would leave you limp with hysteria. Did you know I was here?

CLAIRE: It occurred to me.*(Looks around.)* It's a charming little place. Not my cup of tea, of course.

MEREDITH: I can tell.

CLAIRE: I appreciate you going along with the high school story.

MEREDITH: No problem.

CLAIRE: With Paula here .... well, the upper echelons of Stoddard Industries can be cut-throat. You never know what she might do with the wrong information.

MEREDITH: Our years in New Haven weren't exactly pleasant. I'm not likely to wax nostalgic.

CLAIRE: And Liz, what does she know?

MEREDITH: Nothing about us.

CLAIRE: Life's amazing, isn't it? We both got what we wanted.

MEREDITH: Styrofoam?

CLAIRE: The things styrofoam can buy.

MEREDITH: How'd you manage it?

CLAIRE: Skiing in Switzerland.

MEREDITH: On a music teacher's salary?

CLAIRE: It wiped out my savings, but it was worth it, don't you think?

MEREDITH: I'd have to meet Ralph first.

CLAIRE: He's an angel.

MEREDITH: He must be a saint. Why school in Europe, for Heaven's sake?

CLAIRE: Background. You won't spoil it for me, will you?

MEREDITH: What you do with your life is none of my business, as you used to point out.

CLAIRE: You're a good sport, Merry. You always were.

MEREDITH: Sure.

CLAIRE: Are you doing all right?

MEREDITH: I get by.

CLAIRE: What kind of people come here?

MEREDITH: Climbers, mostly. They use the lodge as a base camp.

CLAIRE: Neither here nor there, hmmm?

MEREDITH: You can go up, or you can go down. *(Pointedly)* Or you can go to bed. *(Turns back to her work.)*

CLAIRE: *(Settling in)* You look well.

MEREDITH: Clean living and mountain air.

CLAIRE: I've thought of you often.

MEREDITH: I really doubt that, Claire.

CLAIRE: You left town so abruptly.

MEREDITH: I stayed around for six months.

CLAIRE: Really? Well, of course I was tied up.

MEREDITH: Of course.

CLAIRE: I tried to call you.

MEREDITH: Gosh, I must have stepped out for a minute.

CLAIRE: Do you miss teaching?

MEREDITH: Not much.

CLAIRE: *(Touches her)* Come on, Merry, loosen up.*(Meredith pulls away)* I didn't come here to disrupt your life.

MEREDITH: Right.

CLAIRE: I really don't want this to be unpleasant.

MEREDITH: Could have fooled me.

CLAIRE: Liz and I got off on the wrong foot. It'll be fine. Who knows, the storm could be a blessing in disguise. It'll give us time to get reacquainted.

MEREDITH: I don't want to get reacquainted, Claire. I want to get back to work.

CLAIRE: There's nothing to be afraid of.

MEREDITH: I've heard that from you before.

CLAIRE: I never made you any promises, did I?

MEREDITH: Not in so many words.

CLAIRE: We weren't right for each other, that's all. It happens.

MEREDITH: It certainly did.

CLAIRE: Nursing a grudge?

MEREDITH: Only on bad days.

CLAIRE: After all this time. You'll get over it.

MEREDITH: If you say so.

CLAIRE: I <u>do</u> say so. See you in the morning, Merry.

> *Claire takes a book at random and exits to kitchen, ruffling Meredith's hair as she passes,waves the book at Natalie and exits to dorm. Meredith tries to get back to work, doesn't have much success, and goes to kitchen.*

MEREDITH: Sorry. I didn't know anyone was up.

NATALIE: It's all right.

MEREDITH: Coffee still hot?

NATALIE: I think so.

MEREDITH: Anything to eat out here?

NATALIE: Some trail bars on the counter.

MEREDITH: *(Shudders)* I'll have enough of nuts and berries toward spring. My kingdom for a Twinkie. *(Gives up)* Oh, well.

NATALIE: I'm not surprised you're hungry.You hardly touched dinner.

MEREDITH: In that atmosphere? There was enough electricity in the air to raise Frankenstein's monster.

NATALIE: Liz and Claire certainly can go at it.

MEREDITH: Liz suffers from a rare form of epilepsy, the major symptom of which is uncontrollable rudeness. I don't know what Claire's excuse is. *(Pours coffee)* Want some?

NATALIE: I'll pass.

MEREDITH: *(Takes a swallow)* My God, what sadist made this?

NATALIE: Paula.

MEREDITH: It's worse than the stuff I serve the tourists. Want to be alone?

NATALIE: Not particularly. It's so quiet here. You can almost hear the snow fall.

MEREDITH: You can, when the wind dies. Nervous?

NATALIE: Not at all.

MEREDITH: What are you doing in this mess?

NATALIE: I didn't think.

MEREDITH: You went out to do a little early Christmas shopping and found yourself halfway up Rockchuck Mountain with winter nipping at your heels.

NATALIE: Something like that. I can't explain.

MEREDITH: It's just as well. It'd probably make me scream.

NATALIE: Liz isn't the only one who's on edge.

MEREDITH: I'm sorry. It isn't you, it's ....

NATALIE: Claire?

MEREDITH: The wind.

NATALIE: *(Decides to let it go)* Do you run the lodge alone?

MEREDITH: I have summer help, college students.

NATALIE: I don't know if I'd have the temperament for it.

MEREDITH: I'm not sure I do, as you might have noticed. But it keeps me in pork and beans. *(Glances out the window)* I hate the first storm. When the tourists leave, silence drifts down like a blessing. But when that snow begins ... Before I know it the roads will be impassable. Then the trails disappear, and the wall of snow grows higher and higher. And no matter how desperately I want to get out, nothing is going to move that snow until spring.

NATALIE: What do you do with yourself?

MEREDITH: Write, and make up imaginary worlds. Once a week I call Liz on the CB. Just to make sure civilization hasn't eaten her alive.

NATALIE: Do you have to stay?

MEREDITH: Not really. It's a low crime-rate neighborhood.

NATALIE: Why do you?

MEREDITH: It's beautiful.

NATALIE: Don't you get lonely?

MEREDITH: Sometimes. Don't you?

NATALIE: Yes.

A brief silence.

MEREDITH: Feel like talking? Or should I go fight with my semi-colons?

NATALIE: Don't go. *(Laughs self-consciously)* I might spill.

MEREDITH: So spill.

NATALIE: I think something's happening to me. I mean, this was really crazy, coming up here the way I did. I've always been so ... normal.

MEREDITH: *(Kindly)* I won't hold that against you.

NATALIE: No, I mean it. All through grade school, high school, dates, proms....

MEREDITH: Adolescent identity crises.

NATALIE: And early twenties, and mid-twenties, and now.... My God, mid-life's probably just down the road.

MEREDITH: Remember when you used to think there'd only be one? I wonder who started that rumor.

NATALIE: I married a man I met in college, at an anti-nuke demonstration. Can you believe it? Consciousness-raising groups. Have you ever been in a consciousness-raising group?

MEREDITH: I always figured I had more consciousness than I could handle.

NATALIE: We settled down into a normal, two-career household. Well, <u>he</u> had a career. <u>I</u> had a job.

MEREDITH: Naturally. What do you do?

NATALIE: I work in a bank.

MEREDITH: You don't go around telling people to have a nice day, do you?

NATALIE: Not in mortgage and loans. Steve wanted children. Two and a half, to be exact. It's lucky we waited.

MEREDITH: Widowed?

NATALIE: Divorced.

MEREDITH: End of normal.

NATALIE: Check the statistics.

Meredith notices Natalie is shivering a little. Gets up, ostensibly for more coffee, takes off her sweater and drapes it, a little awkwardly,over Natalie's shoulders.

Thank you.

MEREDITH: *(Pouring coffee)* I wonder if this stuff can do things to you. Did you have a normal divorce?

NATALIE: It was terribly civilized. Have you ever been married?

MEREDITH: That option hasn't been open to me.

NATALIE: Why not?

MEREDITH: I've never been able to get involved. With a man. The feelings just aren't there.

NATALIE: I see.

MEREDITH: If that shocks you, I'll leave you to ....

NATALIE: It doesn't shock me.

MEREDITH: Right. Your consciousness is raised.*(Quickly)* I still don't understand what you're doing halfway up a mountain with the Wilmington Four. Or is that what one does after a civilized divorce?

NATALIE: Last week I was sitting in my apartment, staring out the window with the day dying and the traffic going by...on and on...as if it would never stop. Picking over memories...trying to discover what went wrong...wanting to blame someone, knowing there was no one to blame...crying over little crushed hopes that should never have been hoped...remembering small disappointments, then larger hurts...and the moments of growing certainty that it was over.

Meredith touches her.

I hadn't let myself remember before. I had to get through the divorce, you know? Put one foot in front of the other and get through it. And then it fell in on me. I thought, "If this doesn't stop, I'm going to die." I wanted to die, to make it stop. *(Pause)* I guess I just started running.

MEREDITH: Why here?

NATALIE: North was the only direction that didn't have memories. I wound up in Anaconda, heard about this trip, and signed on. Maybe I'm having a normal nervous breakdown.

MEREDITH: Better watch out. Destiny may have something in store for you.

NATALIE: All I know is, for the first time in my life I feel as if my clothes fit. Well, I certainly am talkative tonight. It must be the storm.

MEREDITH: Or Paula's coffee.

NATALIE: After one polite half-cup, I swore off Paula's coffee. It's late, and I've bent your ear long enough.

MEREDITH: It's all right.

NATALIE: *(Gets up)* Thanks for the sweater. And for listening. Especially for listening. Good night, Meredith.

MEREDITH: Good night.

Natalie exits to dorm.

BLACKOUT

SCENE 2: The next morning.The wind is howling. Paula and Meredith are finishing up last night's dishes.

MEREDITH: Well, that's that. Now we can start over.

PAULA: It's easy to see how you pass the time.

MEREDITH: I'm strictly an eat-it-from-the-can type. All this is to impress you.

PAULA: I'm impressed. Should I start breakfast?

MEREDITH: Relax for a while. I haven't heard any stirrings from out there.

PAULA: They might all be dead. Depends on who drank coffee last night.

MEREDITH: You heard about that.

PAULA: I heard. I'm sorry about wasting it.

MEREDITH: I've had worse. I've made worse. That's why I carry malpractice insurance.

PAULA: *(Laughing)* You're all heart. *(Listens)* I hate that wind. It's trying to kill me.

MEREDITH: It's only wind.

PAULA: Claire says I'm timid. She's probably right.

MEREDITH: Is she ... I mean, how do you get along?

PAULA: By staying out of her way.

MEREDITH: What's she like?

PAULA: I don't know. She does what she has to, like the rest of us.

MEREDITH: Hey, I didn't mean to put you on the spot.

PAULA: Well, it's hard, you being an old friend of hers ....

MEREDITH: " Friend's" putting it a bit strongly.

PAULA: She likes to be in charge. She likes things to go her way, if you know what I mean.

MEREDITH: I know exactly what you mean

PAULA: She's sort of like a playground bully. Isn't that terrible of me? But there are moments when I feel sorry for her. It must be lonely, don't you imagine?

MEREDITH: That world's pretty far from anything I've even known. Or wanted. It's hard to know how to think about it.

PAULA: It seems to suit Claire.

MEREDITH: Yes. How about you?

PAULA: I get tired of it sometimes. It's so ... homogenized. But right now Mark needs the wall-to-wall carpet. It reassures him. If he ever becomes President of Stoddard Industries, maybe we'll move to the inner city and start a trend—downwardly mobile chic.

Claire enters in nightclothes.

CLAIRE: Good morning, dear hearts.

MEREDITH: You'll freeze like that.

CLAIRE: I'm tired of waiting for Liz to finish in the bathroom. Do you have an FM receiver?

MEREDITH: We're too high up to pick up the signal.

CLAIRE: This begins to feel like a Walt Disney True Life Adventure.

PAULA: Haven't you been camping before?

CLAIRE: Not that I remember. Not that I <u>want</u> to remember. Can we at least turn on the hot water heater?

MEREDITH: I'm sorry. The heater and the lights run off the generator, and the generator runs on gas. What I've got has to last me until spring.

CLAIRE: I'll have Ralph send you more.

MEREDITH: Really, I'm not trying to be unreasonable. If there's a late spring and I run out ... Oh, go ahead. If you can get out, the truck can probably get in.

CLAIRE: If we can get out?

PAULA: You mean we might not get out?

MEREDITH: You'll get out.

CLAIRE: Well, I wish Liz would get out of the bathroom. *(Liz enters)* It's about time. *(Exits)*

MEREDITH: *(To Liz, who looks a little green)* Are you all right?

LIZ: Fine.

PAULA: I'll start breakfast.

LIZ: Oh, God. *(Liz heads for the living room, Meredith follows.)*

MEREDITH: Liz?

LIZ: It'll pass.

MEREDITH: *(The pieces fit)* Are you pregnant?

LIZ: Sure am.

MEREDITH: No wonder you feel rotten.

LIZ: Jesus, Meredith.

MEREDITH: I mean ... You're glad, aren't you?

LIZ: Not until noon.

MEREDITH: You're out of your mind, taking this trip. Tony's out of his ... Tony doesn't know.

LIZ: I wanted it to be special. I was going to tell him, but the damned outfitter called, and we got into that fight, and everything was so creepy after that ... Anyway, we need the money. I want to go home.

MEREDITH: You mean you've been getting up every morning, doing all that work, feeling like this? Liz, that is the most ridiculous ...

LIZ: Want me to throw up all over this room? Because, if you do, just keep it up. I mean, any second now ....

MEREDITH: Can I get you anything?

LIZ: I'll be okay. Leave me alone for a while.

Meredith builds up the fire and exits to the kitchen.

PAULA: I'm not <u>that</u> bad a cook.

MEREDITH: It's just a touch of something. But I don't think scrambled eggs ....

Natalie enters, heads for the coffee pot.

NATALIE: Morning.

MEREDITH: You're very trusting.

NATALIE: It's one of my biggest failings.*(To Paula)* How you doing?

PAULA: Leave me alone and I'll play for hours.

MEREDITH: How did you sleep?

NATALIE: Like a rock. How about you?

MEREDITH: I worried around for a while, thinking about what you said. Sometimes there seems to be so much—living —to do in a single lifetime....

NATALIE: Please! No <u>meaning</u> over breakfast.

Claire enters, takes a seat, and indicates Meredith should sit next to her. Meredith pointedly ignores her and takes the seat next to Natalie.

PAULA: *(Serving)* I don't know how you do it, alone all winter.

MEREDITH: Seven months of solitude won't kill me. Seven months of conversation with strangers would.

NATALIE: You'd make friends.

MEREDITH: Supermarket clerks aren't friends. Gas station attendants aren't friends. Bank teller—no insult intended—aren't friends. You can be dying of terminal life, and they tell you to have a nice day.

PAULA: You could become the Mysterious Anaconda Hermit.

MEREDITH: They come to your door. College students selling newspapers. Boy scouts collecting newspapers. Census takers. Mormons. In all my time up here, I haven't been harassed by a single Mormon. Only a certain Jehovah's Witness who sneaked in under false pretenses.

PAULA: It's dangerous up here.

MEREDITH: It's dangerous down there. It'd be just my luck to be decapitated by a runaway frisbee. Or struck down by some born-again Christian driving home from prayer meeting soused on righteousness. Can't you see them scraping my remains off a bumper sticker that reads *I heart Jesus* ?

PAULA: Seriously.

MEREDITH: I am serious. The world's in a rage. Look at the faces in the crowd at a sporting event. World War III is going to start during the American League Playoffs.

NATALIE: *(Laughing)* Stop it.

MEREDITH: It is all going to blow up. One day there will be a quick,tiny spark—like the sparks struck by freight trains braking in dry leaves—and that'll be it. Goodbye, big blue marble.

NATALIE: You certainly get Biblical when you're aroused.

MEREDITH: If I have to witness the last sunrise, I want it to be over Rockchuck Mountain, not the Anaconda Copper smelter.

NATALIE: I'll trade you the smelter for the Denver smog.

MEREDITH: It's the world's tallest smokestack.

NATALIE: It's the country's tallest smog.

CLAIRE: I'd trade them both for an FM receiver.

PAULA: You haven't really suffered until you've tried Wilmington. Sometimes I think I'm inhaling the same air in September that I exhaled in June.

MEREDITH: Barring the possibility of reincarnation, you know, this is the only life you're ever going to have. The day that thought struck me I decided to leave New Haven and buy this lodge.

CLAIRE: And pass your days neither here nor there.

MEREDITH: After the snow comes, even the birds are silent. On still mornings, I can stand on the porch and hear the water trickling through the beaver dam on Moraine Lake. Nothing moves. Then a pine bough shakes off its load of snow, and ice crystals float through the sunlight like a shower of falling stars.

CLAIRE: You must have gotten that off the back of an old envelope.

NATALIE: *(Quickly)* It sounds like Heaven to me.

CLAIRE: Well, I couldn't bear it. I like to know what's going on in the world.

NATALIE: My ex-husband read a morning paper over breakfast, an evening paper before dinner, and magazines in the bathroom. He watched the six o'clock news and the eleven o'clock news. Sometimes he read the paper and watched the news at the same time. If someone lost their car keys in Tanzania, Steve knew about it. He was obsessed.

CLAIRE: Ralph's obsession is exercise. Every night after work he runs five miles, then sits down and drinks two beers. Before the martinis. *(To Meredith)* What's your obsession?

MEREDITH: What?

CLAIRE: What do you do for amusement?

MEREDITH: Amusement?

CLAIRE: Amusement. You remember amusement.

MEREDITH: Oh, like fun. Sure, I remember fun.

CLAIRE: Well ....

MEREDITH: Well what?

CLAIRE: It's your house. Tell us what to do for fun.

MEREDITH: You could count your fingers. Every time I do it comes out differently.

CLAIRE: How about something we could all do?

MEREDITH: We could all count your fingers.

CLAIRE: Merry.

MEREDITH: *(Gets up)* Whatever you decide on, leave me out. I just got my typing up to tempo.

CLAIRE: It isn't every day you have company.

MEREDITH: It is between June and October.

Meredith exits, taking a trail bar for Liz. Natalie starts clearing up.

CLAIRE: Paula, how about a game of gin?

PAULA: I'll give a hand here first.

NATALIE: I can do it.

CLAIRE: Come on, Paula. *(Exits to dormitory)*

PAULA: I hate gin.

NATALIE: So do I. I never win.

PAULA: I always win. *(Exits)*

MEREDITH: *(To Liz)* Don't argue with me. Eat it.

LIZ: With or without the wrapper?

MEREDITH: You have to eat something.

LIZ: Why?

MEREDITH: Think of the baby.

LIZ: You're not going to be like <u>that</u>, are you? Next you'll be at me to quit smoking.

MEREDITH: You don't smoke.

LIZ: Maybe I'll start, to give you something to carry on about.

MEREDITH: Have you called Tony?

LIZ: They're playing poker. Tony's going to be a rich man after this trip. What the hell kind of Wilderness Experience is that, playing poker? No, I didn't tell him.

MEREDITH: I haven't said a word.

LIZ: But you think at 10,000 decibels. How are you getting along with the old High School chum?

MEREDITH: It could be worse.

LIZ: Meredith....

MEREDITH: I'd better bring in more wood.

LIZ: Let me. It'll take my mind off my problems. Look, pal, this is not a pleasant situation we have here, what with Auld Lang Syne and all. I don't like you going it alone.

MEREDITH: There's nothing to worry about.

LIZ: Then why am I worried? Christ, if it blows up, it'll probably be before breakfast. Sometimes I wonder why I love you.

Liz exits outside. Meredith goes to the kitchen.

MEREDITH: Wood's running low out here.

NATALIE: Want me to ....

MEREDITH: Let Liz do it. Inactivity makes her run in circles.

NATALIE: You two have been friends a long time, haven't you?

MEREDITH: I met her the summer I spent here learning the ropes, before the previous owners retired. Tony and Liz were on their honeymoon, all one week of it. They'll be working out of here as soon as Tony decides they have the capital.

NATALIE: I envy you that friendship.

MEREDITH: We bully each other, but it doesn't mean anything.

NATALIE: You must miss her over the winter.

MEREDITH: I do. But by Thanksgiving I've gone so strange from talking to myself I'm not fit company for anyone.

NATALIE: How do you do it?

MEREDITH: Promise not to tell? I make up imaginary playmates. Seriously.

NATALIE: Is it enough?

MEREDITH: They come when I need them. They don't criticize. They aren't offended by my moods.

NATALIE: They don't touch.

MEREDITH: No.

NATALIE: Can you live without being touched?

MEREDITH: Not very well. But everything has its price. Not being touched is what I pay for solitude, and for that whole spectacular world out there. I got that off an old envelope back.

NATALIE: Claire's a fool. Don't let her get under your skin.

MEREDITH: She brings back memories. Of adolescent awkwardness.

NATALIE: Sure. Meredith, I've known a few people like Claire. Sooner or later, they all put their foot in it.

MEREDITH: Yeah, well I hope she doesn't track up the linoleum. What are your plans for the day?

NATALIE: I don't know.

MEREDITH: If this were September, we could hike over to Moraine Lake. There's a perfect spot for ... *(Catches herself)*

NATALIE: I think I'd better make myself useful.

MEREDITH: You need a vacation. For your nervous breakdown.

NATALIE: Come on, there must be something I can do.

MEREDITH: I'm replacing floorboards in the storage room, but I have all winter.

NATALIE: Perfect. I can hammer out my hostile impulses.

MEREDITH: You have hostile impulses?

NATALIE: I do this morning. Claire snores.

MEREDITH: I know. *(Quickly)* There might be strange little things under the floorboards.

NATALIE: I'm not afraid of strange little things. Only big, two-legged things. Have a nice day. *(Exits)*

BLACKOUT

SCENE 3: That night, after dinner. Meredith is at her typewriter.

Claire enters.

MEREDITH: I thought you were turning in.

CLAIRE: You've been avoiding me.

MEREDITH: I suppose.

CLAIRE: What have you been up to?

MEREDITH: Sorting old envelopes.

CLAIRE: You stayed in your room all day because of that?

MEREDITH: No, I've been working.

CLAIRE: You know me, not at my best in the morning.

MEREDITH: Word around New Haven was you were fantastic.

CLAIRE: You weren't so bad yourself.

MEREDITH: Are you still? Or has marriage changed all that?

CLAIRE: Ralph leaves for work at seven. He plays golf on Saturdays. Sundays we curl up with the Times.

MEREDITH: Whatever turns you on.

CLAIRE: I really wish you'd try to let down a little.

MEREDITH: Why?

CLAIRE: This tension ... well, it's not exactly comfortable for the others.

MEREDITH: Did someone complain?

CLAIRE: Not in so many words, but ... *(Trails off)*

MEREDITH: But what?

CLAIRE: Paula ... I realize she's overly sensitive ....

MEREDITH: I'll try to do better ....

CLAIRE: Good girl.

MEREDITH: ... around Paula.

CLAIRE: *(With a sigh)* Merry ....

MEREDITH: Claire, I have work to do.

CLAIRE: What work?

MEREDITH: I'm writing. So if you don't mind ... *(Waits for Claire to leave. She doesn't. Meredith turns back to her work.)*

CLAIRE: I always liked watching you type. Something about the way you move your hands. Remember how we used to sit in your apartment on winter nights, classical music on the stereo, grading papers together? You always said the only thing missing was a fireplace. Do you ever think of those times?

MEREDITH: No.

CLAIRE: Strange to see the old dinner plates again, and the old silverware. The same plaid bathrobe hanging on the back of the door. I miss the shoe box of loose green stamps. Did you ever get around to pasting them in?

MEREDITH: Probably. I don't remember.

CLAIRE: Do you still keep a journal?

MEREDITH: Yes. Do you?

CLAIRE: I never did. It seemed like a waste of time.

MEREDITH: Claire ....

CLAIRE: I've missed you.

MEREDITH: What?

CLAIRE: <u>Missed</u> you. It's hard to imagine you entertaining the teeming hordes.

MEREDITH: I manage.

CLAIRE: You talk as if you hate it.

MEREDITH: That's end-of-season fatigue. I've met some good people.

CLAIRE: And I'll bet they come back, year after year.

MEREDITH: Some do.

CLAIRE: Anybody special?

MEREDITH: What?

CLAIRE: Never mind. Don't you want to know how I've been?

MEREDITH: *(Wearily)* How have you been, Claire?

CLAIRE: Fine.

MEREDITH: Good.

CLAIRE: Considering. *(Meredith doesn't take the bait.)* Were you surprised? About Ralph?

MEREDITH: I stopped being surprised by you a long time ago.

CLAIRE: I guess you knew me pretty well.

MEREDITH: I thought I did. Then I realized I didn't know you at all.

CLAIRE: You saw what you wanted to see.

MEREDITH: Claire ....

CLAIRE: But I never held that against you.

MEREDITH: It worked both ways.

CLAIRE: Well, it's in the past.

MEREDITH: Right.

CLAIRE: Let's just put it behind us.

MEREDITH: You came a long way to put it behind you.

CLAIRE: Do you ever wonder what it would be like now?

MEREDITH: What?

CLAIRE: The two of us.

MEREDITH: And Ralph?

CLAIRE: *(Laughs)* Still the little Puritan?

MEREDITH:Yeah, I'm into all that obsolete stuff—monogamy, loyalty, honesty, commitment. Silly things like that.

CLAIRE: We had some good times.

MEREDITH: And some very bad ones.

CLAIRE: You see, that's the essential difference between us. I look on the bright side ....

MEREDITH: Right.

CLAIRE: Did you listen to yourself this morning? "If I have to witness the last sunrise ...It's all going to blow up ...." For Heaven's sake, Merry. These people are here to have fun.

MEREDITH: I thought they were here so they wouldn't freeze to death.

CLAIRE: That's exactly what I mean. Life is to be enjoyed.

MEREDITH: A veritable cabaret, old chum.

CLAIRE: It can be.

MEREDITH: And when the dancing ends, somebody's left crying.

CLAIRE: Only if they want it that way.

MEREDITH: It's that simple.

CLAIRE: I've never cried over anyone in my life, and I never will.

MEREDITH: The first time you told me that, I didn't believe you. Boy, do I believe you now. If you'll excuse me ....

CLAIRE: Should I come back later?

MEREDITH: I'll be in bed later.

CLAIRE: I know.

MEREDITH: I'm not interested in that.

CLAIRE: It's going to be a long winter.

MEREDITH: No!

CLAIRE: It wouldn't have to mean anything.

MEREDITH: It never did, did it?

CLAIRE: Of course it did, at the moment. Isn't that what matters?

MEREDITH: It's finished.

CLAIRE: We might never see each other again.

MEREDITH: I pray for that, nightly.

CLAIRE: You never used to be coy.

MEREDITH: You never used to be married.

CLAIRE: Is that the problem? Ralph won't care, he won't even know.

MEREDITH: Claire, I do not want to sleep with you. Not now, not ever.

CLAIRE: It would break the monotony.

MEREDITH: I don't believe this.

CLAIRE: I'll bet it's been a long time. Or does the summer help work nights?

MEREDITH: There are other rooms in a house besides the bedroom.

CLAIRE: There's also the bedroom.

MEREDITH: In which <u>some</u> people <u>sleep</u>.

CLAIRE: Not even curious?

MEREDITH: Not even mildly.

CLAIRE: Taken a vow of chastity?

MEREDITH: Go do the dishes.

CLAIRE: Or do you have your eye on someone else?

MEREDITH: I don't go to bed with people I don't love. I told you that a thousand times.

CLAIRE: You used to love <u>me</u>.

MEREDITH: Well, you took care of that.

CLAIRE: Still blaming me.

MEREDITH: Claire, if you're not out of here in five seconds, I'll call a conference and blow your story wide open.

CLAIRE: I don't think you'll do that.

MEREDITH: Don't push me.

CLAIRE: There are two sides to what went on in New Haven, dear heart.

MEREDITH: Claire ....

CLAIRE: Well, we'll let it go for now. If you change your mind, just say the word. We really could have a very nice time. After all, who knows you better than I do?

Claire exits. Liz enters from Meredith's room to see Claire leave.

MEREDITH: Everything all right at the camp?

LIZ: Snug as bugs in a rug.

MEREDITH: Sometimes you have the most disgusting way of saying things.

LIZ: Sorry. Anything wrong?

MEREDITH: Adverbs. I finally get the semicolons under control, and now the adverbs are running amok.

LIZ: What'd Claire want?

MEREDITH: Cards. She found out she hasn't been playing with a full deck.

LIZ: Meredith, why won't you talk to me?

MEREDITH : I am talking to you.

LIZ: This isn't talking. I'm your friend. In five years you've never lied to me. I've never lied to you. Doesn't that count for anything?

MEREDITH: Of course it does.

LIZ: I'm afraid of this silence between us. Look, I know what kind of person I am. Class clown, gag a minute. People want me around because I make them laugh. But they don't get close to me. They don't confide in me. Outside of Tony, you're the only one who takes me seriously.

MEREDITH: Liz ....

LIZ: And now, because of that ... bitch ... out there, you're pulling away. I don't know what she was to you, but I know what you are to me, and I can see that going down the ....

MEREDITH: Don't, Liz.

LIZ: That high school story is as porous as cheesecloth. If you can't talk about it, say so, but don't close me out. *(Silence)* Damn it, Meredith, I need you.

MEREDITH: *(Touches her)* I'm sorry. Claire and I were lovers. In New Haven. It ended badly. I should have told you long ago, but ....

LIZ: Embarrassed?

MEREDITH: I really didn't mean to hurt you.

LIZ: Yeah, I had a few like that. *(Meredith looks at her in disbelief)* Boys, Meredith.

MEREDITH: Oh, them.

LIZ: Was she your first?

MEREDITH: Yes.

LIZ: You sure know how to pick 'em, pal. Still stuck on her?

MEREDITH: No, but I'm afraid. She can tie me in knots.

LIZ: Knots I understand. If she tries anything with you, I'll use her for target practice.

MEREDITH: She wants me to sleep with her.

LIZ: Why?

MEREDITH: Thanks a lot!

LIZ: You know what I mean. Flattered?

MEREDITH: Are you out of your mind? Please don't let her know I told you.

LIZ: Gosh, Claire and I have become so intimate ... I mean, we share everything. I don't know how I can ....

MEREDITH: My God, don't we learn to keep secrets? You keep secrets from Tony, I keep secrets from you ... I'm really, really sorry.

LIZ: WILL YOU STOP APOLOGIZING?

MEREDITH: Sorry. I do love you, you know.

LIZ: Keep telling me. I think I'm heading into one of my insecure periods.

MEREDITH: You shouldn't be having any periods at all.

Liz gives her a look and exits to dormitory. Meredith starts to build up her fire, finds she's out of wood, goes to kitchen to get some. Natalie enters, in pajamas, carrying a book.

NATALIE: Will it bother you if I read out here? I didn't want to keep the others awake.

MEREDITH: It's cold. Come into the living room.

NATALIE: I won't disturb you?

MEREDITH: Not unless you read out loud.

NATALIE: Have you been outside?

MEREDITH: No.

NATALIE: There are melted snowflakes on your eyelashes. They look like ... tears? Meredith?

MEREDITH: *(Heading for the living room)* Thanks for fixing the floor.

NATALIE: *(Following)* Wait until you've lived with it for a while.That wasn't union help we had out there.

Natalie sits by the fireplace. Meredith goes back to her work. They sneak surreptitious glances at each other.

MEREDITH: Wind's dropped. *(Gets up to put wood on fire)*

NATALIE: Meredith, have you ever loved someone and had it turn sour?

MEREDITH: Anyone our age who hasn't been through that obviously isn't paying attention. Thinking about Steve?

NATALIE: I try to stop, but ... I wish I understood what happened.

MEREDITH: I tell myself everything will be revealed in the last three seconds of my life. If it isn't, I'm going to be madder than hell. *(Touches Natalie reassuringly)* It'll pass.

NATALIE: Steve didn't touch, not really. Oh, we had sex— plenty of sex— but it was ... sex. Impersonal. I don't think he even knew I was there. I tried to tell him ... once in a while I needed to be touched, and held, and ... but every time he did that, it ended up with sex. This is awfully personal. Do you mind?

MEREDITH: Of course not.

NATALIE: You probably don't even know what I'm talking about.

MEREDITH: Sure, I do. Men haven't cornered the market on insensitivity.

NATALIE: They've tried.

MEREDITH: Bitter?

NATALIE: Worn out, I guess. I put so much into that marriage. I don't do well when things break.

MEREDITH: Neither do I.

NATALIE: I even had an affair. I thought, okay, if I can't get what I need from Steve, I'll get it somewhere else and stop trying to change him. How did I ever get that naive?

MEREDITH: What happened?

NATALIE: It was great at first. Well, fine at first. *(Pause)* No, it wasn't. It was awful. I felt so guilty. When I couldn't live with myself any more, I confessed. Do you know what Steve did? He said, "I figured something was up," and rolled over and went to sleep. *(Pause)* I guess something in me died that night. I couldn't love him any more. I could remember loving him, but I couldn't feel it. I'd look at him and remember, and put the memories next to him like two photographs, and try to make them come together, but they wouldn't. *(Pause)* God, if I could only under....

MEREDITH: Stop that.

NATALIE: What?

MEREDITH: Stop blaming yourself.

NATALIE: I can't very well blame Steve. He didn't do anything.

MEREDITH: One of the seven unnatural wonders of the world is the human capacity for cruelty. You have to be a real genius to know when not to notice, not to respond, not to touch.

NATALIE: My friends back in Denver thought I was crazy. I mean, they stood by me, out of loyalty, but ....

MEREDITH: No visible scars.

NATALIE: No.

MEREDITH: But plenty of invisible.

NATALIE: How about you?

MEREDITH: Some. I wanted to spend my life in a plastic bubble, but they wouldn't let me. We're supposed to participate.

NATALIE: Would you tell me?

MEREDITH: *(Hesitates, tempted. Decides against it.)* I've exhausted my quota of self-pity for today. *(Starts to put another log on the fire.)* Damn it!

NATALIE: What's wrong?

MEREDITH: Splinter.*(Tries to pull it out. Natalie takes her hand)* I can do it.

NATALIE: You're making it worse. *(Pulling out splinter.)* This has been hard on you, hasn't it? Why were you crying when I came in?

MEREDITH: I hurt Liz. She's the last person ... Everything happens too fast. I get so inside myself, until all that's real is my own Goddamn, stupid ... I didn't mean to.

NATALIE: Oh, Meredith. *(Holds her)*

MEREDITH: *(After a moment, afraid of what she's feeling, pulls away)* Nothing quite like the late-night willies.

NATALIE: Is there anything ....

MEREDITH: I have work to do. I'll see you in the morning.

NATALIE: *(Hesitates)* Well, goodnight, then.

MEREDITH: Goodnight.

Natalie hesitates again, finally exits, leaving Meredith alone.

God damn it, NO!

<u>BLACKOUT</u>

END OF ACT I

ACT TWO

SCENE 1: The next morning. It is still snowing. Paula and Natalie are having a quiet cup of coffee in the kitchen.

Liz bursts in with a load of wood which she drops by the stove.

LIZ: America Held Hostage, Day Three. Good morning, glories.

NATALIE: You're certainly cheerful for this time of day.

LIZ: Been up for hours. *(Starts making herself a sandwich.)*

CLAIRE: *(Entering from dorm.)* What's for breakfast?

LIZ: Anything you can scrounge.

CLAIRE: What are you having?

LIZ: Breast of peanut butter,*Cordon Bleu.*

CLAIRE: Are you a manic-depressive?

LIZ: Only in Real Life.

CLAIRE: I hope we can expect a downswing soon.

LIZ: Do your damnedest, Princess. I'm not taking the bait.

Natalie pours a mug of coffee and goes to the living room. Meredith enters from her room.

CLAIRE: *(Looking after Natalie)* Room service?

LIZ: *(Holds out silverware)* Maid service?

NATALIE: *(To Meredith, handing her coffee)* Good morning.

MEREDITH: Morning.

NATALIE: Strange night, wasn't it?

MEREDITH: Look, I'm sorry I....

NATALIE: I was honored.

MEREDITH: *(Unable to look her in the eye)* Thanks for the coffee.

NATALIE: You're welcome. Why did you send me away?

MEREDITH: Did you make this? *(Coffee)*

NATALIE: Yes. Meredith....

MEREDITH: It's very good.

NATALIE: Can we talk about it?

MEREDITH: Coffee?

NATALIE: Last night.

MEREDITH: I broke the first rule of hotel management: "Always make a good impression."

NATALIE: You made an impression.

MEREDITH: Please, overlook it.

NATALIE: I can't overlook it, Meredith.

LIZ: *(Pokes her head in)* Hey, you two, better get out here before Claire pigs all the Cap'n crunch.

Meredith makes a bee-line for the kitchen, grabs the seat next to Paula. Natalie follows.

CLAIRE: If I leave here alive, I'm going to have my entire gastrointestinal system replaced.

LIZ: Garbage up, Sweets. It won't hurt a tough old bird like you.

Natalie gets up to get something, touches Meredith's shoulder as she passes. Claire notices.

CLAIRE: Sounds as if you two had a fun time in the wee small hours. You should have called us. We could have made popcorn and had a real slumber party.

LIZ: Not me. I forgot my fuzzy slippers.

PAULA: *(Nibbling on burnt toast)* This is vaguely reminiscent of some of my early barbecues.

CLAIRE: The less said about your early barbecues, the better.

PAULA: Charred steak was my specialty. The neighborhood dogs loved us. As soon as the smoke began to rise, they'd gather outside the fence and drool. One Sunday the Johnsons' St. Bernard nearly drowned the Calleys' Pomeranian.

LIZ: That did it. *(Exits to dorm)*

PAULA: Oh, dear, I am sorry.

MEREDITH: She was only holding herself together with baling wire.

PAULA: I felt that way, too, especially with my first. I know a few tricks. *(Exits after Liz)*

MEREDITH: Paula hides her light under a bushel.

CLAIRE: Isn't she a dear?

An uncomfortable silence. Meredith is trying not to meet Natalie's eye.

MEREDITH: *(To Claire)* If you don't want to eat that, don't worry. Clementine loves it.

NATALIE: Clementine?

MEREDITH: The raccoon.

CLAIRE: You keep animals in here?

MEREDITH: Only under duress.

Another awkward silence.

NATALIE: Do you think this weather means we'll have a White Christmas?

CLAIRE: *(To Natalie)* What time did you finally come to bed last night?

NATALIE: I don't know. Did I miss bed-check?

CLAIRE: I must have drifted off three or four times before you got in.

NATALIE: I hope I didn't disturb you.

CLAIRE: I'm a light sleeper. I couldn't imagine what in the world you were doing out there, at that hour. *(No one answers)* Weren't you cold?

NATALIE: Not by the fire.

Meredith cringes.

CLAIRE: I love a fire on a winter night, don't you? It's so cozy.

MEREDITH: Up here, it's a necessity.

CLAIRE: The perfect atmosphere for shared confidences.

MEREDITH: Actually, Natalie read a book and I worked.

CLAIRE: That must have been cozy, too.

MEREDITH: *(Can't stand it any more)* I was on the verge of a new paragraph. I'd better get it down.

CLAIRE: You work too hard. Why not relax today?

MEREDITH: Want to run down to Anaconda and see a movie?

CLAIRE: What's playing?

MEREDITH: *Wilderness Family.*

CLAIRE: Very cute. Isn't she, Natalie?

NATALIE: What?

CLAIRE: Cute. Don't you think Meredith's cute?

NATALIE: No, that isn't the word I'd use.

CLAIRE: What word would you use?

MEREDITH: Jesus. *(Exits to living room)*

CLAIRE: Did I say something wrong?

NATALIE: Sorry. I wasn't listening.

CLAIRE: And what are your plans for today?

NATALIE: Staying out of Meredith's way.

CLAIRE: Did you have a falling-out?

NATALIE: She was nice enough to let us stay here. The least we can do is respect her privacy.

CLAIRE: You'd think she'd welcome the company. If I had to stay in this place year 'round, I'd slit my throat. *(Claire heads for the living room)* It's your turn to do the dishes.

Claire exits to living room. Natalie considers doing the dishes, exits in disgust.

MEREDITH: *(Annoyed)* You have the kitchen, the dormitory, the bathroom, the outbuildings, and all of Rockchuck Mountain.

Do you have to be in here?

CLAIRE: You didn't mind visitors last night.

MEREDITH: What?

CLAIRE: Oh, Merry, you are so transparent.

MEREDITH: What the hell are you ....

CLAIRE: Come off it. She's falling all over herself waiting on you.

MEREDITH: Look, Claire ....

CLAIRE: She's exactly your type.You always were attracted to the innocent and vulnerable.

MEREDITH: Really? I wasn't your first lover, or your last. Or the only one at the time, as a matter of fact.

CLAIRE: That still galls you. How you do hold on.

MEREDITH: If you're bored, go read a book.

CLAIRE: One of yours?

MEREDITH: No, not one of mine.

CLAIRE: You're wasting your time. She may be padding after you like a housepet now, but when push comes to shove, she'll run for cover.

MEREDITH: Don't you have anything better to do?

CLAIRE: I don't want you to get hurt.

MEREDITH: Since when?

CLAIRE: Merry ....

MEREDITH: Please don't call me that.

CLAIRE: You used to like it.

MEREDITH:When I was still innocent, and vulnerable.

CLAIRE: My, my, aren't we defensive today?

MEREDITH: Go away.

CLAIRE: You're afraid of me, aren't you? *(Silence)* That really hurts, Merry. After all the things we shared.You took all the good and just threw it away, as if it never existed.

MEREDITH: For God's sake, don't you remember what went on?

CLAIRE: More than you do, I think.

MEREDITH: I remember enough.

CLAIRE: But none of the fun. The dances? The trips to Provincetown? The picnics.

MEREDITH: The fights?

CLAIRE: People argue, Merry. It's a part of life.

MEREDITH: Not like that.

CLAIRE: So we had a few tiffs. So things didn't work out. That....

MEREDITH: Happens.

CLAIRE: It's in the past.

MEREDITH: You're bringing it all back.

CLAIRE: Merry, Merry, let it go.

MEREDITH: Just leave me alone, Claire, okay?

CLAIRE: Didn't you learn anything from our years together?

MEREDITH: Yes. I learned that when your lover leaves you, you feel unloveable.

CLAIRE: Sometimes, dear Meredith, your lover leaves you because you are unloveable.

Claire exits. Meredith goes into her room, slamming the door.

BLACKOUT

SCENE 2 : That night. The wind has stopped. Liz is in the kitchen, mending a piece of equipment.

Natalie enters.

NATALIE: Are you concentrating?

LIZ: What's on your mind?

NATALIE: I think I need to talk.

LIZ: To me?

NATALIE: If it's all right.

LIZ: Hey, yeah, sure. Sit down.

NATALIE: *(Sits. Doesn't know how to start)* Liz, if you hadn't married Tony ...I mean, did you ever think ... I mean, well ....

LIZ: Spit it out, kid. I don't bite.

NATALIE: How do you know...I think I'm attracted to women.

LIZ: Is that a fact?

NATALIE: I never thought about it before. I mean, I thought about it, but not seriously, kind of in the way you'd wonder what you wanted for dinner or something. I had a friend in high school—and a couple in college—and I know the things I felt about them weren't the same as the things they felt about their friends or the things I felt about my other friends ... And I figured that was just adolescent stuff and I'd outgrow it, and anyway I was too busy following the road maps other people had made for my life...and when that didn't work out I thought it was just one of those things that don't work out, like things don't work out sometimes, you know ... HELP ME WITH THIS.

LIZ: Gosh, I don't know what to say.

NATALIE: Liz....

LIZ: I thought you were going to tell me something I didn't know.

NATALIE: What?

LIZ: I knew it the minute I met you.

NATALIE: Well, I didn't. You could have told me.

LIZ: Walk up to someone I never met before and say, "Hi, I'm Liz Raymo, your climbing guide, and I can tell you're attracted to women"? That can be bad for business. So what are you going to do about it?

NATALIE: Do about it?

LIZ: Do about it.

NATALIE: How should I know what to do about it? I just figured it out. I wouldn't know where to start to know what to do about it.

LIZ: Look, maybe I'm not the best person to talk to about this.

NATALIE: Who am I going to talk to? Claire? Paula? She's very sweet and all, but I don't think this is up her alley. And I sure can't talk to Meredith about ....

LIZ: How come? *(Light dawns)* Oh.

NATALIE: "Oh" what?

LIZ: *(Casual)* Just "oh."*(Gets up quickly)* Gotta check with the Forest Service. *(Exits to living room)*

NATALIE: What are you talking about? Liz....

Liz exits through the living room toward Meredith's room, bumps into Meredith.

LIZ: Hi-hi.

MEREDITH: *(Puzzled and amused by Liz's good mood)* You just win the lottery?

LIZ: Better than that, pal.

Liz exits to Meredith's room before Meredith can respond. Meredith goes to kitchen, where Natalie is still contemplating Liz's last remark.

NATALIE: Liz, I ... *(Glances up quickly, is stunned by her own visceral reaction)* Oh, my God.

MEREDITH: Excuse me?

NATALIE: Nothing.

MEREDITH: *(Looks around the kitchen, avoiding Natalies's eye)* How are we fixed for leftovers?

NATALIE: I'm not sure what it was, but there should be some around. Why did you miss dinner?

MEREDITH: Heard it was Paula's turn to cook.

NATALIE: Meredith ....

MEREDITH: I had letters to write.

NATALIE: All day?

MEREDITH: I have a lot of pen pals. They call me the sweetheart of the Postal Service.

NATALIE: Meredith, last night ....

MEREDITH: Forget it.

NATALIE: Something happened ....

MEREDITH: Nothing happened.

NATALIE: ... between us. Don't turn away, please. I felt something, knew something. You needed ... Meredith, how can you live without ....

MEREDITH: Television? Self-discipline.

NATALIE: Love.

MEREDITH: I have Liz and Tony. That's not a disposable plastic friendship.

NATALIE: The make-breakfast-for-each-other kind.

MEREDITH: Love, love, love. The whole damn world's one monstrous Valentine.

NATALIE: You don't mean that.

MEREDITH: Care to hear about the great tragedy in my life? The one that left me bleeding and embittered?

NATALIE: I certainly would.

MEREDITH: My goldfish died.

NATALIE: For God's sake.

MEREDITH: I was very attached to that goldfish. I'd given it a name, though it escapes me at the moment. One bright spring morning I toddled down the stairs, trembling with childish anticipation at the thought of seeing my What's-his-name. And there it was, floating upside down at the top of the water. My tiny heart cracked with a deafening retort. I vowed never to love again.

NATALIE: Meredith, what did I do?

MEREDITH: I'm sorry. I'm not handling this well.*(Natalie goes to touch her)* Don't, please.

NATALIE: What did Claire say to you this morning?

MEREDITH: Nothing of value.

NATALIE: Really? *(Meredith shrugs)* You two shared a squalid history, didn't you?

MEREDITH: Something like that.

NATALIE: My God, isn't <u>this</u> the ultimate nightmare?

MEREDITH: I suppose.

NATALIE: We all have our share of squalid history, but who expects to be trapped in a blizzard with it? It's hard to imagine, the two of you.

MEREDITH: I've never been famous for my good judgment. She was different. Or I was different. <u>One</u> of us <u>must</u> have been different.

NATALIE: Some people change once they're sure of you.

MEREDITH: I'd never be that sure of anyone.

NATALIE: Neither would I. Love's the most fragile, the most precious thing in the world to me. I couldn't treat it roughly.

MEREDITH: You shouldn't say things like that in public.

NATALIE: I don't. You sure get prickly under stress.

MEREDITH: Beneath this tougher-than-nails exterior, there beats a heart that weeps over abandoned luggage. There was a time when I couldn't bear to throw anything away. That's why I took up writing—to make unemployed scraps of paper feel useful.

NATALIE: That isn't funny.

MEREDITH: I guess it isn't.

NATALIE: I'd like to read one of your books.

MEREDITH: I'm sorry. The only people I can show them to are Liz and Tony, and faceless editors I might never meet. If I didn't think I was only talking to myself, I'd freeze.

NATALIE: You're a private person, aren't you?

MEREDITH: You noticed.

Liz comes bursting in.

LIZ: It's over. Clearing by morning. *(No response)* Don't thank me.

It's all in a day's work. *(Draws Meredith aside)* Rocks your boat a little, doesn't she, pal? *(Exits to dormitory, calling)* Hey, Claire, stop polishing your Guccis. I have news.

NATALIE: It seems as if we just got here.

MEREDITH: Does it?

NATALIE: There are a thousand things I want to ask you. A thousand things I want to say, but it's all so ... unformed. Meredith, how do you know when something's right for you?

MEREDITH: I guess it's when you feel your clothes fit. *(They look at each other)* You'd better go.

NATALIE: I suppose.

MEREDITH: You don't want to spend half the night packing, and have to stumble down the mountain with gravel in your eyes.

NATALIE: I guess not. *(Turns to go)*

MEREDITH: Natalie? Whatever destiny has in store for you .... I hope it's the very best. Sleep well.

NATALIE: Good night, Meredith.

Impulsively, Natalie embraces Meredith who exits quickly to the living room. Paula enters the kitchen.

PAULA: Did you hear? We're leaving tomorrow.

NATALIE: Yes.

PAULA: Good news, isn't it?

NATALIE: Back to civilization and central heating.

PAULA: No more snow and wind and trail bars.

NATALIE: No more heating water on the stove.

PAULA: So why aren't we celebrating?

NATALIE: I'll miss it. And Liz ... and Meredith. And Claire, of course.

PAULA: I'm lucky. I can see Claire any time I want. And other times as well.

NATALIE: Do you think you'll come back here?

PAULA: Probably not. How about you?

NATALIE: I don't even know what I'll be doing the day after tomorrow.

PAULA: *(Picking up some of her things)* Well, I'd better pack before I get any more sentimental. Mark says I'd get sentimental about Hell if I spent two days there.

Paula exits. Natalie starts to gather her things, sits at the table to think. Claire enters.

CLAIRE: Are my gloves out here.

NATALIE: I haven't seen them.

CLAIRE: Turning in soon?

NATALIE: In a while.

CLAIRE: It's been quite a couple of days, hasn't it?

NATALIE: Yes.

CLAIRE: You and Meredith seemed to hit it off.

NATALIE: I suppose.

CLAIRE: She's an interesting person. Tricky, but interesting.

NATALIE: You should know.

CLAIRE: What does that mean?

NATALIE: *(Realizes she let something slip)* Nothing.

CLAIRE: Has she been talking about me?

NATALIE: Not to me.

CLAIRE: What did she tell you?

NATALIE: *(Exasperated)* For God's sake, Claire, you're not the center of the Universe.

Claire storms off to the living room in a huff. Natalie starts to follow, changes her mind, stays in kitchen.

CLAIRE: Well.

MEREDITH: That's a deep subject.

CLAIRE: We're leaving tomorrow.

MEREDITH: I heard.

CLAIRE: Can't you drag yourself away from that typewriter for one night?

MEREDITH: I'm married to my work.

CLAIRE: *(Decides to try a softer approach)* I'm sorry we didn't have a chance to work through our differences.

MEREDITH: It happens.

CLAIRE: But you had a lot on your mind, didn't you?

MEREDITH: What?

CLAIRE: Oh, come off it, Meredith. How stupid do you think I am?

MEREDITH: Claire, I don't know what you're talking about.

CLAIRE: You just <u>had</u> to tell her, didn't you?

MEREDITH: Tell who? What?

CLAIRE: Meredith the Misunderstood, Patron Saint of Innocents.

MEREDITH: What?

CLAIRE: I suppose your precious Liz knows all about it, too.

MEREDITH: About <u>what</u>?

CLAIRE: New Haven.

MEREDITH: I mentioned it to Liz. I was having a hard time, and she knew it.

CLAIRE: "Having a hard time."

MEREDITH: Yes, having a hard time. I never wanted to see you again, Claire.

CLAIRE: Well, it's the same old story. Poor, dear, unhappy, sensitive Meredith.

MEREDITH: Claire ....

CLAIRE: Gets them every time, doesn't it?

MEREDITH: *(Confused)* What?

CLAIRE: It's a great line. I have to grant you that. Five minutes of pathetic and they're hooked.

MEREDITH: I don't know what you think's happening, but ....

CLAIRE: I know the routine. How much did you tell her?

MEREDITH: Who?

CLAIRE: The little Denver divorcee.

MEREDITH: She asked if we had shared a history. I told her we had.

.CLAIRE: That's all?

MEREDITH: That's all.

CLAIRE: Liar.

MEREDITH: Claire ....

CLAIRE: I'll bet you spilled your pathetic little guts all over her.

MEREDITH: I didn't.

CLAIRE: I know how you operate, Meredith.

Paula enters kitchen looking for a game of cards.

And how much of your pitiful story did you just have to tell Liz?

MEREDITH: *(Her voice rises)* I told her we had been lovers. I told her you wanted to sleep with me. She wasn't impressed, all right?

Natalie and Paula are about to leave the kitchen when they hear Meredith's outburst.

NATALIE: We'd better ... *(Motions Paula out)*

PAULA: Are you kidding? I wouldn't miss this for the world. *(Settles down to eavesdrop.)*

NATALIE: Paula ....

PAULA: Shhhhh.

Natalie gives up politeness and sits with Paula.

CLAIRE: So you sat in here with Calamity Jane and had a grand old gossip.

MEREDITH: We didn't gossip.

CLAIRE: Merely whiling away the time on a snowy evening? Nothing worth watching on television, so let's get our kicks out of trashing Claire Stoddard.

MEREDITH: It wasn't like that at all.

CLAIRE: Of course it wasn't.

MEREDITH: I was upset, Claire.

CLAIRE: That's right, you'd never break a promise, would you? But if you're upset, and the story just happens to come out, in all innocence, of course ... I'll give you credit for one thing, Meredith. You are one champion manipulator.

MEREDITH: Damn it, I never wanted to see you again.

CLAIRE: You've made that clear enough. No wonder everybody's talking.

MEREDITH: Nobody's talking.

CLAIRE: Except you. And Liz. And Natalie. Poor Paula must feel left out. Or did you "have to" tell her, too.

MEREDITH: I haven't even had a conversation with Paula.

CLAIRE: Really? It seems to me things got awfully quiet, awfully fast when I walked into the kitchen yesterday morning. What were you talking about?

MEREDITH: Nothing. The wind ....

CLAIRE: *(Dripping sarcasm)* The wind. I can't believe it. I come all this way to be friends with you, and you can't even wait twenty-four hours to try to turn everyone against me.

MEREDITH: I didn't try to ....

CLAIRE: Of course not. You were just upset. So you let a little slip here, leak a little there ... Why didn't you send out an All-Points Bulletin? But that wouldn't be subtle enough, would it? Someone might be able to blame you for that.

MEREDITH: Please, Claire, I'm not very good at this.

CLAIRE: Oh, yes, you are, Meredith. You're very, very good at it.

MEREDITH: I didn't mean to ....

CLAIRE: You never mean to, do you?

MEREDITH: *(Her voice rising)* Do we have to go through all this again?

CLAIRE: You started it.

MEREDITH: Well, let's both end it.

CLAIRE: So you can have one more free "fuck you"?

MEREDITH: What?

CLAIRE: You can say anything that comes into your head. Any time. But let me call you on it, you want to drop it.

MEREDITH: Okay, I'm sorry. Will that do it?

CLAIRE: No, that won't "do it".

MEREDITH: Then what the hell do you want?

CLAIRE: My God, it hasn't changed a bit.

MEREDITH: I don't even know what you're talking about.

CLAIRE: You want <u>me</u> to tell <u>you</u> what to say, so you don't have to put your <u>real</u> feelings on the line. If you <u>have</u> any real feelings.

MEREDITH: Claire ....

CLAIRE: You have all the right words, and you know how to use them. It took me along time to realize there was nothing underneath.

MEREDITH: Claire, I loved you.

CLAIRE: You were dependent on me. That isn't love.

MEREDITH: I <u>did</u> ....

CLAIRE: You wanted someone you could control. Someone who'd come running any time you called.

MEREDITH: I called you once. <u>One time</u>, I needed you. Because I had the flu and couldn't walk as far as the kitchen. I asked you to come over and put a TV dinner in the oven. Do you remember what you said?

CLAIRE: It was always something.

MEREDITH: "I'm going out tonight. You'll have to fend for yourself."

CLAIRE: If it wasn't the flu, it was some emotional trauma ....

MEREDITH: Later you got around to telling me who you'd gone out with.

CLAIRE: Or something I'd said that you couldn't "understand" and it was so upsetting ....

MEREDITH: And that you'd been sleeping with her for the past two months.

CLAIRE: All you really cared about was keeping me under your thumb.

MEREDITH: *(Blowing up)* Goddamn it, Claire, you made it into half the beds in New Haven, while I sat home and wondered where you were. And if I as much as had coffee with a friend, you accused and berated until I wasn't even sure wh....

CLAIRE: Because you're a liar.

MEREDITH: I never lied to you.

CLAIRE: You lied to yourself. You don't know the difference between the truth and that lovely picture of yourself you carry in your head.

MEREDITH: No matter what I said, you wouldn't believe me.

CLAIRE: How could I? Everything you said or did was to tighten the noose around my neck.

MEREDITH: Claire ....

CLAIRE: Everybody felt sorry for you, didn't they? Poor, sweet Meredith.

MEREDITH: Stop it!

CLAIRE: And now you have to run to Natalie with your sad stories. I wonder what she'd think if she knew you had ulterior motives.

MEREDITH: *(Shouts)* Damn it, I don't have ulterior motives!

Natalie starts to get up, to stop the argument. Paula stops her.

PAULA: Let her do this.

NATALIE: But I ....

PAULA: If you stop it now, Claire wins.

Natalie sits down.

CLAIRE: All open and above-board? Like your so-called "friendship" with that History teacher, what was her name ....

MEREDITH: What?

CLAIRE: I'll bet it didn't take you long to get her between the sheets.

MEREDITH: I never slept with her.

CLAIRE: Right.

MEREDITH: She was a friend.

CLAIRE: Right.

MEREDITH: She was straight.

CLAIRE: I suppose you hear from her weekly, if not daily.

MEREDITH: I don't hear from her at all.

CLAIRE: Really? I'm amazed. You two were so tight back in New Haven.

MEREDITH: I stopped seeing her.

CLAIRE: Why?

MEREDITH: My God, don't you remember? Every time I spent ten minutes with her you went into a jealous rage.

CLAIRE: It was my idea for you to see her in the first place.

MEREDITH: I don't know why.

CLAIRE: You were too dependent on me. It wasn't healthy. I should have known you couldn't just be friends with her.

MEREDITH: I never slept with her, Claire.

CLAIRE: Oh, give me a break. We're not involved any more, Merry. You don't have to lie.

MEREDITH: I never slept with her.

CLAIRE: You might as well have. Talk about obvious. The way you looked at her was obscene.

MEREDITH: I wasn't attracted to her.

CLAIRE: You really believe that? No wonder I couldn't trust you.

MEREDITH: *(Beginning to lose it)* You told me to be friends with her, and then accused me of sleeping with her. What was I supposed to do?

CLAIRE: I've often wondered what kind of lies you told her about me.

MEREDITH: I never even <u>talked</u> about you.

CLAIRE: Like you didn't talk about me to Liz, or to Natalie, or....

MEREDITH: *(A little hysterical)* Why are you <u>doing</u> this?

CLAIRE: You really are a fucked-up bitch, Meredith.

MEREDITH: What did I do? I don't know what I did.

CLAIRE: From the day I met you, you had your hands around my throat. Offering me your little hurts, one by one, like flowers. All your embarrassing moments. All your secret longings. All the tiny joys and tragedies of your pathetic life.

MEREDITH: I told you those things because I <u>loved</u> you.

CLAIRE: You never loved me. You used me. You spun your web around me until I couldn't breathe....

MEREDITH: <u>Stop it, Claire!</u>

CLAIRE: And when I tried to get away, to save myself, you made me out to be the villain.

MEREDITH: *(Losing control)* Why are you doing this?

CLAIRE: But nobody really knew you, did they? Nobody ever guessed that beneath that sweet, sensitive, clever façade you were nothing. NOTHING. NADA. ZERO.

MEREDITH: What do you want from me?

CLAIRE: I want you to tell the truth.

MEREDITH: <u>What</u> truth?

CLAIRE: Any truth. Anything that isn't one of your imaginary worlds populated by imaginary playmates. What do you call your free-lance autobiography, "A Made-Up Life"?

MEREDITH: Claire.

CLAIRE: Behold the tragic heroine, hidden away on her mountaintop too fragile to live in the real world. Writing drivel that has all the depth of a greeting card, and feeding off of other people's lives like a vampire.

MEREDITH: Did you read my ....

CLAIRE: Enough to know you haven't changed. *(Laughs)* Back in New Haven, we used to sit around and read those asinine stories you wrote for me and laugh ourselves sick. Our favorite game was "guess who this one's about."

Devastated, Meredith starts for her room, but Claire blocks the way.

That's right, run out into the darkness. Make everyone look for you in the cold.

Meredith starts for the kitchen.

Go cry on Liz's shoulder. Get Natalie to kiss it and make it well. It always worked before.

Meredith reaches the kitchen just as Natalie unfreezes and heads for the living room to stop the fight.

MEREDITH: *(Stops short when she sees Natalie.)* Oh, Christ.

CLAIRE: Well, isn't this cute?

Meredith heads for her room. Natalie catches her.

NATALIE: Meredith ....

MEREDITH: <u>Leave me alone!</u>

CLAIRE: Careful, dear heart. She might take you at face value, and then what would you do?

NATALIE: *(Won't let Meredith go)* Crawl back under your rock, Claire.

CLAIRE: *(Takes a piece of Meredith's writing from her desk)* Want to hear something touching? I believe this is from her journal. "Every time N looks at me, I want to scoop her up and put her in my pocket." Who's "N," Meredith?

Meredith shakes Natalie off , grabs the paper, and runs to her room.

CLAIRE: She'll get over it.

NATALIE: You really are trash.

CLAIRE: Look out for her. She may be all sweetness and light now, but once she gets her hooks into you, she hangs on and hangs on ....

NATALIE: Get out of here before I throw up on you.

CLAIRE: *(As she exits to kitchen, with a shrug)* Forewarned is forearmed, dear heart.*(To Paula)* When you come to bed, try to be quiet for a change. *(Claire exits to dormitory.)*

BLACKOUT

SCENE 3: The next morning. Liz is sitting in front of the fireplace. Paula is in the kitchen.

Natalie enters the living room.

NATALIE: Where is she?

LIZ: Outside.

NATALIE: Have you talked to her?

LIZ: I tried. She ran.

NATALIE: I should have stopped it sooner.

LIZ: We all should have. We didn't. Damn Claire. When I first met Meredith, she had so many walls ... I got angry at her for lying to me. I wish I hadn't.

NATALIE: Come on, Liz. This isn't your fault.

LIZ: I can organize a party of ten for a week in the wilderness. I can pitch a tent in a high wind. But this—I'm a dead loss.

NATALIE: You love her tremendously, don't you?

LIZ: Yeah, I love her tremendously.

NATALIE: I think I do too.

LIZ: After three fun-packed days in a snowstorm?

NATALIE: I can't help it. Destiny had something in store for me.

LIZ: Why couldn't you have come here before Claire?

NATALIE: I wish I had. Is there anything we can do about Our

Lady of Perpetual Plastic?

LIZ: That I can handle. I have Divine Torture planned.

NATALIE: After we leave, will Meredith be all right?

LIZ: I think so. She survived Claire once, I guess she can do it again. Jesus, I hate to go like this.

NATALIE: I know. I'll do what I can.

LIZ: Listen, there's one thing .... I don't want anyone messing her up.

NATALIE: I had that impression.

LIZ: Just want to be clear about that.

NATALIE: It's clear.

LIZ: Just want to be sure it's clear.

NATALIE: *(With a laugh)* Don't worry, Liz.

LIZ: Let somebody else don't worry. Me, I worry. Well, time to get cracking. I have a long day ahead. So do you, I suspect. *(Liz exits to dormitory)*

Natalie calls out the front door.

NATALIE: Meredith. Meredith, come in here.

MEREDITH: *(Offstage)* I'm mowing the lawn.

NATALIE: Very funny. Stop acting like a jerk and get in here. *(Meredith enters)* God, you look awful.

MEREDITH: Thank you. *(Natalie gives her a look.)* It was a long night. We're probably due for Daylight Savings Time.

NATALIE: I should have stayed with you.

MEREDITH: And read me nursery rhymes?

NATALIE: Don't do this.

MEREDITH: What do you want me to do? Go about my business humming and whistling as if nothing had happened? Fling myself weeping into your arms? I'm humiliated, I don't like myself very much, and I'm handling it the best I can.

NATALIE: Scream. Throw things. Go out there and tear her apart eyelash by eyelash. But, please, Meredith, don't close me out.

MEREDITH: Forget last night ever happened.

NATALIE: Swell. That woman drops a load of manure in your living room, and I'm supposed to pretend it's a Christmas tree?

MEREDITH: That's very good. May I quote you?

NATALIE: You do that.

Natalie and Meredith go to opposite sides of the room. Claire enters the kitchen, where Paula is cooking with a vengeance.

CLAIRE: *(Glancing into the pan)* Better take that off. It'll burn.

PAULA: *(Pleasantly)* Good morning.

CLAIRE: You're in a sunny little mood. Where did you get that shirt?

PAULA: From Liz.

CLAIRE: It looks silly.

PAULA: Fried eggs, is that all right.

CLAIRE: Fine.

PAULA: If you'd rather have soft-boiled, I don't mind the extra trouble.

CLAIRE: Fried are fine.

PAULA: How about hot cereal?

CLAIRE:*(Beginning to get suspicious)* Do you have something up your sleeve?

PAULA: It's a cold day, and we have a long way to go. I wouldn't want you to be uncomfortable.

CLAIRE: I see.

PAULA: *(Serves Claire her breakfast, sits down with her, watches her eat for a moment. Still pleasantly)* I could have anything I wanted from you right now, couldn't I?

CLAIRE: Excuse me?

PAULA: *(Still pleasant)* I'll bet you'd screw the Calleys' Pomeranian if I told you to.

CLAIRE: What?

PAULA: Screw the Calleys' Pomeranian, Claire.

CLAIRE: Now, wait a minute.

PAULA: You know, dear heart, you handed me the Ace of Trump last night. And I know exactly how to play it.

CLAIRE: All right, now we're down to brass tacks. What do you want? A vice-presidency for hubby?

PAULA: You underestimate me, dear heart.

CLAIRE: I'm in a position to do a lot for you. And for Mark. Let's work something out.

PAULA: I could have a lot of fun with this.

CLAIRE: *(An uneasy laugh)* So, the worm finally turns.

PAULA: I dropped the first shoe. You can wait for the second.

Liz enters.

LIZ: Grab your coat, Claire. You're coming with me.

CLAIRE: Where?

LIZ: To pack a trail to the camp.

CLAIRE: Let one of the rugged outdoor types do it.

LIZ: I want you.

CLAIRE: Why?

LIZ: Because it's impossible to hate someone and freeze to death at the same time.

CLAIRE: Don't be an idiot.

LIZ: Move your buns, Sweet Cakes, before I forget I'm a lady. *(Claire exits. To Paula)* You can relax. I'll take it from here.

Liz exits after Claire. In the living room, Natalie turns to Meredith.

NATALIE: Damn it, I didn't do anything to you.

MEREDITH: You're right. I'm sorry. Really, I'm sorry.

NATALIE: Great! I finally work up a perfectly beautiful anger, and you ruin it.

MEREDITH: Sorry.

NATALIE: We may not get another chance to talk. I want to tell you ... I'm glad I met you.

MEREDITH: So am I.

NATALIE: I'd like to ... Meredith, I love you.

MEREDITH: *(Not understanding)* You're a rare person, Natalie. Don't let them eat you alive.

NATALIE: Oh, Christ.

MEREDITH: Please go now.

Reluctantly, Natalie turns to leave

Natalie. *(Meredith gets one of her notebook-bound manuscripts, hands it to Natalie, and exits to her room.)*

BLACKOUT

SCENE 4: Later that morning.Meredith is alone in the living room.

Liz enters from outside.

MEREDITH: That was quick.

LIZ: Snow thinned out at the spruce woods How you doing, pal?

MEREDITH: I'm all right.

LIZ: I'll take the campers out the back way.

MEREDITH: Thank you.

LIZ: I don't like leaving you.

MEREDITH: I'll be okay, really.

LIZ: Well, we'll be back in May. Bag, baggage, and papoose, if the offer's still open.

MEREDITH: What about Tony?

LIZ: I'll try a different approach. Soft lights, romantic music, sexy negligee ... *(Sees the look on Meredith's face)* Think I can't do it? I'll drive him mad with lust.

MEREDITH: Liz, this isn't because of ... you know?

LIZ: Let's say Claire put things into perspective for me. I spent my childhood proud and miserable. I want my kid in debt and happy. There's an opening for a godmother. Interested?

MEREDITH: Isn't that for you and Tony to ....

LIZ: We decided. Long before this infant was a twinkle in our eyes. Well?

MEREDITH: No reservations?

LIZ: To tell you the truth, we were hoping for someone a little more articulate.

MEREDITH: All right, all right I'll miss you, Liz.

LIZ: Yeah. Would you give the boys a call in a while? Tell them we're on the way. For all I know, they could be over there trying on women's dresses. So long, pal.

Liz and Meredith embrace. Claire walks in from outside.

CLAIRE: For Heaven's sake, Liz, we're freezing ... *(Sees them)* I despise women. *(Exits, slamming the door.)*

LIZ: Gosh, I always wanted to make an exit like that.

MEREDITH: Be my guest.

LIZ: "I despise women."

Liz exits, slamming the door. Natalie enters the kitchen. Meredith goes to kitchen.

MEREDITH: I thought you'd left.

NATALIE: I guess I should.

MEREDITH: Don't want to miss the wagon train.

NATALIE: Will you be all right?

MEREDITH: Sure.

NATALIE: I'm worried about you.

MEREDITH: The way people worry about me, I should write my autobiography. I'd make every school of social work in the country.

NATALIE: It doesn't seem right, leaving you ....

MEREDITH: Better move along. It could snow again any time.

NATALIE: I know.

MEREDITH: If you don't show up at the bank, they'll think you ran off with someone's trust fund.

NATALIE: Meredith ....

MEREDITH: Next thing you know, an FBI agent behind every bush.

NATALIE: I'm serious.

MEREDITH: You're crazy, but I appreciate the offer.

NATALIE: Damn it, I <u>want</u> to stay.

MEREDITH: The lodge is closed. Try us in June.

NATALIE: June's a long way off.

MEREDITH: Not for me. Around January all of us weirdo-hermit-odd-balls get together and whoop it up until ice-out.

NATALIE: You don't understand. I want to ....

MEREDITH: It's seven months of cold, and silence, and claustrophobia. Dawn is a major event.

NATALIE: I love this place. I think I love you.

MEREDITH: Don't let my warm, cuddly exterior fool you. I picked it up from greeting cards.

NATALIE: Why did you give me your book?

MEREDITH: Farewells make me maudlin.

NATALIE: Can't we have a reasonable conversation?

MEREDITH: Sorry, I've had enough conversation to last me the rest of my life.

Liz creeps into the living room and eavesdrops.

NATALIE: Will you let me explain?

MEREDITH: It was a long season, and I've had recent difficult house guests. I'm not in the mood for explanations.

NATALIE: Meredith, I don't want to do it this way.

MEREDITH: I don't want to do it at all. You have a life down there. Go back to it.

NATALIE: The life I have down there can be settled with a few phone calls. Anything I need I can get in one trip to Anaconda. I can get a job with the Forest Service, and a snowmobile, and be with you on weekends. I only want to try, to see if....

MEREDITH: I want you out of here.

NATALIE: Not until you listen to me.

MEREDITH: *(Heads for the front door, calling)* LIZ!

LIZ: Hi.

MEREDITH: Get her out of here.

LIZ: You handle it, Meredith. I'm on her side. *(Exits)*

MEREDITH: Liz!

NATALIE: If there were time, I could be gentle. I could reach out to you and make it safe for you, and you could learn to trust me. But Claire stole what little time we had. I know what I'm asking, but ....

MEREDITH: You don't know what you're asking. You can't stay here, Natalie. Not now, not in June, not ever.

NATALIE: Why?

MEREDITH: Because, damn you, I've fallen in love with you.

NATALIE: So am I. I feel awkward. I don't know what to do with my hands. I want make breakfast for you, to carry you around in my pocket. I'm not asking you to marry me, just to give it a little time, to see....

MEREDITH: NO!

NATALIE: So, Claire wins again.

MEREDITH: What?

NATALIE: When she didn't have you, she wanted you. When she got you, she didn't want you. She came here wanting you again, and when you didn't want her, she made sure you'd never want anyone. It's as simple as that, Meredith. It's the oldest game there is, and you let her win.

MEREDITH: Natalie, I ....

NATALIE: I'm afraid, too, you know. Of caring, not caring, loving, being loved, being left. But until that last sunrise, what else do we have?

MEREDITH: You don't know what you're asking.

NATALIE: I'm asking you to love me. Just the way I am. Rough edges, insecurities, moodiness. I think too much. Sometimes I talk too much. I'm compulsive about dishes, and not very handy with a hammer. But I know how to love, and when to let go. I wouldn't be jealous of your friends, or your imaginary worlds, or your writing. And I'd never, ever treat your love roughly.

MEREDITH: I can't do it.

NATALIE: Not even try?

MEREDITH:You don't understand. I can't go though that again.

NATALIE: Then tell me how it was, for God's sake. Tell me <u>something</u> that makes sense.

MEREDITH: *(Reluctantly, at first)* It was almost perfect in the beginning. I opened myself to her, She opened herself to me. Claire could listen. So hard, so completely that you thought you were the most fascinating, important person in the world. That the things you said were so new and exciting ... Then, one day, I was telling her something I'd seen ... I don't remember now ... something that moved me. And she laughed. She lit a cigarette and laughed. After that, when I tried to ....

NATALIE: Are you cold? *(Takes Meredith's sweater from the chair and puts it around her)*

MEREDITH: I wanted to ask why, but I was afraid. And when I finally did, she said, "You know." Nothing more. She sat there and stared at me, with the smoke from her cigarette drifting between us and hatred in her eyes, and said, "You know."

NATALIE: Meredith, it wasn't you.

MEREDITH: Toward the end ... there would be good times now and then, but I never knew. I tried to do what she wanted. I tried to <u>be</u> what she wanted, but it was never right. I'd try to reach...to touch what had been... and I'd think, "If I can only find the key, the words ... if I can figure out what I did wrong ..." And all the while there was a terror, gnawing at me... One night, driving to her house, the world tore apart and I screamed, and went on screaming...Oh, Christ, I'm so <u>empty</u>.

NATALIE:*(After a moment)* I want to touch you, to warm you.

There is so much in you to love ....

MEREDITH: There's nothing in me to love.

NATALIE: Meredith ....

MEREDITH: *(Distraught)* Don't you understand ? I'm hollow. I'm empty. I don't feel!

NATALIE: You don't ... *(Wants to comfort her, but finds herself beginning to laugh)* I ... I'm sorry, I can't help it. *(Tries to get control of herself, fails)* If you're empty, if you don't feel ... Meredith, what the hell is going on here?

MEREDITH: *(Glares at her for a second, then realizes the ridiculousness of it. Starts to laugh)* Listen, this isn't funny. *(Both are laughing, unable to stop, partly from released tension)* This is pain and suffering we have here.

NATALIE: Right, pain and suffering.

MEREDITH: Agony.

NATALIE: Misery.

MEREDITH: Tragedy.

NATALIE: Definitely, tragedy.*(Pause)* Meredith, for the last time, may I stay?

MEREDITH: Of all the mountains you could climb, you had to climb this one. Of all the days you could have left home, you chose the one you did. The storm ... there wasn't a chance in a million this would happen.

NATALIE: It happened.

MEREDITH: We have to believe in what happens, don't we? If anything is going to mean anything in this life, we have to help that meaning to happen.

NATALIE: I offer you love, and you give me back philosophy. *(Takes her hands)* Look at me, and tell me what you want.

MEREDITH: I want .... Are you going to stand around all winter in that coat?

BLACKOUT

THE END

Backward, Turn Backward

"Backward, turn backward,
O time in your flight,
Make me a child again,
Just for tonight."
From an old photograph album

Introduction

This play always inspires controversy. I've overheard it described (as I lurked about anonymously in theater lobbies) as "better than anything I saw on Broadway this year." I've also been confronted by a woman who angrily demanded to know why I bothered to write about child abuse "since it's already been done." (If "never been done" is our criterion for art, why, I ask myself, are there so bloody many shows about heterosexual relationships? Hasn't that "been done"?)

If you don't like dark comedy, or speaking ill of the dead, or criticizing fathers, skip this play. It's an angry play, and I wrote it out of the frustration all of us feel when someone treats us badly, but is judged a saint by the rest of the world.

I also wrote it to see if I could capture a particular type of psychological manipulation—control by passivity. My father raised this to an art form, and left a trail of shattered psyches wherever he went, while he came up smelling like a rose. So, this play is for all those women who find themselves saying, "You'd know what I mean if you had to live with him."

The question often comes up, "Is Monroe really there, or is Rae hallucinating?" To be perfectly honest, I don't know. I'm not trying to be coy; I really don't know. I know he—the actual living, breathing Monroe—doesn't come downstairs. But something happens, and most of the time I don't think Rae hallucinates him. I think, strange as it may sound, that strong emotion makes things happen, and that Rae's anger toward Monroe makes him materialize in some way. Or maybe it's just her memories that she fights with. I've deliberately left it ambiguous. In the long run, I don't think it really matters. People who can do us in, can do us in whether they're in the same room or half a continent away.

"Monroe the ghost" has provided us with some interesting discussions about how he/it would be presented onstage. Do you use a real actor? A cardboard cut-out? Someone even suggested a hologram, which led us into a rousing game of "unlimited budget"—a game similar to that popular parlor game "The Mysterious Millionnaire Lesbian Benefactor." It's irrelevant for us in the long run, since we're an all-woman company (though one of our actors does a terrific Disgusting-Old-Man imitation).

This is a "kitchen play." Kitchen plays are terribly hard to produce, and terribly tempting to write. In most families, a lot goes on in the kitchen. It's traditionally the woman's room. Men don't feel very comfortable in kitchens, unless they're playing cards. But the kitchen was (and probably still is in most homes) the room in which the woman is In Charge. My mother and I felt safe in our kitchen. You might say it gave us the Home Court advantage.

Kitchens are also casual rooms, unlike living rooms and dining rooms, which are more polite rooms. "Family rooms" (which used to be called "rumpus rooms" until television quieted everyone down) are usually rooms in which everyone faces in the same direction, either toward the TV or behind the newspaper. Interaction is at a minimum, and not much drama takes place there.

There are tables in kitchens. People feel safe behind tables. Tables, particularly round or square tables without a discernible Head or Foot, equalize the power. If you're going to get down to the bare bones of something, chances are you'll do it in the kitchen. (Or the bedroom, but that creates a whole different dynamic.)

Try an experiment. Take a conversation you've had recently in the kitchen, and imagine having it in the bedroom, living room, back yard, a crowded restaurant, an empty restaurant. See how it changes.

The only thing wrong with kitchens is that they require so much set-building. And, once built, tend to be static. I have promised myself, and the Theater, Too production staff, that I'll never write another Kitchen Play. I suspect I'll break that promise more than once.

Porches are almost as good as kitchens, and almost as crazy-making to build.

Anyway, this is a Kitchen Play.

It's also a play about families, and how they can reduce us to the age of four before we even know what hit us.

And, yes, it's about child abuse. And injustice, and unfairness.

But it's also about women's hearts, seeking each other out, finding each other.

And healing.

CAST OF CHARACTERS

RAE JEGHELIAN, a woman in her thirties. She owns and works a farm in Vermont. Her clothing is functional, her manner straightforward, and her conventions her own. Her anger covers a deep-seated fear of her father, a fear which has been with her since childhood.

LYNDA STRATTON, Rae's younger sister, is married to a real estate agent. She has settled into a conventional life in Barnesville, and now spends her days looking after her family, and caring for her comatose father. Her devotion to duty hides an ugly past. She wants to be closer to Rae, but is sometimes impatient with her.

LEONA KOPKE, the elderly "family retainer" who cared for Rae and Lynda's mother and now looks after Monroe. A warm, uncomplicated, shy woman, she has lived a life of hardship and hard work, but it would never occur to her to complain.

IRIS WINTERS, the neighbor from across the street, is middle-aged and a busy-body. Her attitude is typically Barnesville, and utterly conventional. She never speaks ill of the old, the dying, or the dead, but feels free to trample the feelings of the young and alive.

MONROE JEGHELIAN, the father, is old, and was always old in his heart. A stubborn, self-centered man with a streak of cruelty, he is absolutely convinced of his own rightness. He has been successful in business, and has used his money to control the lives of those around him.

PLACE: in the kitchen of the Jeghelian home, an upper-middle-class home in Barnesville, PA, outside of Philadelphia.

TIME: is the present, mid-September.

ACT ONE

SCENE 1: A night in mid-September.

SCENE 2: Late that night, and the following morning.

ACT TWO

SCENE 1: That evening.

SCENE 2: A little later.

SCENE 3: The next morning.

ACT ONE

SCENE 1: The kitchen of the Jeghelian home. It is clean and tidy to the point of sterility. No amiable clutter, all cupboards and drawers carefully closed. Objects of hospitality (coffee mugs, dishes, etc.) are present, but lined up like soldiers, giving an institutional and slightly eerie effect.The appliances are slightly outdated, the clock on the stove doesn't work, and there are a few tacky touches (Pennsylvania Dutch stencils on the backs of the kitchen chairs). A large table stands in the exact middle of the room, a philodendron in the exact middle of the table. African violets in indifferent health grace the windowsills. A refinished dry sink serves as a liquor cabinet.

When Rae and Lynda's mother was alive, the kitchen was always a mess: neighbors in and out, unwashed glasses in the sink, bits of unidentifiable food tucked away in corners of the refrigerator, bent paper clips and unopened junk mail littering the table. When she took to her bed ten years ago with terminal cancer, the kitchen was cleaned up and put in its proper place. It has not changed since. A door leads directly to the outside, another to the interior hall. Rae's suitcase stands, dropped, near the back door. As the play progresses, Rae will gradually return mess and clutter to the kitchen.

TIME: Night, mid-September.

Rae enters in a state of shock and horror.

Lynda follows.

RAE: Jesus Christ!

LYNDA: I should have warned you.

RAE: He looks like something that came out of a dead 'possom the dogs brought home. Has he been like that since the accident?

LYNDA: More or less.

RAE: Does he speak, or feed himself, or anything?

LYNDA: He's what's loosely known as a vegetable.

RAE: Our father, the turnip.

LYNDA: Sometimes he mumbles a little, but it's hard to make out.

RAE: You've been waiting on <u>that</u> all this time?

LYNDA: Eight months, one week, and two days, to be exact. I don't stay over, of course. Leona takes the night shift.

RAE: Loved your telegram: "Come at once Father dying."

LYNDA: I wanted to have it sung, but they don't have that service up your way.

RAE: In Vermont we communicate by rumor and innuendo. Is it true, or did you do it to give me a lift?

LYNDA: He's dying.

RAE: I should have come sooner.

LYNDA: He wouldn't have recognized you.

RAE: I was thinking of you.

LYNDA: I'm used to it.

RAE: Eight months. Leona, too?

LYNDA: It's part of the job to her. She cleans the house, scrubs the sink, waters the African violets, and takes care of Monroe.

RAE: Shouldn't there be <u>machinery</u> or something? It's been a long haul, hasn't it?

LYNDA: That first day, in the hospital ... I stood and looked down at him. At his shrunken old man's arms, his legs like lumps under the sheet, his fingers ... maggots. Everything was white. The room, his face, cotton blankets, all so white. I was afraid of all that white. I counted the seconds until I could decently leave. I kept thinking, "Don't let him open his eyes. Please, God, don't let him open his eyes." His arms began to move, a kind of swimming motion. I turned and ran.

RAE: How could you go back?

LYNDA: *(Shrugs)* It was the thing to do.

RAE: Do you bring Eric and Cindy to see him?

LYNDA: They're too young.

RAE: I'm too young.

LYNDA: They'll be breaking down the door when they know you're in town. It's all I hear, "When's Auntie Tink coming?"

RAE: I wish they wouldn't call me that.

LYNDA: They learned it from Monroe. By the way, sister dear, I have a bone to pick with you about Eric.

RAE: Whatever it is, I didn't do it.

LYNDA: The tractor.

RAE: He squealed. Never swear a blood oath with an 8-year old.

LYNDA: He's not going to Vermont again until you promise not to let him up on that tractor.

RAE: I was holding him.

LYNDA: Promise.

RAE: I promise.

LYNDA: I'm surprised you didn't have Cindy up there, too.

RAE: She didn't want a ride.

LYNDA: The mother-child relationship is a state of siege. I don't need you giving aid and comfort to the enemy.

RAE: All right.

LYNDA: Maybe I'll come along next time, to make sure.

RAE: Better think twice. Farms are kind of cruddy.

LYNDA: *(Gestures toward upstairs)* I'm no stranger to crud. I hope this wasn't a bad time for you to be away.

RAE: It isn't your fault. Monroe's one aim in life is to cause the greatest inconvenience for the greatest possible number of people.

LYNDA: Rae, I haven't told Leona about him dying. I'd like her to have a little time off. She won't go if she thinks we need her. Do you mind?

RAE: Of course not. When's the Big Event.

LYNDA: It could be any time.

RAE: Do you realize Leona's been waiting on this family, on him, for nine years? Ten, if you count the year before Mother died.

LYNDA: *(Hesitantly)* You'll have to help me feed him, and turn him. He has to be changed.

RAE: Changed?

LYNDA: He's incontinent. We have to change his ... diaper. And check for bed sores.

RAE: Oh, Christ.

LYNDA: We have to clean his teeth....

RAE: He smells of rot and stale cigars.How can he smell of cigars when he hasn't smoked for eight months?

LYNDA: Please, Rae. I need your help.

RAE: Why isn't he in a nursing home?

LYNDA: It wasn't possible.

RAE: That bastard has enough money to keep himself in nursing homes for the next three generations.

LYNDA: After the accident, we found out he'd drawn up a paper ... it said we could only do it if it was necessary to save his life.

RAE: So what? We're next-of-kin. We have rights.

LYNDA: He gave power of attorney to the bank.

RAE: The bank?

LYNDA: I guess he felt closer to the bank than he did to us.

RAE: What about nurses?

LYNDA: You can't get round-the-clock nurses in Barnesville. They all move to Philadelphia.

RAE: It wasn't a problem when Mother ....

LYNDA: *(Sharply)* I don't want nurses.

RAE: Why not?

LYNDA: For my own reasons.

RAE: What reasons?

LYNDA: My own reasons, Rae.

RAE: I can't touch him. He's disgusting.

LYNDA: He's only an old man. A pathetic, dying old man.

RAE: Please, Lynda.

LYNDA: You do what you have to do, like on the farm. It isn't so bad.

RAE: Animals are different.

LYNDA: Why can't anything be easy with you?

RAE: All right, all right. I'll do what I have to do.

LYNDA: That's all I ask. How have you been, Rae?

RAE: Great. We might break even this year, if the weather holds.

LYNDA: Do you need money?

RAE: If we didn't need money, I'd think something was wrong.

LYNDA: It doesn't seem right. Monroe had so much. Did you ever ask him for help?

RAE: Sure. You know Dear Old Dad. "I ain't puttin' nothin' in no Goddamn farm." Do it his way or not at ... *(Sees something pass in the hall)* What was that?

LYNDA: I didn't see anything.

RAE: Someone went past the door.

LYNDA: Maybe it was Leona coming down.

RAE: We'd hear Leona. She thunders.

LYNDA: Well, the house is full of shadows. Have you had dinner?

RAE: Ever check out the food in a bus depot?

LYNDA: I'll get you something.

RAE: I can find the refrigerator, nothing changes around here. I'll bet that's the same philodendron Mother bought before she took to her bed. Can a philodendron live ten years?

LYNDA: I've never outlived one.

RAE: The kitchen's still the way she left it.

LYNDA: I tried to talk Monroe into having it painted, but he wouldn't.

RAE: *(Browsing in the refrigerator)* And the refrigerator's exactly the way he left it.

LYNDA: He hasn't entertained much lately.

RAE: He always had the most boring refrigerator on the Eastern Seaboard. Every time I visited, I'd roll in half starved and find one egg, a pat of butter, half a pint of milk, and a bowl of canned peaches. Always a bowl of canned peaches. I wonder if it was the same bowl of canned peaches.

LYNDA: He liked to walk to the Handi-Mart for what he wanted.

RAE: When Mother was alive, we could have opened an all-night diner.

LYNDA: When Mother was alive, we had to throw out so much food we could have kept pigs.

RAE: *(Indicates the ceiling)* The old stain's still there.

LYNDA: What is it?

RAE: She blew up the pressure cooker. While we were trying to clean up that mess, the bathtub overflowed and brought down the dining room ceiling. We sat in the rubble and laughed ourselves sick. She wouldn't admit it, but I know she did it on purpose. Where were you that day?

LYNDA: Probably at the Country Club, screwing behind the fourteenth hole.

RAE: *(Remembering her mother has reawakened her anger at Monroe)* I thought he'd be gone by the time I got here. Christ, he can't even die with involving everyone. That son-of-a-bitch has been sucking at this world for seventy years.

LYNDA: "That son-of-a-bitch" is our father.

RAE: Who art not, but should be, in Heaven.

LYNDA: Don't start.

RAE: Are you sure he's dying? Or did he dream it up to get me here?

LYNDA: He's dying.

RAE: I know he shuffled in front of that pick-up truck to punish me for staying away at Christmas.

LYNDA: He punished me for that. We had tears over turkey. It's just not Christmas unless it's maudlin.

RAE: Damn it, every time I took a stand, you had to pay for it. First it was the baseball games ....

LYNDA: *(Sharply)* What baseball games?

RAE: Don't tell me you've forgotten those golden childhood Saturdays at Veterans' Stadium.

LYNDA: It wasn't called that back then.

RAE: Every weekend, crammed into the box seats with old Constant Comment. *(Gives a Monroe chuckle)* "You girls wearin' your red jackets today, are ya'?" *(Chuckle)* "Eatin' a hot dog, are ya'?" "Goin' out to the bathroom, are ya'?" Jesus. And when I refused to go, you were stuck with it. And with his bad mood.

LYNDA: It didn't matter.

RAE: What did they call it? Connie Mack Stadium. How could I forget that? I must be going senile.

LYNDA: *(Getting up her courage to tell Rae something)* Rae....

RAE: Why doesn't he let go? What's he doing up there, playing with himself?

LYNDA: For God's sake.

Leona clatters into the room, carrying a tray with a couple of small dishes.

LEONA: I tried to get him to take some chocolate ice cream. He always liked chocolate ice cream. He took some egg custard, though.

RAE: Swell.

Leona starts cleaning up.

LYNDA: We can take care of that. There's an extra chicken in the freezer for you.

LEONA: Thanks. *(Putters around)* I'll come by in the morning and give him his bath.

LYNDA: You're taking tomorrow off.

LEONA: I don't mind.

LYNDA: Rae and I can handle it. Or we can call Iris.

RAE: *(At Iris' name)* God help us.

LEONA: I'd better. He's used to me. *(To Rae)* Is it fall yet up your way?

RAE: There was a touch of frost in the lower fields last week, but the cabbages like it. We're getting the tomatos in now.

LEONA: I remember how that was. My folks had seven acres of tomatos. Us kids had to stay out of school and pick them.

RAE: What did you do with the green ones? We're going to have bushels.

LEONA: Mostly we threw them at each other.

LYNDA: *(Eager for Leona to leave)* Can I give you a ride?

LEONA: No, thanks. My man and I went to New England when we got married. It was nice.

RAE: Come up to the farm sometime. I'll bet there are places in Vermont that haven't changed since you were there.

LEONA: *(Pleased, but shy)* Oh, well ....

LYNDA: Is there anything else you need, Leona?

LEONA: *(Checks her belongings)* No. I made the coffee ready. Plug it in if you want some. I always did that way for him.

LYNDA: That's fine.

LEONA: *(To Rae)* How's your friend?

RAE: She sends her best. Said to tell you to think of us if you ever want to go back to farming.

LEONA: Oh, I'm too old for that.

LYNDA: Are you sure you want to walk? It's getting dark.

LEONA: It's no bother. Well, I'll see you in the morning.

LYNDA: It really isn't necessary.

LEONA: If he's uneasy in the night, give him a little warm milk.

RAE: And don't come straight from Mass, okay? I'll never understand how you can pray at the crack of dawn.

LEONA: *(With a laugh)* Good to see you again.

Leona exits.

RAE: If that woman doesn't go to Heaven when she dies, I'll know there's no God.

LYNDA: I thought you already knew that.

RAE: Sometimes. Sometimes I figure he's just an old fart like Monroe.

LYNDA: I made up your bed in our old room.

RAE: I'll sleep down here.

LYNDA: Why?

RAE: He might wake up.

LYNDA: He doesn't wake or sleep, not the way we think of it. You have to be there in case something happens.

RAE: He can die without my encouragement.

LYNDA: He might fall out of bed.

RAE: What do I do then? Roll him down the stairs?

LYNDA: Call me. For Heaven's sake, Rae.

RAE: I can't ... *(Lynda looks at her helplessly)* I'll stay up there.

LYNDA: I'd do it myself, but Neil and the kids ....

RAE: Does he still snore?

LYNDA: Like a drowning elephant.

RAE: I hope you're paying Leona a king's ransom.

LYNDA: The bank pays her what Monroe gave her, eighty dollars a week.

RAE: She should tell them to stick it up their vault.

LYNDA: Leona? I slip her a little extra when I can, but she usually won't let me. Sometimes she'll take food.

RAE: Did you ever see her house? It's a shack. She tacks plastic over the windows for insulation. She used to do her laundry— and his, by the way—in a hand-wringer that belongs in the Smithsonian.

LYNDA: She still does.I suggested he buy her a new one, as a Christmas present, you know? *(Shrugs)*

RAE: When he dies, maybe we can set her up. You should get a mint for this barge.

LYNDA: It's our house, too.

RAE: You can have it, Baby Sister. You've earned it. Though I did have dreams of selling it to a racially mixed gay couple who'd turn it into a halfway house for drug users. I don't suppose you'd consider ....

LYNDA: I don't think so.

RAE: Pity.

LYNDA: The neighborhood's zoned.

RAE: Even the flower gardens are zoned in this town. How's the real estate business, anyway.

LYNDA: Slow, but we get along. And keep up appearances.

RAE: Yeah, I noticed the tan. Golf? Or screwing behind the fourteenth hole?

LYNDA: Golf. I've reformed.

RAE: Hey, I brought you something. *(Gets a jar of pickles from her suitcase)* Just to let you know I was thinking of you.

LYNDA: While you were making pickles? How am I supposed to take that?

RAE: Lynda, if you didn't have Leona to help, would you have put him in a nursing home? It takes more than paper to bind you to this.

LYNDA: Well, he's an old man.

RAE: Not that old.

LYNDA: He's my father.

RAE: What are you getting out of it?

LYNDA: Not eighty dollars a week.

RAE: Bucking for sainthood?

LYNDA: I don't question the way you live, Rae.

RAE: I'm sorry. Do the locals make it hard for you because of me?

LYNDA: Their attitude toward me is generally sympathetic where you're concerned.

RAE: There must have been talk when I didn't come after the accident, but I didn't trust myself.

LYNDA: You'd probably have pulled the plug on his life support system. Don't worry about the talk. It goes past me.

RAE: Lynda, before we get involved with wills and whatever, would you mind if I take a couple of Mother's things? Nothing much, just the blue ceramic dish she kept on her dressing table, one or two things like that? If you'd rather I didn't ....

LYNDA: They aren't here.

RAE: What?

LYNDA: It's all gone. Everything of hers. He got rid of it.

RAE: He did what?

LYNDA: And everything of ours. All that's left in the house belongs to him.

RAE: The attic?

LYNDA: Every box up there is filled with his old notebooks, cancelled checks and receipts. Even his high school compositions.

RAE: When did he do that?

LYNDA: Over the years, I guess. He was always cleaning out. Didn't you notice?

RAE: I figured he'd stored them.

LYNDA: So did I. I don't know what he did with them.I didn't find out until after the accident. I'm sorry, Rae.

RAE: It isn't your fault.

LYNDA: Sometimes I'm afraid ... maybe I didn't notice because I didn't, I didn't care about her the way you did.

RAE: She changed over the years. Living with him. She got crazier, and more bitter ... she thought people were laughing at her. She thought everything I did was to hurt her. When she died, all I felt was relief.

LYNDA: You?

RAE: She nagged, she criticized, she hated my friends. We couldn't spend two days together without fighting. Being around her made me raw. But when I saw her in her coffin, the pain and tension gone from her face, it was like going back fifteen years. I remembered what was lost.

LYNDA: I wish I could.

RAE: You were too young. This was the only room in the house that was really hers. There should be some ... feeling of her. I guess that's what it means to be dead.

LYNDA: I guess it is.

RAE: Everyone felt sorry for Monroe. Good old steady, hard-working, long-suffering Monroe. They'll probably build a monument to him in the middle of the town square.

LYNDA: That should please you. The place is rampant with pigeons.

RAE: He had a wife who knew she had breast cancer for four years, and wouldn't see a doctor. One daughter who can't stand to be in the same room with him. And another who had a private office behind the fourteenth hole at the Country Club when most kids were still playing dodge ball. And no one ever asks what <u>he</u> did.

LYNDA: What did he do to you?

RAE: That's the hell of it. There's nothing I can point to and say, "I hate my father because he did this, or this." Sometimes I think I'm as crazy as Mother was.

LYNDA: You're not crazy, Rae.

RAE: I was afraid to come for Christmas. I was afraid to be alone with him. The year before, we were out here having dinner. He was talking at me. Talking. Talking. I tried to eat, but he wouldn't stop talking. I had a glass of water in my hand. I wanted to throw it in his face. But I knew, if I let go,I wouldn't be able to stop until ....

LYNDA: It's alright. I understand.

RAE: Lynda, do you know of anything ....

LYNDA: I know you're not crazy. I mean, hate doesn't come out of nowhere, does it?

RAE: Apparently. *(Looks around)* She's gone.

LYNDA: *(Gently)* She's been gone for nine years.

RAE: There has to be something of hers ....

LYNDA: There's nothing.

RAE: Do you mind if I look?

LYNDA: It's your house, too.

RAE: *(Explodes)* It's his house. It's Goddamn, fucking Monroe's house.

LYNDA: *(Uncomfortable with Rae's fury)* Rae, if you don't need me, I'd better go. I'll bring the kids over after school tomorrow.

RAE: They can help me dress for the funeral. I bought a red Bikini for the occasion.

LYNDA: I half believe you.

RAE: Wait and see.

LYNDA: Will you be all right here?

RAE: Sure, I'll play with the ghosts of my childhood.

LYNDA: Call me if you want anything?

RAE: I'll be okay, really.

LYNDA: As soon as the kids are off to school, I'll be over.

RAE: Are you going to leave, or are we going to stand around and discuss it?

LYNDA: I am sorry about Mother's things. God, I'm glad you're here. Good night, Rae.

Lynda exits. Rae roams the kitchen, looking for something of her mother's. Giving up, she opens a can of soup and puts it on the stove. Monroe enters. Rae doesn't see him. He sits at the table waiting to be served.

MONROE: *(Chuckles)* Soup's on.

RAE: *(Startled)* What? Monroe?

MONROE: Huh? What'd you say?

RAE: What the hell are you doing here?

MONROE: Come to see your old man, eh?

RAE: You're supposed to be up there, ebbing away.

MONROE: Come all this way to see the old man, did ya'? What you got in that kettle?

RAE: Damn her!

MONROE: I said, what you got ....

Rae heads for the door.

Where you goin'?

RAE: Out.

MONROE: The hell you say.

RAE: I'm going to Lynda's.

MONROE: Plannin' to walk? Take you three days. *(Chuckles)*

RAE: That little bastard.

MONROE: Custard? You got custard in that kettle?

RAE: Bean soup.

MONROE: Pea soup?

RAE: Bean.

MONROE: Just a cup for me. Green peas upset my bowels.

RAE: It's bean.

MONROE: And some of them wafers.

RAE: It's bean soup. Bean soup.

MONROE: Beef stew? Better pick out the corn. I'm not supposed to eat corn.

RAE: BEAN SOUP!

MONROE: *(Fiddles with his hearing aid)* Goddamn son-of-a-bitch.

RAE: What are you doing down here?

MONROE: Huh? What'd you say?

RAE: What ... are ... you ... doing ... down ....

MONROE: *(At his hearing aid)* Goddamn things never work right.

RAE: Here. How did you ....

MONROE: No beer for me, but you go ahead. Some of that Heineken in there. You girls always liked Heineken. *(Chuckles)*

RAE: You and Lynda cooked this up ....

MONROE: *(Stabs his cigar at the stove)* Soup's on.

Giving up, Rae gets cups of soup for herself and Monroe, gets soup spoons, and sits. Monroe looks at his spoon, puts it down, and stares at her.

RAE: Now what?

Monroe holds up his soup spoon. Rae gets up, gets him a teaspoon, and sits.

MONROE: Never liked them Goddamn round things. Thought I told you that.

RAE: Well, you've told me so much through the years, some of it got lost in the shuffle. *(Rae has her spoon halfway to her mouth when Monroe slurps loudly. Rae stops.)*

MONROE: Thought you said this was beef stew. This ain't beef stew. *(More slurps.)*

RAE: You'd better turn down the volume. Don't want to wake the philodendron.

MONROE: What'd you say?

RAE: Talking to myself.

MONROE: *(At his hearing aid)* Put new batteries in last week.

Goddamn thing. *(Monroe slurps a few more times, then points to counter.)*

RAE: Want something?

MONROE: Wafers.

Rae gets the tin of crackers and parks it in front of him..He fumbles endlessly with it.

Goddamn son-of-a-bitch.

Exasperated, Rae grabs the tin and pulls the lid off and hands it to him. He points to the table. She puts it down.

MONROE: Can't do things the way I used to, Tinker girl. Old age is a terrible thing.

RAE: You were <u>born</u> old.

MONROE: You say somethin'?

RAE: Pack it in. Don't say goodbye, farewells break my heart.

Monroe goes back to slurping and munching. Rae gets a soda from the refrigerator.

MONROE: Havin' a soda, are you? *(Chuckles)*

Rae puts the soda down unopened. Starts to eat a cracker.

MONROE: You get wafers like that up your way?

RAE: Vermont isn't a foreign country.

MONROE: Whata you wanta live in a dump like that for? Full of Canadians.

RAE: We smuggle them across the border for cheap labor.

MONROE: What'd you do with the morning paper?

RAE: You don't get one. I hear you've lost interest in current events.

Monroe: Bet Iris took it. Goddamn woman, Always pokin' around. I wanted to look at the funnies. You seen those boys of hers? Fine boys. *(Chuckles)* That young Ted sure did like to go to the ball game with me. Ate all the time. *(Slurp)* Fine, polite boys. *(Slurp)* That other one. What the hell's his name? Had cancer of the prostate. We lost your mother to cancer.

RAE: Not of the prostate.

MONROE: Yep, lost her nine years ago last January ... January... what the hell was the date? *(Pulls out a pocket notebook and leafs through it)*

RAE: Are you sure she's lost? Maybe you only misplaced her.

MONROE: *(Finds his entry)* January 17th. She had that lump in her breast for four years. Didn't see a doctor. Now, why would she do a thing like that?

RAE: Maybe you put her out with the newspapers.

MONROE: Can't understand why she'd do a thing like that.

RAE: How do you know she's gone? You never noticed her when she was here.

MONROE: Get me another of those Goddamn wafers.*(Rae does)* I have an appointment with Doc Snyder every six weeks.

RAE: I thought he retired before they discovered penicillin.

MONROE: His mother was my history teacher back in High School. Ain't that somethin'? *(Slurp)* Your old man isn't as strong as he used to be, Tinker. Some days I have to lay down and take a nap right in the middle of lunch.

RAE: Better watch it. You might drown in the beef stew. *(Breaks a cracker into her soup)*

MONROE: Puttin' wafers in your soup, are ya'?

Rae loses her appetite completely. Monroe looks blankly around the kitchen.

RAE: Lose something?

MONROE: Right knee keeps goin' out on me. Had to get one of them lifts made for my shoe.

RAE: I hear that old pick-up truck gave you a real lift.

MONROE: Damn near took a spill on the ice last winter. Borough doesn't keep the sidewalks shovelled. I called and gave them hell about it. They said it was the individual homeowners' responsibility. Now ain't that a hell of a note?

RAE: I never could understand why you went into business. With your command of the language, you should have been a writer.

MONROE: Plug in that coffee pot. Leona sets it up so all I have to do is plug it in.

RAE: *(Plugging it in)* What do you do with the other half of the day?

MONROE: Don't want too much.Goddamn stuff keeps me awake. *(Lights his cigar)* Can't get a decent cigar any more. Trouble started when Roosevelt let them railroad workers go on strike. Goddamn Communists.

RAE: Who do you think makes those black market Havanas you smoke, the John Birch Society?

MONROE: Shoulda bombed the shit outa that Castro S-O-B. Don't see no Kennedy doin' that. Whole damn Vatican's a bunch of Communists. You got that coffee made yet?

RAE: Try to hang on.

MONROE: Shit. Want anything done right around here, you gotta do it yourself. I want to come visit you in ... what's the name of that joint you live in?

RAE: Dover Depot.

MONROE: Denver Dee-pot. *(Chuckles, pulls a railroad schedule from his pocket.)* I can take the 4:10 train out of Philadelphia. You meet me in White River Junction at .... *(Peers at schedule)*

RAE: I haven't invited you.

MONROE: Eleven-fifty. I got reservations for us at that Holiday Inn. I want to spend a couple of days alone with you.

RAE: Dream on.

MONROE: Some things I want you to explain to me. Things that trouble my mind. I got a list right here. *(Leafing through notebook)* What happened to the son-of-a-bitch? *(Finds the page, tears it out)* You look this over and give me your answers. *(Holds it out. Rae, fed up and furious,refuses to take it. He lets it drop on the table)* Ain't no hurry. I want you to get them answers clear in your mind. That damn coffee ready yet? *(Rae gets up and pours it. He slurps, shudders)* Hot. Any of that chocolate ice cream left? *(Rae doesn't answer)* Goddamn it, I told Leona to get me some. Never gets anything right. Your mother was the same way. *(Slurps his coffee)* Little things worry you when you're old. *(Consults his notebook)* Weekend of the twenty-fifth. Phillies have a home stand. I'll come up from there. You still livin' with that girl from Omaha? That one you went to college with? She still sends me one of them Christmas letters every year. Now, that pleases me. I want you to see it. *(Goes through his pockets)* What'd I do with the Goddamn thing? *(Finds the letter, pulls it out and goes to stand over Rae)* That's her husband and children. What the hell are their Goddamn names? *(Shoves the letter closer to Rae)* See if you can make out those names. *(No response from Rae. Peers at the letter again)* Kansas City? Thought you said she was from Omaha. *(Belches)* I'm gonna lay down a while. When you find that chocolate ice cream, bring me a dish. Not too much. You can't eat too much when you get to be my age.

Monroe shuffles out. Rae crumples list of questions angrily, throws it in the garbage, goes to the phone and dials.

RAE: Lynda, get the hell over here. *(Hangs up)*

<u>BLACKOUT</u>

SCENE 2: Later.

Rae is pacing the kitchen in a fury. Lynda enters, a coat thrown hurriedly over her nightclothes.

LYNDA: What happened?

RAE: He came down here.

LYNDA: Who?

RAE: Monroe.

LYNDA: Have you been drinking?

RAE: I haven't been drinking.

LYNDA: You got me out in the middle of the night for some kind of sick joke?

RAE: What are you trying to pull, Lynda?

LYNDA: <u>Me</u>?

RAE: You. There's not a damn thing wrong with him, is there?

LYNDA: This isn't funny.

RAE: Playing, *Night of the Living Dead*, or just *Let's Scare Rae to Death*?

LYNDA: Do you really expect me to believe he came down here?

RAE: Do you expect me to believe he didn't?

LYNDA: There's no way he could ....

RAE: "Come at once, father dying." You did that to get me here, didn't you?

LYNDA: Rae ....

RAE: I'll bet the two of you had a grand old chuckle cooking this up.

LYNDA: He couldn't ....

RAE: I've seen some sleazy tricks in my time ....

LYNDA: <u>There's no way he could come downstairs</u>.

RAE: How did you get Leona to play along?

LYNDA: My God, don't I have enough to worry about?

RAE: Apparently not.

LYNDA: Rae ....

RAE: *(Indicates dishes)* Don't deny it. We broke bread together.

LYNDA: Anyone can put out an extra dish.

RAE: *(Holds up the match)* I don't smoke.

LYNDA: You never light matches?

RAE: You want hard evidence? *(Starts going through the waste-basket)*

LYNDA: Don't root through the garbage.

RAE: There's a note, in <u>his</u> handwriting. *(Can't find it)* A list of things that "trouble his mind".

LYNDA: <u>Stop it</u>! Settle down and tell me what this is about.

RAE: Monroe, our father ... you remember our father? ... came into this room, ate a bowl of soup in his usual disgusting manner, and talked at me.

LYNDA: That's impossible.

RAE: I saw him, I heard him, and I smelled him. I'm sorry your little game backfired, but he's never been too quick on the uptake.

LYNDA: This is nuts, Rae. Nuts.

RAE: If you were so desperate to get me here, you could have said so. You didn't have to lie.

LYNDA: I've asked you a dozen times. There's always some excuse.

RAE: So you did do it.

LYNDA: He didn't come down here. He's a vegetable. He's ....

RAE: Dying. I don't believe the way your mind works.

LYNDA: Rae, I swear, there's no way you could have seen him.

RAE: I saw him.

LYNDA: You imagined it. You had a long trip. You're strung out.

RAE: I'm strung out, all right.

LYNDA: Call his doctor. Go up and pinch him. Poke him. You won't get a response.

RAE: I've gotten all the response I need.

LYNDA: *(Wearily)* Oh, Christ.

RAE: God damn it, Lynda. I left Val on the farm with the harvesting, canning, and selling. It means a sixteen hour day for her—or hiring someone, which we can't afford. We ain't sittin' around the pool swilling gin and tonics like you, baby sister.

LYNDA: Look, don't take this attitude.

RAE: We have a mountain of tomatos in the field, and they don't give a damn what my attitude is, as long as we pick them before they freeze. So don't talk to me about attitude.

LYNDA: *(Blows up)* I've had it, Rae. You come into this town like an avenging angel, puffed up with rage and righteous indignation. Well, I take care of our father every day. Every day. Which, by God, is more than you've done.

RAE: It was your choice.

LYNDA: If you gave a damn about what goes on around here, you'd know I didn't have a choice.

RAE: I do give a damn.

LYNDA: You have a funny way of showing it.

RAE: I'm afraid of this town. I'm afraid of him.

LYNDA: So am I.

RAE: Lynda ....

LYNDA: All right, I lied. He isn't dying. Satisfied?

RAE: Why did you ....

LYNDA: Because I can't take it any more. Can you understand that, Rae? I can't take it any more.

RAE: Yeah, I can understand that.

LYNDA: I'm sorry. I didn't think about the farm.

RAE: It's okay.

LYNDA: I only wanted you to do your part.

RAE: I have to stay here eight months? No time off for good behavior?

LYNDA: What good behavior? Forgive me?

RAE: For what?

LYNDA: Being selfish.

RAE: You can't help it. I can't help it. It runs in the family.

LYNDA: I guess it does.

RAE: But I refuse to eat one more meal with him.

LYNDA: Come on, Rae. Enough is enough.

RAE: I didn't make it up. Why would I want to drag you over here in the middle of the night? You're not that much fun. Lynda, he sat here, at this table ....

LYNDA: I've been running all day. By the time I get home, I'll have to wake the kids for school ....

RAE: He sat here, at this table ....

LYNDA: Maybe you fell asleep.

RAE: How could I sleep with the social life around here. Lynda, you admitted ....

LYNDA: He isn't dying. But he sure isn't prowling the house. You saw him up there. Did he look like he could ....

RAE: You made him up to look like that.

LYNDA: Do you think I have the mentality of a six-year old?

RAE: *(Beginning to get frightened)* What the hell's going on?

LYNDA: Don't ask me. Did you get any dinner?

RAE: The ambience was wrong.

LYNDA: How about some breakfast? As long as I'm here ....

RAE: Don't you do anything but cook and look after him?

LYNDA: I play golf and have babies. What would you like?

RAE: Canned peaches.

LYNDA: All right, Rae.

RAE: I'm sorry. I'm having a hard time.

LYNDA: So am I. You're not teasing?

RAE: No.

LYNDA: You really believe you saw him.

RAE: I ... I think I believe I saw him. I mean, if I didn't see him, if he wasn't here....*(Indicates Monroe's dishes)* all of this....

LYNDA: You were pretending, the way we did when we were kids ... and, being tired and upset ... maybe it got out of hand.

RAE: This isn't "out of hand". This is major psychosis.

LYNDA: Not necessarily.

RAE: Necessarily.

LYNDA: Maybe you sat down to think or something, and kind of drifted off for a while, and walked in your sleep. You used to walk in your sleep.

RAE: I haven't walked in my sleep in twenty years.

LYNDA: People have done stranger things.

RAE: I don't do strange things.

LYNDA: *(Laughs)* Care to take an opinion poll on that around town?

RAE: Well, maybe ... this place is creepy enough.

LYNDA: And you hate him enough.

RAE: Yeah, I hate him enough.

LYNDA: Do you spend all your time hating Monroe?

RAE: Once a month I light a black candle and project evil thoughts. The rest of the time he doesn't exist.

LYNDA: *(Laughing)* How did you come up with that?

RAE: I was brooding about him one day and plowed under half a field of broccoli. I had to do something.

LYNDA: I don't think your evil thoughts had much of an impact.

RAE: Don't forget the pick-up truck.

LYNDA: Rae, would you like me to stay with you until Leona comes?

RAE: You have to get the kids off to school.

LYNDA: Neil can do it. God knows what they'll look like, but he'll do it. Once he let them dress themselves, and Eric went to school in one of Cindy's skirts. I told the teacher I was raising them androgynous. *(Notices Rae is staring at the dishes, clears them out of the way as she talks)* Do you do the cooking, or does Val?

RAE: We both do. We're androgynous. You're afraid of him?

LYNDA: Sometimes, I have been.

RAE: But you don't hate him.

LYNDA: He's my father.

RAE: That kind of thinking has kept the human race in a constant state of neurosis for thousands of years.

LYNDA: I can't help what I don't feel.

RAE: And I can't help what I do feel.

LYNDA: We never really talk to each other, do we? All we do is argue about Monroe. All the time we were growing up, we never talked.

RAE: You didn't sit still long enough.

LYNDA: And you were always angry.

RAE: I guess I was. I tried to talk to you once, about why you weren't going to college.

LYNDA: And Monroe came in and asked you to drive him to the bank.

RAE: He told me to drive him to the bank.

LYNDA: You didn't have to leap up and go like a trained dog.

RAE: And have him stand in the doorway and stare at us? You could have waited for me.

LYNDA: I did, nearly two hours.

RAE: You know how he was about the bank. Every month, down to the First National Mecca of Barnesville to clip the coupons on his bonds. Then he had to record every cent in his notebook. Those damn coupons paid the same amount every month, but he had to write it down.

LYNDA: It hasn't changed, has it?

RAE: What?

LYNDA: Nothing.

RAE: I did what he wanted because of Mother. So he wouldn't take it out on her.

LYNDA: I was pregnant.

RAE: I didn't know.

LYNDA: They didn't want you to know. They kept my secrets from you, and yours from me.

RAE: What happened?

LYNDA: When you were safely back at Penn State, and Mother

had recovered from her hysteria, she whisked me away to New York for an abortion. I was pretty messed up, and Monroe claimed he wouldn't waste his money on any damn slut of a kid who'd shack up with any damn hippie that looked my way. So I hung around here for a while, under house arrest, and then married Neil.

RAE: Was he the father?

LYNDA: I'm not sure who the father was, but it wasn't Neil.

RAE: Does he know?

LYNDA: I told him a couple of years ago.

RAE: What did he say?

LYNDA: That no one should be held responsible for their adolescence.

RAE: Did you want the baby?

LYNDA: Yes, but my whole life would be different. I don't even know how to think about that.

RAE: You were pregnant, and I didn't even ....

LYNDA: Would it have made a difference?

RAE: Of course it would. We really are strangers, aren't we?

LYNDA: Yes.

RAE: There must be other families like us.

LYNDA: I suppose.

RAE: Oh, my God, I just had a horrible thought. Maybe we're <u>normal</u>.

LYNDA: I doubt it. You didn't like me very much, did you? *(Rae hesitates)* It's okay. I didn't like me very much, either. Those were the worst two days of my life, that trip to New York with Mother.

RAE: She loved you.

LYNDA: Sure.

RAE: It's true. One night, we were sitting up late watching television, waiting for you to come in from a date. We did that a lot. As soon as the car pulled up out front, she'd run to bed so you wouldn't know.

LYNDA: Why?

RAE: You'd have accused us of spying. That night, as she was starting up the stairs, she turned to me and said, "I love her, Rae, and I don't know what to do."

LYNDA: I wish she'd said it to me, just once.

Lynda is crying a little. Rae gets a box of tissues from the counter and offers them to her, touching her a little awkwardly.

RAE: Life's a bitch, isn't it? But, hell, who wants to sit around holding hands like the Waltons? *(Notices something on the tissue box)* What's that?

LYNDA: What?

RAE: Those numbers.

LYNDA: Monroe always wrote the date on a box of tissues when he opened it. Guess we don't do much crying around this house.

RAE: He did what?

LYNDA: Wrote the date on the box, so he'd know how long they lasted. He dated everything. His filing cabinet is full of envelopes with receipts in them. The envelopes are dated. And there are envelopes that used to have receipts in them, with the dates he moved the receipts to new envelopes.

RAE: Empty envelopes?

LYNDA: And all those envelopes are in a big manila envelope with the date on it. Just before the accident I found a slip of paper on his dresser. Every time he changed the blade in his razor, he made a note of it, and kept track of the number of shaves he got.

RAE: Comparison shopping?

LYNDA: He only used one kind.

RAE: The man's a lunatic.

LYNDA: I added a few marks at random, to confuse him.

RAE: That's why he wandered in front of the pick-up truck. His razor blades troubled his mind.

LYNDA: I thought you arranged that.

RAE: Not me. He lived. As Monroe always says, "If you're gonna do something, do it right." *(Finds a pencil and writes on box)*

LYNDA: What are you doing?

RAE: He might come to and want to know when we used one.

IRIS: *(Offstage)* Yoo-hoo!

RAE: What's that?

LYNDA: Iris.

RAE: Mother of God.

LYNDA: Rae.

Iris sweeps in like royalty.

IRIS: Tink, dear, so lovely to see you.

RAE: Mrs. Winters, you look like a breath of spring.

IRIS: Why, thank you, dear.

RAE: But, mercy, you gave me a turn. I didn't hear the doorbell.

IRIS: Nobody stands on ceremony around here. I've been popping in on Monroe for years.

RAE: Lucky he didn't startle easily.

LYNDA: *(To Iris)* You'll have to forgive Rae. She had a long trip.

IRIS: You must be glad to be home.

RAE: Words fail me.

IRIS: It's been long enough. Well, I can't stay, just wanted to say hello and welcome. I happened to glance out the window last night and saw someone in Monroe's room, and I said to myself, "Why, I do believe that's Tink." What's new on your little farm?

RAE: Eight hundred and fifty-nine giant zucchini.

IRIS: I don't know how you girls manage.

RAE: We've had to give up *kaffee klatches*.

IRIS: And how is our patient today?

LYNDA: We're expecting Leona.

IRIS: You mustn't keep him waiting.

RAE: Does he have an appointment?

IRIS: Routine, Tink. Routine is very important for a man in his condition.

RAE: Really?

LYNDA: Leona will be along soon.

IRIS: I suppose she's at Mass. Catholics! She has fourteen grandchildren, you know. Well, she doesn't know any better. Poverty, ignorance, and the Pope. Birds of a feather. How do you find Monroe, Tink?

RAE: Top of the stairs, take a right, first door on the left.

IRIS: We were certainly taken aback when you didn't come home after the accident. It could have been your last chance to see him alive.

RAE: I know.

LYNDA: She was snowed in.

RAE: Ten-foot drifts.

IRIS: It breaks my heart to see that poor man lying there day after day, just shriveling away. We never dreamed he'd come to this. It's a miracle he lived.

RAE: A miracle.

IRIS: The inside of his head was completely filled with blood, you know. It was running out his ears when they brought him into the emergency room. The police didn't even charge that boy who ran him down.

RAE: He didn't "run him down," Iris. Monroe walked out in front of the truck.

IRIS: Nevertheless.

RAE: Where was he going, anyway?

LYNDA: To the bank.

Rae cracks up. Lynda has a hard time restraining herself.

IRIS: Now, any little thing I can do while you're home ... How long will you be with us? More than your usual two days, I hope. Any little thing at all, you just give me the high sign. I have some detective stories I borrowed from your father, ages ago. I'm terrible about returning things. But I don't suppose it makes much difference now. I'll bring them for you when I stop over later.

RAE: You're stopping over later?

IRIS: Twice a day, like clockwork. Leona is coming, isn't she?

LYNDA: Any minute.

IRIS: I'll run up and see Monroe.

RAE: Better knock. He might be on the toilet.

IRIS: You know, Tink, sometimes your brand of humor isn't funny.

Iris exits.

RAE: *(Sheepish)* You going to kill me?

LYNDA: No.

RAE: My God, it's barely light.

LYNDA: She probably saw my car. After the accident, she stuck to me like a barnacle. Every time I turned around she was hovering. There's a proper tone one must maintain in time of tragedy around here: distraught but not devastated, competent but not cheerful, grateful but not needy. One must, in a word, "hold up well."

RAE: And did you?

LYNDA: In all modesty, it was a virtuoso performance.

RAE: You know what?

LYNDA: What?

RAE: You're not bad. For a sister. Are you comfortable in those clothes, or would you like some of mine?

LYNDA: I'm fine.

RAE: I don't know what Iris is going to think.

LYNDA: But I'll bet we'll find out. Well, it'll give her something to gossip about over the produce counter at the A and P.

RAE: Wait'll she spreads the word I'm in town. We'll have traffic backed up for miles. "Hey, guys, let's go see the freak."

LYNDA: You really couldn't have stayed in Barnesville, could you?

RAE: I didn't want to. At least up in old Denver Dee-pot nobody cares how you dress, as long as you pay your taxes on time and show up for Town Meeting.

LYNDA: Denver Dee-pot?

RAE: Monroe's little .... *(Remembering, breaks off)*

LYNDA: He wasn't here, Rae.

RAE: Sure.

IRIS: *(Offstage)* Lynda.

LYNDA: I'd better get up there.

RAE: Right. He might be out of Pampers.

LYNDA: Eat something, will you?

Lynda exits. Rae starts to tidy up the kitchen. Monroe enters, dressed to go out.

MONROE: Don't bother making lunch for me. I'll have a sandwich at the Elks' Club. Tell your sister to pick me up at the bank at three. *(Monroe exits through back door.)*

In a few seconds Leona enters.

RAE: Did you see him?

LEONA: Excuse me?

RAE: Monroe. Did you see him?

LEONA: Not yet.

RAE: You passed him on the porch.

LEONA: What? *(Decides Rae is teasing)* Oh, you.

RAE: You walked right by him.

LEONA: There's nobody out there, except the paper boy.

RAE: *(Beginning to get frantic)* Not the paper boy, Monroe, my father.

LEONA: Now, Rae, your father's ....

RAE: Out there. I saw him go out there. Leona, for God's sake.

Lynda and Iris enter.

IRIS: *(To Leona)* You finally got here.

RAE: *(To Lynda)* He was here again.

IRIS: Not again.

RAE: What?

IRIS: That crazy old man from the State Hospital. He wanders all over town peering in windows. God knows I've complained long and hard, but they let anyone roam the streets nowadays.

RAE: It wasn't any crazy old man. It was Monroe.

IRIS: *(Disgusted)* Oh, really. *(Goes to refrigerator)*

LYNDA: What are you doing?

IRIS: He needs his custard.

RAE: He isn't up there.

LYNDA: Rae, you know he's ....

RAE: He went out. Leona saw him, didn't you? Didn't you, Leona?

IRIS: I don't know how you can stand there and rave like a maniac, while that poor old man upstairs ...

RAE: Tell them, Leona. Please, tell them.

LEONA: I just saw the paper boy.

RAE: Leona, please tell them.

IRIS: You haven't an ounce of consideration, none of you.

LYNDA: Iris, don't.

RAE: Please, Leona.

LEONA: Now you come sit down, Rae. Calm yourself.

RAE: Leona ....

IRIS: Go upstairs and see for yourself.

RAE: He isn't up there, is he, Lynda?

IRIS: Of course he's up there.

LEONA: Listen to me, Rae. This isn't a bad thing.

RAE: What?

LEONA: I saw my husband, too. After he died. He came in my room one night. He told me not to worry.

IRIS: That is the silliest thing I've ever heard.

LEONA: Father Driscoll said that happens sometimes.

IRIS: Peasants!

LEONA: He said don't think about it and it won't happen again.

RAE: You saw your husband?

LEONA: He looked good, except it scared me.

IRIS: This is absurd. *(Starts out of the room with the custard)* Come, Leona.

Iris exits.

LEONA: If you don't want him to come again, just don't think about it.

IRIS: *(Offstage)* Leona.

Leona exits.

RAE: She believes me.

LYNDA: Leona believes a lot of things.

RAE: What about you?

LYNDA: I don't know how to think about it.

RAE: Think. Hold it in your mind until something occurs to you.

LYNDA: I don't want to.

RAE: Please, Lynda.

LYNDA: *(Hesitantly)* You might have seen something. There have been times ... Sometimes the house ... feels funny. *(Pulls herself together)* For crying out loud, Rae. You don't *even* believe in God.

RAE: I've never seen God. *(An idea begins to take shape)* Maybe, if I can get him to appear again ....

LYNDA: Leona says ten words, and all of a sudden it's real to you.

RAE: It was real before.

LYNDA: You're an intelligent woman, Rae. You can't ....

RAE: If I can get him to talk to me ....

LYNDA: Talk to you?

RAE: Well, listen to me. I have a few things to say to the old....

LYNDA: Even if you did see him, to try to make it happen ....

RAE: Maybe I should light candles. Do you think Father Driscoll makes house calls?

LYNDA: You want to turn this place into the Barnesville Horror.

RAE: This place is the Barnesville Horror.

LYNDA: Rae, that ... thing you saw isn't real.

RAE: I don't care if it's real. I don't care if it's animal, vegetable, or ectoplasm.

LYNDA: I shouldn't have brought you here.

RAE: Lynda, all my life he's been like a rock in my chest. All the things I never said to him, if I can find the courage to say those things now, maybe I can be free of him.

LYNDA: His life's nearly over. The past is ancient history.

RAE: The past is unfinished business.

LYNDA: Put it behind you.

RAE: Is that what you did? Is that why you come running over here twice a day to check the remains? What have you put behind you, Lynda?

Lynda goes to liquor cabinet to make herself a drink.
Iris and Leona enter, Leona carrying the tray.

IRIS: He wasn't hungry, poor dear. You can try later.

Leona begins gathering up her things.

RAE: Leaving, Leona?

LEONA: If you don't need anything.

RAE: We're fine. And I don't want to see you back here today. This is to give you a break, you know.

LEONA: I don't want to cause a fuss.

RAE: Set one foot in this house in the next twenty-four hours, and you'll see a real fuss. Go visit your children. They probably think they're orphans.

LEONA: I can stop back and help you this evening.

RAE: Leona, if you don't get your butt out of here, I'm calling the police.

LEONA: *(Laughs)* Well, all right, then.

RAE: Goodbye, Leona. *(Leona exits).* My God, she's tenacious. Reminds me of one of our goats. *(Iris is going through the cupboards)* Taking inventory?

IRIS: He might like a little oatmeal.

LYNDA: This is crazy, Rae.

RAE: Ranks right up there, doesn't it?

IRIS: Don't you have any without raisins? He can't digest raisins.

RAE: Persevere, Iris.

LYNDA: It could be dangerous.

RAE: What can he do? He's not even real.

LYNDA: What you're doing to yourself.

RAE: It beats running out again.

IRIS: Maybe some vanilla pudding ....

RAE: Oatmeal! Egg custard! Vanilla pudding! Warm milk! You're going to bland him to death.

IRIS: He has a very sensitive digestion.

RAE: Let's slip him some chili.

IRIS: God will punish you for this.

RAE: God owes me.

LYNDA: Stop it, Rae. Iris, we'll take care of it later.

IRIS: Do you want him to starve?

RAE: It's a thought.

LYNDA: *(To Iris)* She's only trying to provoke you.

IRIS: You can do anything you like on that farm of yours, but in Barnesville we don't speak ill of the dead.

RAE: He isn't dead.

IRIS: Or the dying. I'd think, at a time like this, you'd make an effort to be civil.

RAE: Sorry.

IRIS: *(To Lynda)* Drinking? At this hour?

RAE: Suburban housewife syndrome. Or maybe I drive her to it. I drive myself to drink sometimes. *(To Lynda)* Unless you're planning to tie one on, it's time for you to go.

LYNDA: Are you sure you'll be all right?

RAE: Soon as I tend to my personal hygiene.

IRIS: It wouldn't hurt either of you to tidy up a bit.

RAE: Oh, my God, is my fly unzipped?

LYNDA: I don't know if I dare leave the two of you alone.

IRIS: Don't worry about me. I raised two boys.

RAE: Fine boys, from what I hear.

IRIS: Thank you.

RAE: *(To Lynda)* See? All hearts and flowers. Scoot along, now.

LYNDA: I don't like this, Rae. *(Lynda exits.)*

RAE: With all the traffic around here, we're going to have to hire a crossing guard to get to the bathroom. Would you like some coffee?

IRIS: Just a touch. I have to be off.

RAE: *(As she pours coffee)* I'm sorry about being such a smart ass, Iris. I don't know what gets into me.

IRIS: *(Thinks she's being kind, willing to let bygones be bygones)* Well, you're a square peg in a round hole around here.

RAE: That's about it.

IRIS: But you ought to be more thoughtful, for Lynda's sake.

RAE: I know.

IRIS: She's been through a lot.

RAE: I'll try to do better.

IRIS: God knows what Leona thinks. That kind of behavior sets a bad example for the help.

RAE: Leona's part of the family.

IRIS: Oh, don't be silly.

RAE: What's the official word on Monroe? I mean, how long?

IRIS: He could go tomorrow. He could linger indefinitely. Lynda's a pillar of strength.

RAE: I'll tell her you said so.

IRIS: You could take a few lessons from her.

RAE: I don't know, Iris. It's kind of complicated.

IRIS: Your trouble is you think too much.

RAE: I suspect you're right.

IRIS: Your mother always said too much thinking makes a mess of things.

RAE: She was a great one to talk about mess. When she got through with a room, it looked as if 20 hyperactive kids had been turned loose in it.

IRIS: It was her nerves, you know. It drove your father wild. He's so deliberate and fastidious.

RAE: Must have been a relief to him to have her out of the way.

IRIS: He was devoted to her.

RAE: He should be in a nursing home. This is asking too much of Lynda.

IRIS: He'd hate a nursing home. You could do your share.

RAE: The farm eats up my time pretty well.

IRIS: Nonsense. You stick things in the ground, and when they come up you yank them out.

RAE: *(Laughs)* Well, not quite. There's always a crisis. As soon as we finish planting, along comes a rain and washes it out and we have to start over, and by then we're into weeds and beetles.

IRIS: I can't imagine why you'd want to live like that.

RAE: Someone has to. There is no Jolly Green Giant.

IRIS: A girl with your background and education.

RAE: Why, Mrs. Winters, I believe you're a snob.

IRIS: Oh, I'm a terrible snob. Isn't that dreadful?

RAE: More coffee?

IRIS: I have to get along.

RAE: Iris, did you know he got rid of Mother's things?

IRIS: He did? Are you sure?

RAE: Lynda says they're gone.

IRIS: Why, I believe you're right.

RAE: Doesn't that strike you as odd?

IRIS: I suppose he couldn't bear to be reminded. He must have suffered terribly, and he never let on.

RAE: Yeah, he's a brick. That's "brick" with a "b".

IRIS: He must have thrown them away, or given them away. He kept her jewelry for you girls, of course, but everything else was worthless.

RAE: Well, I kind of wanted ... well, something worthless ... for sentimental reasons.

IRIS: There are all these dishes and silverware. I'm sure he wouldn't mind.

RAE: Dishes aren't very personal.

IRIS: My goodness, if it means so much to you, I have something right here. *(Gets her handbag and takes out a key ring with St. Christopher medal)*

RAE: *(As Iris is removing keys)* I don't want to take your ....

IRIS: Don't be silly.

RAE: *(Taking it)* Thank you, Iris. Thank you very much.

IRIS: Whatever did she want with a St. Christopher Medal?

RAE: For luck, when she was driving.

IRIS: I can see why, the way young people behave these days, like a bunch of wild Indians. Every time I hear tires squeal, my heart jumps up in my throat. I never knew you were sentimental.

RAE: I get that way sometimes, at the full moon.

IRIS: Your mother and I had wonderful talks in this kitchen. I do miss her. With her gone, and Monroe lying up there, the house is so empty.

RAE: Not to me.

IRIS: You know, sometimes when I walk through that front door, I get the oddest chill, right between my shoulder blades.

RAE: You do?

IRIS: Almost as if someone or something had been prowling around. Can you keep a secret?

RAE: My lips are sealed.

IRIS: Once, I was so sure of it I went through every room. I tell you, it was absolutely chilling.

RAE: Maybe it was Monroe.

IRIS: I have to admit, it crossed my mind. But the doctors say he'll never leave his bed again.

RAE: They're sure of that?

IRIS: Absolutely. He has no brain any more. Next thing you know,

I'll be seeing spooks, like Leona. It's probably the Change of Life.

RAE: Probably.

IRIS: Well, I'd better run. I have a little shopping to do. Can I get you anything?

RAE: I'll shuffle up to the Handi-Mart later.

IRIS: You mustn't leave him alone for long.

RAE: I won't.

IRIS: You'd better pick up more egg custard. Your father seems to enjoy it. Oh, he always hated the boxed kind. Why don't you make him up some real? It would be such a nice surprise.

RAE: I thought he'd lost the capacity for surprise.

IRIS: Oh, dear. I still walk in here expecting to see him sitting in that easy chair in his den, smoking a cigar and watching the ball game. Isn't that silly?

RAE: Not as silly as you think.

IRIS: I wish things would never change. Listen to me. I'm getting old.

RAE: *(Kindly)* Maybe it's the full moon. Iris, would you mind not coming back today? I'd like to spend some time alone, with my father.

IRIS: I understand completely.

RAE: Thank you. And thank you for this. *(Key ring)*

IRIS: Don't give it another thought.

Iris exits. Rae straightens things up a little, delaying her confrontation with Monroe, apprehensive now that she's alone. Finally steels herself.

RAE: Monroe? *(Silence)* Hey, Monroe, come on down. I want to talk to you. *(Silence)* <u>Monroe.</u> *(Silence)* Son-of-a-bitch never was around when you needed him.

<u>BLACKOUT</u>

END OF ACT I

ACT TWO

SCENE 1: That evening.

Rae sits at the table, poring over the contents of a large cardboard box. Lynda enters.

LYNDA: Everything all right?

RAE: Swell. Pull up a box of clutter and sit down.

LYNDA: Monroe's papers?

RAE: Uh-huh.

LYNDA: What are you looking for?

RAE: Signs of intelligent life. Kids mind my putting off our date?

LYNDA: Disappointed, but they forgive you. *(Picks up the Christmas letter)* What's this?

RAE: Betty Shackleford's Christmas Press Release.

LYNDA: Hasn't she bored herself to death yet?

RAE: Watch that kind of talk. It doesn't sit well in Barnesville. Monroe thinks I live with her. And her husband and children, I presume.

LYNDA: Did you see him?

RAE: He didn't show. Probably still downtown terrorizing the bank tellers. I shoved a little coconut custard down his mortal remains, by the way. That should warm Iris' heart.

LYNDA: He hates coconut custard.

RAE: Yeah. We could make a fortune renting him out to Overeaters' Anonymous. Prop him up at the table and you never want to eat again. *(Reads from a notebook)* He had the oil changed in the car on April 16, 1975. There were 24,378 miles on it. Remember that. We might be quizzed on it later.

LYNDA: Rae ....

RAE: *(Still reading)* Your living room rug measures 8 feet 6 inches by 10 feet 6 inches. Is that with or without the fringe?

LYNDA: With. Rae ....

RAE: Did he get down on the floor with a ruler?

LYNDA: I did it for him.

RAE: And you call me crazy. Jesus, his notebooks are even more depressing than his refrigerator.

LYNDA: Rae, I'm really worried about you.

RAE: So is Monroe. "Troubled in his mind", I believe he said. I wonder if trouble in the mind shows up on an EEG. *(Pulls a paper from the box)* Aha! The Now-Famous, Soon-to-be-a-major-motion-picture nursing home document. *(An envelope)* "Funeral service, void." He doesn't want a funeral service?

LYNDA: He gave it to the minister. He didn't trust us.

RAE: He shouldn't trust me, but why you?

LYNDA: I sided with you about Christmas. That's when he had the nursing home paper drawn up, and gave power of attorney to the bank.

RAE: Think they'll let us pick out the casket?

LYNDA: I guess so. If he hasn't already.

RAE: They'd better. I've been looking forward to that all my life.

LYNDA: There's something I need to tell you.

RAE: Better do it now, while I'm in a good mood.

LYNDA: When Mother died .... Well, remember how he put her jewelry in his Safe Deposit box and gave us access to it? We don't have access to it now.

RAE: Lynda, how far would he go?

LYNDA: What?

RAE: Have you seen his will?

LYNDA: I couldn't find it.

RAE: There must be a copy in the house.

LYNDA: No, I went through everyth....

RAE: Uh-huh. Crazed with grief and shock, you ransacked the

joint.

LYNDA: There were things we had to know.

RAE: Did you check the liquor cabinet? Behind the poker chips?

LYNDA: No, why?

RAE: *(Going to cabinet)* Heavy-duty stuff there.

LYNDA: How did you know about that?

RAE: I was a sneaky kid. You should have hung around the house more. This was where you learned real survival techniques.

Rae finds the will as Iris enters.

IRIS: *(Offstage)* Yoo-hoo! *(Entering, she goes directly to the refrigerator and puts a box of ice cream in the freezer)* I know it's late, I know you want to be alone, I won't stay a minute. They're having a sale on chocolate ice cream at the A and P. *(Spots the papers)* Aren't those his papers?

RAE: If they're in this house, they are.

IRIS: I really don't think you should ....

RAE: He won't mind. Iris, I asked you to stay away.

IRIS: Somebody has to tend to his little needs. *(Browsing in the refrigerator)* Did you feed him?

RAE: Yes, I fed him.

IRIS: I don't see any custard. Did you make custard?

RAE: Shucks, I clean forgot.

IRIS: What's this?

RAE: Pudding.

IRIS: *(Tastes it)* Coconut. He doesn't like coconut.

RAE: Really?

IRIS: Have you given him a moment's thought?

RAE: Several.

LYNDA: I'll make custard.

RAE: Lynda, <u>sit</u>.

IRIS: Not even a little bit of custard. I wonder if you care about him at all.

RAE: Not so you'd notice.

IRIS: Well, that shouldn't come as a surprise. You don't care about your sister, you didn't care about your mother.

RAE: I loved my mother.

IRIS: You could have fooled her. Selfish, that's what she thought you were. "I try my best with her," she used to say, "but she'll never be anything but selfish."

LYNDA: Iris, this is unnecessary.

IRIS: The one thing she wanted was for you to make peace with your father, but you wouldn't even do that for her.

RAE: Iris ....

IRIS: He stood by her all those years. All those years when she was sick and in pain, he never left her side. And where were you?

RAE: She understood ....

IRIS: You turned your back on her when she needed you. <u>That's</u> what she understood.

LYNDA: You have the instincts of a rattlesnake.

IRIS: *(To Rae)* Someday, when you're old and lonely, I hope you remember what you did to her.

LYNDA: If you're finished, I wish you'd leave.

IRIS: And <u>you</u> always stand up for her. All the concern she's ever shown you would fit in a thimble.

LYNDA: *(Furious)* You don't have the slightest idea what went on in this house, Iris. So either shut up or get out.

IRIS: *(Leaving)* You killed her, Rae, just as much as the cancer. I hope you're satisfied.

Iris exits.

LYNDA: *(Trying to minimize it)* That's what Neil calls an Iris Blessing.

RAE: Don't.

LYNDA: She's a vindictive woman. Everyone in town knows it.

RAE: Did Mother really say ....

LYNDA: She was on morphine, she was half out of her mind.

RAE: I have so many memories, contradictions. She's all in pieces.

LYNDA: People change. Life eats them up.

RAE: I don't know her any more. I'm losing her. Iris was her closest friend, she must be telling the truth.

LYNDA: Nobody tells the truth about the dead, especially Iris.

RAE: Lynda, did she know I loved her?

LYNDA: I don't know. Rae, she was crazy.

RAE: I wanted to tell her, but I'd look at her and the words would die.

LYNDA: You did the best you could. It doesn't matter now.

RAE: I should have gotten her out of here.

LYNDA: If she'd wanted to leave, she'd have gone. Don't do this to yourself. *(Picks up the will)* Hey, big sister, what do you say we read this thing?

RAE: Do you really want to?

LYNDA: I'm dying of curiosity.

Lynda drops the will on the table. They stare at it.

RAE: Do you think it's legal?

LYNDA: The will?

RAE: Reading it.

LYNDA: I don't know. Does that bother you?

RAE: Well ...I'm funny about the law. If my parking meter expires, I have an anxiety attack.

LYNDA: Me, too.

RAE: Must be the way we were brought up.

LYNDA: Must be.

They hesitate.

RAE: Hell, who's going to know? We'll take a quick peek and put it back where we found it.

LYNDA: Okay.

They hesitate again.

RAE: Well ....

LYNDA: You do it. You're older.

RAE: Oh, brother. *(Picks up the will and starts reading)* Make us a drink and watch for intruders.

LYNDA: *(As she makes drinks)* Know what this reminds me of? The first time I sneaked a cigarette in the house.

RAE: I hope you're wrong. I got caught.

LYNDA: What happened?

RAE: Mother cried, and Monroe got troubled in his mind. What about you?

LYNDA: They didn't dare do anything to me. They were afraid I'd go get pregnant again.

RAE: Wish I'd thought of that. *(Reading)* This is pure Monroe. His first bequest, of primary concern, is to the cemetery. For perpetual care of his grave. He must have been afraid you wouldn't pick the dead blossoms off the petunias.

LYNDA: I wouldn't.

RAE: Leona, for all her years of faithful service, gets five thousand dollars.

LYNDA: That's inhuman.

RAE: You have to admire the old bugger. He has a style all his own. Fifty thousand to the High School. To endow the Monroe Jeghelian Memorial Men's Room, no doubt. *(Reads on)* Well, well.

LYNDA: What does it say?

RAE: In a nutshell, the remainder of his estate ... all property, real and imaginary ... is to be sold. The proceeds therefrom will be placed in trust. The income from said trust is to be divided between us, equally. When we die, the whole ball game goes to the church.

LYNDA: Eric and Cindy?

RAE: Not a cent.

LYNDA: *(Shaky)* Every little bit helps, I guess.

RAE: He's even going to run things from beyond the grave.

LYNDA: Were you counting on it for the farm?

RAE: I haven't counted on Monroe for years. Did you have any plans?

LYNDA: I sort of wanted to move in here. We're so crowded.

RAE: Can't you swing it?

LYNDA: Not at today's prices. We could have managed to buy out your half, but ....

RAE: And that would have gone a long way toward getting us out of debt. It's a kick, isn't it? We can't afford to buy <u>our</u> home from the bank. Good thing we don't have a sentimental attachment to it. Or do you?

LYNDA: No.

RAE: I'm sorry, Lynda. That was one expensive Christmas.

LYNDA: It probably didn't have anything to do with Christmas.

RAE: Want to bet? The will's dated December 16, the day after I told him I wasn't coming.

LYNDA: Who'd expect him to do this over one holiday? I don't even know how to think about that.

RAE: I never knew what you meant by that. I sure do now. We should have had him declared incompetent years ago.

LYNDA: Not around here. They'd say we were doing it because he's an inconvenience.

RAE: Then we should have had him declared inconvenient.

LYNDA: Well, it's his money.

RAE: He went down to that factory and kissed the boss' ass, knowing he could come home and suck the life out of Mother. If you want to know who really earned that money, dig her corpse out of your memory and take a look.

LYNDA: It's only money, I guess.

RAE: Doesn't this bother you?

LYNDA: Bother?

RAE: As in annoy, irritate, make frantic?

LYNDA: I don't know.

RAE: <u>You don't know</u>! Christ Almighty, what do you <u>do</u> with it?

LYNDA: He's our father.

RAE: He <u>killed</u> our mother. Why do you think she was the way she was? Do you think she'd have wanted to die if she'd had a <u>life</u>? Do you think you'd have done the things you did if there'd been <u>love</u> in this house?

LYNDA: I don't want to think about that.

RAE: For God's sake, Lynda, <u>wake up</u>.

LYNDA: Leave me alone.

RAE: He used us, and he screwed us.

LYNDA: Don't.

RAE: He screwed Mother, he screwed Leona, he screwed me.

LYNDA: Rae, please.

RAE: And he screwed you.

LYNDA: No.

RAE: When you needed a mother, he made her crazy. When you were in trouble, he turned away from you. And for the last nine years he's let you wait on him, and slobbered over the Christmas turkey because he couldn't get what he wanted from me. And now you trot over here twice a day to wipe his ass and shovel egg custard into him. And all the time he's been screwing you, Lynda. <u>Screwing you</u>. And you don't even know it.

LYNDA: I know it! I knew it when I was six. I knew it at the ball park, and in hotel rooms, and on the living room couch.

RAE: Lynda?

LYNDA: I know when I'm being screwed, Rae.

RAE: What do you mean?

LYNDA: What the hell do you think I mean?

RAE: You ... with Monroe ....

LYNDA: Not at first. At first it was just grope and fondle. But we moved on to other things.

RAE: Did you ... want ...?

LYNDA: Of course I didn't want. Why do you think I spent half my life in the bathtub? You thought I was vain, didn't you? I was trying to wash away the feel of him, and what I had let him do. It isn't very pretty, is it?

RAE: How long did it ...?

LYNDA: I stopped it when I was twelve. That's when he went elsewhere for his creature comforts, and so did I. At a loss for words?

RAE: Yes.

LYNDA: And I thought there were no miracles any more. Every day I go up to that room and look at him and remember. I remember the first time, how he came at me very slowly, his hand touching my dress, then my knee. I thought it was an accident, because he was staring out at the ball game. He touched my leg. His fingers started creeping under my skirt, but I didn't believe it, because I was only six years old, and he was my father, and things like that don't happen. When he .

... I knew. And I knew I had known all along, and I let him, and I couldn't stop him because I hadn't stopped him when I knew.

RAE: Don't, Lynda.

LYNDA: You're going to hear it! For once in your life, you're going to listen to me! He never looked at me. Not once. All the time he was touching me, he never looked. I made myself very small inside. I made myself go away, far away, away from the ball park and the game and that other thing that was happening. I thought about water, and what it would be like to be clean again. But I knew I'd never be clean again. Now I look at him, I look at him long and hard, and I remember, and I hate him. I hate him, and I hate Mother, and I hate you. Because I needed you then, and you didn't give a damn.

RAE: Lynda ....

LYNDA: I used to watch you with Mother. Your love made a magic circle around the two of you, and there was no way in for me. And there's no way in for me now. When you're not hating him, you're loving her, and there's no way in.

RAE: *(Touches her)* I love you, Lynda. Right now, this minute I love you. I'm sorry, sorry I didn't know, sorry I closed you out. I'm sorry for my whole damn life.

LYNDA: *(Shaky humor)* Well, there's no need to get carried away.

RAE: Does anybody ... did anybody ... did Mother know about this?

LYNDA: Yes.

RAE: Oh, Christ.

LYNDA: I told her, at the beginning. It was the only time she ever hit me. Rae, tell me what to do.

RAE: I don't know what to do.

LYNDA: Sometimes I look at Neil, and I think ... he's such a good person. I wonder if it's fair to him. Maybe I should leave, disappear. But I can't. Neil and Eric and Cindy ... I can't give them up. And I can't tell him, because ... because I don't want him to think of it every time we make love.

RAE: He wouldn't.

LYNDA: I'd never be sure.

RAE: We have to get Monroe out of here. You can't keep doing this.

LYNDA: What if he talked? What if he talked to strangers?

RAE: An old man, rambling ....

LYNDA: There were others. Didn't you ever notice how many children he took to the ball games? And how many of them lost interest in the middle of the season? *(Pause)* Well, now you know.

RAE: Now I know.

LYNDA: What do you ... think of me?

RAE: Oh, Lynda, do you even have to ask?

LYNDA: Sometimes I wonder ... if I had stopped him when it first started ... all those others ....

RAE: I don't think it would have made any difference.

LYNDA: Rae, what the hell am I going to do?

RAE: I don't know right now. I'll think of something. We'll think of something. I won't leave you in this.

LYNDA: Please stay away from him.

RAE: Why?

LYNDA: I'm afraid of what you might do.

RAE: I won't do anything. I promise. I won't do anything that involves you without your okay.

LYNDA: *(Checks her watch)* Oh, God, I have to go.

RAE: Frightened? Then stay here. We'll talk.

LYNDA: I don't want to talk any more.

RAE: You'll have to sometime. Things like that are poison. You can't ....

LYNDA: Not tonight.

RAE: Then we'll play Monopoly. With all your real estate experience, you'll beat the pants off me.

LYNDA: Neil's out of town. The sitter has to get home. *(Hesitates)* Everything's different.

RAE: Nothing's different, except you're not alone. Lynda, did he ever try anything with Eric or Cindy.

LYNDA: Do you think I'd leave them alone with him?

RAE: If he'd done this to Cindy, would you blame her?

LYNDA: Of course not.

RAE: Well, take that to heart.

LYNDA: It's not that easy.

RAE: I know. You're a good mother, you're a good wife. You're a hell of a sister. But, just between you and me, you're a lousy bartender.

LYNDA: Doesn't this disgust you?

RAE: Not about you. Where Monroe's concerned, I think I can find room in my heart for a little more disgust.

LYNDA: Will you be all right?

RAE: Sure.

LYNDA: I'm sorry I dumped this on you.

RAE: That's the silliest thing you ever said. Call me if you need me, I love you, go home.

Lynda exits. Rae watches her go.

All right, Monroe, this is war.

<u>BLACKOUT</u>

SCENE 2: A little later. Rae is alone in the kitchen. She plays with her mother's key ring as if it were a kind of talisman, keeping it with her until Monroe takes it away. Throughout the confrontation, Monroe keeps up a constant stream of activity, fumbling with objects, puttering, etc. His actions are never motivated by anything Rae says or does.

Monroe enters in pajamas, bathrobe, and slippers.

MONROE: Thought I saw a light on down here.

RAE: It's time we had a talk.

MONROE: You got those answers I wanted?

RAE: I've been thinking of having a little celebration, a ceremony, to commemorate what you've meant to this family over the years. If we were at the farm, I could toss you on the compost heap and let you freeze or rot, whichever comes first. However, the climate here's too temperate, and the only compost heap around is the one inside your skull. *(Tracks him around the kitchen)* I could drive you to the bank parking lot on Saturday morning, seal the windows, and let your brains boil over the weekend. But you'd probably be found before <u>rigor mortis</u> set in, if it hasn't already. Damn you, light somewhere and listen to me.

Monroe takes a bottle of scotch from the liquor cabinet, drinks straight from the bottle, and shudders.

MONROE: Jesus, that's strong stuff. Iris' boys gave me this scotch for Christmas. *(Shoves it at her)* See if you can make out the date on that label.

RAE: *(Retreating)* Now, if we accept the assumption that you're human, all evidence to the contrary, we must also consider the possibility that you're capable of insight.

Monroe drinks again, shudders, puts bottle away.

MONROE: Fine boys, those boys of Iris'. Real baseball fans.

RAE: Nothing deep or penetrating. I wouldn't want to cause you undo mental strain. Just a simple acknowledgement of the mess you've made of life.

MONROE: Worked my way up from the shippin' room to general manager. Just doin' my job.

RAE: You did a great job on Lynda.

MONROE: Your sister leave? Thought I heard her down here.

RAE: I know what you did to her.

MONROE: She bring me any chocolate ice cream?

RAE: Don't play dumb with me. I know.

MONROE: Yak, yak, yak. You sound like a tree fulla starlings. *(Chuckle)*

RAE: <u>Monroe.</u>

MONROE: Goddamn birds shit all over the front walk.

RAE: We're not talking about bird droppings. We're talking about child abuse.

MONROE: Ross Tatum, across the street, goes out every evening, bangs a couple of wood blocks together to scare them off. Goddamn things come right back. Circle around and come right back. You got starlings up your way?

RAE: How could you <u>do</u> that?

MONROE: Probably got Canadian starlings, squawkin' in French. Probably can't tell 'em from nuns.

RAE: Who gave you the right to put your hands on her?

MONROE: Huh? That what you got? Canuk starlings?

RAE: She'll remember that every day for the rest of her life.

MONROE: That boy of hers sure is growin'.

RAE: The rest of her life.

MONROE: Gonna be a real baseball fan.

RAE: In case you hadn't heard, incest is frowned on in this culture.

MONROE: Vultures? You got vultures? Must be somethin' dead on that farm of yours. *(Chuckle)* Find that morning paper yet?

RAE: Know what happens to people like you, Monroe?

MONROE: Goddamn kids nowadays, callin' parents by their first names. It ain't respectful. Let me have some of that coffee.

RAE: They put you in jail and let the other cons beat the shit out of you.

MONROE: We ain't outa coffee. Leona keeps an extra can in the pantry. I don't let her serve that Goddamn powdered stuff. Gives me gas.

RAE: You don't care what you did to her, do you?

MONROE: You got a turd crossways today? *(Chuckles)*

RAE: Is that what you're going to say to your precious God when he asks you? "You got a turd crossways today?"

MONROE: I want you to drive me out to the water dam. Stop at the bank and the liquor store on the way home.

RAE: Sooner or later, you have to pay for what you do in this world.

MONROE: Take my car. More comfortable than that damn outfit you drive.

RAE: Maybe you'll come back as a tape worm.

MONROE: You got them answers to my questions?

RAE: Do you have the answers to mine?

MONROE: I want you to help me understand why you didn't come home for Christmas. Now, that hurt me, Tink.

RAE: Good.

MONROE: *(At his hearing aid)* You're gonna have to talk up. Goddamn thing.

RAE: I said "good."

MONROE: That was a terrible thing, leavin' your old man alone on Christmas. Just can't understand that kind of thinkin', leavin' your old man alone. You gonna get me that Goddamn coffee.

RAE: No, I'm not gonna get you that Goddamn coffee.

MONROE: You write that letter I told you to?

RAE: What?

MONROE: That letter.

RAE: What letter?

MONROE: The letter I told you to write. It was on the list. Didn't you read the son-of-a-bitch?

RAE: As a matter of fact, I didn't.

MONROE: What's the matter with you? Spend so much time with the chickens you forgot how to read? *(Chuckles, amused with himself)* I want you to write to those people in Philadelphia I stay with when I go to the ball game. They're mighty good to your old man.

RAE: Do they have any children?

MONROE: One girl, couple of fine boys. Whata you wanta know that for? You ain't writin' to <u>them</u>. I want you to thank them for takin' care of your old man.

RAE: The only thank-you note I'm going to write is to the incompetent who ran you down.

MONROE: Send them some of that maple syrup from up your way. It'd mean a lot to your old man, Tinker.

RAE: How can you ask anyone to do anything for you after what you did to Lynda?

MONROE: Damn little slut, prancin' all over town in tight pants. Gonna get herself raped.

RAE: She doesn't have to go downtown for that. She can get it right in Daddy's house. Why didn't you try it with me? I'd have cut off your balls and fed them to the umpires.

MONROE: Women are always carryin' on nowadays. Bellyachin' about this, bellyachin' about that. Dress like whores, carry on when they get raped. When we get back from downtown you can drop me at the Handi-Mart. I'll walk home from there. When you get to be my age, you need a little exercise regular.

RAE: Are you listening to me? I <u>know</u> what you did to Lynda.

MONROE: You forget that coffee? Oughta write things down. You never could remember things.

RAE: I remember plenty. Not as much as Lynda remembers, but plenty.

MONROE: Your mother'd tell you to do something, half the time you wouldn't remember. Never could get you to remember to lock the back door.

RAE: I wanted to make sure I could escape.

MONROE: The hell you say. What'd you wanta do that for?

RAE: So I wouldn't have to talk to you.

MONROE: First you're goin' on about talkin', now you're goin' on about about not talkin'. Make up your mind.

RAE: Now that I have your attention, let's talk about Lynda.

MONROE: I don't know nothin' about your sister. Bringin' up the children is the mother's business.

RAE: You have pus for brains.

MONROE: Huh? What'd you say?

RAE: You have pus for brains.

MONROE: Don't look like rain to me. *(Lights his cigar)* Your mother was always at me to get this room painted. Goddamn woman, always wantin' somethin'.

RAE: She should have papered it with your old check stubs.

MONROE: Wantin' to go here, go there. Always had her bowels in an uproar to go to that Mardi Gras business. *(Chuckles)* One time I told her I'd take her. Christ, she was up half the night, callin' everyone, talkin' about that Goddamn trip. Madder'n hell when I said we weren't goin'. *(Spots the key ring)* What's that you're foolin' with?

RAE: Something of Mother's you overlooked.

MONROE: Piece of junk. You want a key holder, get one out of my desk drawer.

RAE: Gosh, I don't know what to say. Are you sure you can afford to part with it?

MONROE: Your mother was always buyin' junk. Anything new, she had to have it. Used to sit up and watch them Goddamn talk shows, order every damn gadget she saw.

RAE: She had to get <u>something</u> from you. What's seven bucks for a Veg-O-Matic?

MONROE: I played gin rummy with her every night that last year. Every night. She owed me *(Consults his notebook)* four dollars and twenty-six cents when she passed on.

RAE: Why didn't you yank out a couple of her gold fillings?

MONROE: You want gold fillings? You got no use for gold fillings. Goddamn kids.

RAE: *(Wearily)* You know, Monroe, we can trade insults all night, but ....

MONROE: I had to go to the dentist a couple months back. Had some tenderness in my gums. When the hell was that? *(Searches through his notebook)*

RAE: Just tell me one thing. Satisfy my curiosity. Did you love us?

MONROE: Told me to rinse my mouth with salt water. You ever hear of a thing like that?

RAE: I mean love <u>us</u>. Or were we just a means to an end for you.

MONROE: See if Leona remembered to get me more salt. *(When Rae doesn't move, he shuffles to the cupboard, takes out a box of salt)* What the hell's this junk? That ain't the kind of salt we use.

RAE: Did you love Mother?

MONROE: Bet she's been shoppin' at that Goddamn A and P outfit.

RAE: Did you love Mother? Did you feel anything when she died?

MONROE: Never looked at another woman but your mother.

RAE: Except Lynda.

MONROE: Yep, never looked at another woman.

RAE: Did she ever look at another man?

MONROE: Why would she do a thing like that? Why would you say a thing like that about your mother?

RAE: I was hoping I was illegitimate.

MONROE: You oughta settle down. Ain't right, a girl of your age runnin' around.

RAE: Well, I would, but I'm spoiled. There aren't many men like you out there.

MONROE: You look like a bum in them clothes. Bet Leona kept the money I gave her for that chocolate ice cream.

RAE: Considering what you pay her, you'd better count the silverware. Monroe, why didn't you tell us you were getting rid of Mother's ....

MONROE: How much you got invested in that farm? That other girl put any in?

RAE: We're equal partners.

MONROE: You make sure the deed's in your name. You don't want her sellin' it out from under you. Better get yourself an attorney. 'Course, you'd probably go out and hire some Goddamn lady lawyer.

RAE: Okay, we're going to talk about Lynda.

MONROE: What'd you say?

RAE: No more monologues. No more games. Starting now, we're going to have a conversation.

MONROE: I already told you I made the reservations through the Holiday Inn in Philadelphia. Get the wax outa your ears.

RAE: *(Boils over)* You can rise like Lazarus from the dead. You can be the Miracle of Barnesville, and pilgrims can come from the four corners of the earth and leave their crutches on your doorstep. But you are never, ever coming to Dover Depot again.

MONROE: Let me have that bowl of canned peaches in the ice box.

Rae gets the peaches, puts them in front of him, but doesn't get a spoon. He waits. She waits. He taps the table to get her attention. She just stares at him. He pushes the peaches away and opens the pickles.

RAE: Those belong to Lynda.

MONROE: *(Bites one)* Sour. *(Puts it back in the jar)* It could have been my last Christmas, Tink. I don't know why you didn't want to be at my side. It would have meant a lot to me, to have my daughter at my side.

RAE: What for? So you'd have someone to complain to about how your hearing aid doesn't work and your gums are rotting and your bowels don't move on schedule?

MONROE: Better see if your mother wants anything. She had a bad night.

RAE: Mother hasn't had a bad night in nine years.

MONROE: I'll be a lonely old man when she goes.

RAE: She's gone. Souvenirs and all. You saw to that.

MONROE: Had that lump in her breast for four years before she saw a doctor. I don't understand why she'd do a thing like that.

RAE: She did it to get away. From you, from this town. When she told me she had cancer, and they couldn't do anything, she laughed.

MONROE: You oughta come see her more, Tink. It troubles her when you don't come see her.

RAE: I couldn't watch her die, and remember how she used to be. There was nothing in her eyes any more. I couldn't look at her eyes.

MONROE: We play gin rummy every night.

RAE: She hated gin rummy. She hated playing cards with you. She wanted to throw them in your face.

MONROE: Every night. It's a great comfort to her.

RAE: We used to laugh at how cheap and stupid you are.

MONROE: No matter how tired I am, I play gin rummy with her.

RAE: She said playing cards with you was like being on an elevator, stuck between floors.

MONROE: You say somethin'?

RAE: I begged her to get out. She could have lived with me. I'd have taken care of her. She loved Vermont, and farms, and animals. I used to drive her out in the country to look at the animals.

MONROE: Night she died, I stood in the doorway to her room and she waved at me, like she knew she was goin' away.

RAE: I wish she'd lived long enough to see the farm. The goats would have come up and nibbled at her hands, and she could have touched them. If she'd been able to touch the goats, maybe she'd have wanted to live. *(Begins to cry)*

MONROE: You should have stayed with me longer after the funeral. I needed my family at my side. *(Notices her crying)* What the hell's the matter with you.

RAE: I miss her.

MONROE: Yep, four dollars and twenty-six cents she owed me. You gonna make me some of that coffee?

RAE: Why didn't you love her, Monroe? She was so much fun ....

MONROE: I heard you down here in the kitchen last night after I went to bed. I don't like you sneakin' around the house. When I shut out the lights, I don't like you sneakin' around turnin' them back on.

RAE: We used to be silly together. We'd make funny noises, and giggle until we nearly choked. Nobody's ever made me giggle the way she did.

MONROE: *(As he fumbles in his pocket for a match to light his cigar)* Think you can run a Goddamn farm, don't even have the sense to shut out the lights.

RAE: Even when I was in college, and thought everything in the world had to be serious, she could make me giggle.

MONROE: Your mother was the same damn way. Never saw anybody who could waste so much damn electricity.

RAE: *(Heads for the door)* Go fuck yourself.

MONROE: Where do you think you're goin'?

RAE: Home.

MONROE: *(Strikes the table violently)* You get your ass back here. *(Rae freezes)* This here's your home. You ain't runnin' out on me like you ran out on your mother. I ain't cryin' over you like she did. While you're up, look and see if Leona remembered to get me that chocolate ice cream.

RAE: *(Automatically)* There's chocolate ice cream.

MONROE: Get me a dish. Not too much. And put these peaches up. *(Rae takes the peaches)* Goddamn women, always leavin' stuff layin' around.

RAE: Look, Monroe, you don't really need me here. Can't I go ....

MONROE: Huh? What'd you call me?

RAE: Monroe.

MONROE: Huh?

RAE: Monroe.

MONROE: Huh?

RAE: Dad.

MONROE: Well, whata you want?

RAE: I want to go home.

MONROE: I told you, this here's your home. *(Chuckles)* Your mother was always talkin' about leavin'. Any time something didn't suit her, she was gonna leave. Never went anywhere. Damnedest woman for not doin' what she was gonna do.

RAE: *(To herself)* She knew about Lynda.

MONROE: Huh?

RAE: Nothing.

MONROE: Talk like you got a mouth full of mush.

RAE: Please. Go away now. You can have the house to yourself, and the memories, and Mother.

MONROE: You got somethin' to say, talk up. What'd they teach you in that Goddamn college? Take your money, don't even teach you to talk right.

RAE: Please, let me have this room.

Monroe gets up, walks toward door.

Thank you.

He stops at the cupboard, brings out a pack of matches.

MONROE: You see these matches? Got the company insignia on them. *(Shoves them at her)* Whata you think of that? Ain't that somethin'? You hear me? I said, ain't that somethin'?

RAE: Yeah, swell.

MONROE: What'd you say?

RAE: I said they're very nice.

MONROE: Got these last Christmas from the men in the shippin' room. Why'd you say you didn't come home last Christmas?

RAE: I told you at the time. I was tired of being treated like furniture.

MONROE: Talk up.

RAE: You ... *(Giving up)* We were snowed in.

MONROE: Wouldn't get snowed in if you lived here. Your sister don't get snowed in for Christmas. Don't know what you want that Goddamn farm for. You got no use for a farm.

RAE: I like the farm.

MONROE: Just like your mother. Always some pipe dream. Front yard's full of dandelions.

RAE: That doesn't matter.

MONROE: Looks like a nigger farm. You put any corn in that stew you made?

RAE: No.

MONROE: Pick the seeds out of them tomatos before you put them in?

RAE: No.

MONROE: I ain't supposed to have roughage. Upsets my digestion.

RAE: I'm sorry.

MONROE: You grow them tomatos yourself?

RAE: Yes.

MONROE: Bring some of them along next time you come home. I want to show Iris. She don't get nothin' like that outa her garden. Heat me up some of that Heinz Chicken Broth.

RAE: I don't have any.

MONROE: What the hell kind of a joint is this? Let me see that thing of your mother's. *(Rae gives him the key ring)* What's that medallion?

RAE: St. Christopher Medal.

MONROE: Whata you want that for? You ain't no Goddamn Catholic. Less them Canadians got you all mixed up. *(Chuckles. He tosses the key ring on the table.)*

Rae doesn't touch it.

What's that girl do?

RAE: Val?

MONROE: What kind of people she come from?

RAE: What?

MONROE: You ever meet her people?

RAE: Her family?

MONROE: What kinda business her father in?

RAE: He works in a factory.

MONROE: What kinda factory?

RAE: A factory. They make things.

MONROE: Goddamn it, gettin' yourself mixed up with people, don't know nothin' about them. Look out she don't take advantage of you. *(Lights his cigar)*

RAE: I'm tired, Dad. Can't we call it a day?

MONROE: What kinda grades you gonna get this term?

RAE: Semester. We call them semesters.

MONROE: Well, what kinda grades you gonna get?

RAE: Okay, I guess. I have to drop chemistry.

MONROE: What for?

RAE: I'm not going to pass it.

MONROE: What'd you take it for if you're gonna drop it? Didn't drop it last term, did you?

RAE: No.

MONROE: Your mother ain't gonna like this. You gotta start applying yourself to your work.

RAE: I try, Dad. I really do. But I feel so mixed up all the time ....

MONROE: Probably runnin' around half the night. You ain't dumb. Not like your sister.

RAE: Lynnie isn't dumb.

MONROE: Better get herself married off, anyone that dumb.

RAE: She's only fourteen, Dad.

MONROE: Dumb just like your mother.

RAE: Dad?

MONROE: Whata you want now?

RAE: Maybe I should take some time off. Get a job for a while. The Dean said I could have a leave of absence ....

MONROE: You only got three terms to go.

RAE: I'd only lose one semester. I could graduate in January.

MONROE: Goddamn it, you start somethin' you finish it.

RAE: I'd finish, I promise.

MONROE: Never heard of a thing like that, grad-gee-atin' in January.

RAE: I'm really messed up, Dad.

MONROE: If you're messed up, take a bath. *(Chuckles)*

RAE: Depressed. Sometimes I want ... I want to die.

MONROE: Whata you got to be depressed about?

RAE: I don't know. If I could take some time off ....

MONROE: You wanta kill your mother? That what you want? She ain't well.

RAE: What's wrong with her?

MONROE: Nervous. You know damn well she's nervous. Whata you wanta upset her for?

RAE: I don't want to upset her. This doesn't have anything to do with her.

MONROE: Always thinkin' about yourself.

RAE: Dad, please.

MONROE: You drop outa school, don't come around here lookin' for nothin'. Wanta go to school, somethin' doesn't go your way, you wanta quit. I don't understand that kind of thinkin'.

RAE: All right, forget it.

MONROE: What'd you say?

RAE: Forget it.

MONROE: And you forget about droppin' that course. Straighten yourself out and apply yourself. You got the brains.

RAE: Sure, Dad.

MONROE: You gotta make your mother proud, ain't that right?

RAE: Right.

MONROE: What'd you say?

RAE: I said, that's right.

MONROE: That's the ticket, Tinker girl. All you gotta do is apply yourself. *(Relights his cigar)* What's this I hear about you goin' to Penn State? Thought you were goin' to Bryn Mawr.

RAE: I didn't send the application.

MONROE: Whata you mean you didn't send it?

RAE: I didn't send it.

MONROE: Thought you told me you sent it.

RAE: Well, I didn't.

MONROE: Sneakin' around, lyin'. What the hell's the matter with you? Huh?

RAE: I want to study agriculture.

MONROE: Agriculture? You gonna be some Goddamn florist?

RAE: I'd like to have a farm some day.

MONROE: Must think you're a man. You dress like one.

RAE: Could we drive over to State College on Sunday? We could look around, maybe go in some of the buildings? I know you'd like it. Could we, Dad?

MONROE: Jesus Christ, I don't know what we're gonna tell your mother. Goddamn cow college.

RAE: Couldn't we just look at it, Dad? Please?

Monroe puffs on his cigar for a moment.

MONROE: Saw you comin' out of that Mayflower soda shop this afternoon.

RAE: *(Guilty)* We just went in for a Coke.

MONROE: I don't like you hangin' around that cheap joint.

RAE: Everybody was going.

MONROE: Everybody? You mean the entire Junior High School?

RAE: Some of us.

MONROE: Thought you said everybody.

RAE: I only meant ....

MONROE: Always gotta be exaggeratin'. *(Pause)* You set this table?

RAE: *(Proud)* Uh-huh. Mama let me do it myself.

MONROE: You got the silverware all ass-backward.

RAE: I did?

MONROE: If you're gonna do somethin', do it right. Now, you fix that.

RAE: *(Stares at the table)* I don't know how.

MONROE: You oughta plan things out. You think of that from now on, Tinker girl. Never go into a situation without plannin' things out.

RAE: Don't call me that. I don't like it.

MONROE: Say please.

RAE: Please.

MONROE: Yep, you remember that, Tinker. You gotta plan things out. Don't wanta be silly like your mother.

RAE: She isn't silly. She isn't.

Monroe chuckles and relights his cigar.

Please don't smoke, Daddy. It makes me sick. *(Monroe puffs away)* Please, Daddy? *(Pause)* Daddy?

MONROE: Whata you want now?

RAE: I ... I don't know.

MONROE: Always wantin' somethin', don't even know what you want. Jesus Christ. *(Picks up the key ring)* You tell me what hand this is in, you can have it. *(Makes fists and mixes them up, holds them out to her)*

RAE: Uh ... uh ....

MONROE: Don't take all day.

RAE: Uh ... right.

MONROE: Your right or mine?

RAE: Yours.

MONROE: You sure about that?

RAE: I ... think so.

MONROE: You gotta be sure.

RAE: Right hand.

Monroe opens his left hand, which is empty.

That's your left hand.

MONROE: No, it ain't.

RAE: Yes, it is. Isn't it, Daddy? Isn't it?

MONROE: *(Puffs on his cigar)* Nothin' wrong with my hearing. Never was. Specialist over in Philadelphia said so. Said the only thing wrong was I didn't listen. Wanted me to see some Goddamn hearing therapist. *(Chuckles)* Your mother sure was mad when I wouldn't go. Don't know why. She never said a Goddamn thing worth listenin' to. *(Gets up and dangles key ring in front of Rae)* You don't need this. *(Puts it in his pocket)* Leave those dishes in the sink. Leona can wash them in the morning.

Monroe exits. Rae puts her head down on the table and starts to cry.

BLACKOUT

SCENE 3: The following morning, early. Everything is as it was, including Rae.

Lynda enters.

LYNDA: Rae, are you all right? *(Shakes her)* Come on, wake up. Time to plug in the coffee. What's the idea, falling asleep in the kitchen? You know Monroe likes things in their proper place. Did you see him.

RAE: Yes.

LYNDA: Well? What happened?

RAE: Not much. How are you doing?

LYNDA: All right, considering I sat up thinking all night. I've never done that before in my life. Now I know why. I guess I'd better start putting myself together. I'm too old for the fourteenth hole.

RAE: That isn't funny.

LYNDA: It never was. It's going to be hard, isn't it?

RAE: Probably.

LYNDA: How do you feel about 3 a.m. phone calls?

RAE: Fine.

LYNDA: I can imagine the long distance bills.

RAE: It won't be long distance.

LYNDA: *(A moment for this to sink in)* You're not staying here.

RAE: Why not?

LYNDA: A thousand why nots. You hate it here. Val needs you. The tomatos need you. The farm ....

RAE: We'll never make a go of that farm.

LYNDA: You will. Rae, you will.

RAE: *(Starts to get Monroe's breakfast)* Funny, isn't it? We think, if we want something, we have to do something to get it. That's what they teach us. But Monroe knows. Do nothing, and sooner or later you get what you want.

LYNDA: Stop it.

RAE: He doesn't care. He really doesn't care.

LYNDA: You knew that.

RAE: He's like the snake that swallows its tail. Everything begins with him, and ends with him. Whatever happens, deep inside wherever consciousness lives, that infinitesimal spark goes around and around ....

LYNDA: Damn it, Rae.

RAE: He has it all. He'll lie up there and be fed, and cleaned, and turned, and have his family at his side on holidays. And it won't really matter. We're never going to be free of him, are we?

LYNDA: We'll be free of him.

RAE: How can you be free of someone who doesn't care?

LYNDA: Walk out. Now. Turn your back and leave.

RAE: I really thought I could .... Well, as Monroe would say, there's no fool like a damn fool.

LYNDA: You tried. That's more than I ever did.

RAE: I'm no hero.

LYNDA: You are to me. I love you, Rae.

Leona enters through back door.

LEONA: I know you said not to come, but it didn't seem right.

RAE: Habits of a lifetime?

LEONA: I guess.

LYNDA: I'm going to check on Monroe. Leona, please help Rae clean up here. *(Lynda exits. Leona and Rae start cleaning up.)*

RAE: Val had an old dog when I met her, so old his muzzle was soft as a puppy's. The vet thought we should have him put to sleep. But he wasn't in pain, just old. One day he stopped eating. He lay under his favorite bush, where he could see if anyone came up the drive. We'd take water and bits of food to him, but he'd wag his tail to let us know he was glad to see us, and politely turn his head away. By evening he couldn't stand. We carried him from room to room with us, so he'd know we still loved him. He'd look at us and smile, the way some dogs do. But mostly he seemed to be somewhere else. He didn't wake up the next morning. *(Pause)* I'm glad I could see that.

LEONA: Dying's like that sometimes. They just go peaceful.

RAE: Did Mother?

LEONA: No, she had a lot of pain. And the drugs, the morphine, it made her see things. Things that scared her.

RAE: Monroe won't suffer.

LEONA: They say he'll go in his sleep, like that old dog.

RAE: It doesn't make any sense.

Lynda enters.

LYNDA: Leona, you'd better call an ambulance. There's something wrong with his breathing. And stay with him until they come, please.

Leona exits.

RAE: Lynda?

LYNDA: *(Touching Rae)* No questions.

RAE: Lynda ....

LYNDA: Rae, if I try to break the will, to use what he did to me to prove he was crazy, will you stand by me?

RAE: Of course.

LYNDA: I'd like to come up to the farm with you, to walk with you down the path between the field and the woods, and hear the wind in the trees. Vermont must be beautiful in September. We can go over to the covered bridge and throw chocolate ice cream in the river. *(Gives Rae the key ring)* This belongs to you.

RAE: Lynda.

LYNDA: Our father's dead.

RAE: When?

LYNDA: Just now.

RAE: Was it because of me? Last night?

LYNDA: No.

RAE: *(Slowly understanding)* Lynda, what did you do?

LYNDA: What had to be done. It's over, Rae. Let's get on with our lives.

BLACKOUT

THE END

This Brooding Sky

Introduction

During the early years of our theater company, we used to spend hours "discussing our politics." It was hard but important work, even though we sometimes became impatient and tired and it was a miracle we had the energy left over to actually put on a show. Anyway, during one of those horrible impasses common to political groups, when no one can see anyone else's point of view, and everyone's drained and depressed because we used to be friends and we don't know how we can be now that we've pushed each other to opposite Horns of the Dilemma—when it's darkest, and there is no dawn—when no cloud has a silver lining—when you feel as lonely and bleak as the last buzzard in the world, perched on the last remaining fence rail, friendless in the dark—I decided we needed something to lighten things up. So I wrote this play for us to read.

It's a Gothic Romance. Obviously. I love Gothic Romances. I devour them by the dozens, usually in the tub. Of course, I change the hero/villain to a woman in my head. (don't we all?)

This play is for fun. It has no message. It's to play with, and be outrageous with. It can be performed on an empty stage, or with elaborate sets and costumes. It lends itself to cardboard scenery. The characters can be doubled-up, or expanded to include anyone who ever wanted to be on stage. There can be three twins, or one twin, or fifteen twins. The sound effects person can be a part of the on-stage action. It makes a great fund-raiser.

Use your imagination. Enjoy.

CAST OF CHARACTERS

NARRATOR, the narrator

MARY BETH, our heroine

VILLAGER, the wizened crone

MRS. GRAVES, the kindly housekeeper

SALLY, the slovenly servant girl

STEPHEN, the moody mistress of Seven Chimneys

COLLEEN, the stable hand

EMMALINE, the friendly neighbor

HAZEY, DAISEY, MAISIE, the twins

GRANNIE SEMPLE, Stephen's old governess, gone senile

AUNT LILLIAN, Stephen's aunt, locked in a closet

Other characters—living trees, crows, strange creatures, etc.—may be added or subtracted, as desired.

THE SET can be simple or complex. This play has been performed with elaborate cardboard sets, on empty stages, and with various sets in between.

Narrator enters with a stack of books. Opens a book and prepares to read,

NARRATOR: "1801—I have just returned from a visit to my landlord—the solitary neighbor that I shall be troubled with."

Dissatisfied, puts the book down and tries another.

"There was no possibility of taking a walk that day. We had been wandering ...."

Rejects this one, tries another.

"Last night I dreamt I went to Manderly again."

Rejects this one, tries one more.

Even the mist that swirled around her ankles spoke of evil. The sky overhead, what she could see of it through the twisted leaves of the ancient, brooding oaks, was dark and threatening. Somber clouds boiled relentlessly toward the sea. Gray dust lay dismally on the road, and coated the wilting leaves of stinging nettle and deadly nightshade.

Mary Beth enters.

She straightened her shoulders, shifting the simple knapsack that contained all of her worldly belongings. She glanced about apprehensively. Poor but honest, she was in her mid-twenties, but hardship had made her wise beyond her years, and she displayed a determined and optimistic demeanor.

Villager enters.

MARY BETH: Pardon me. Is this the road to Seven Chimneys?

VILLAGER: *(Draws back in horror)* Aye, but I wouldn't be goin' there if I was you.

MARY BETH: Indeed! May I ask why?

VILLAGER: 'Tis an evil place, that 'un. Cursed, they say. Bad doin's.

MARY BETH: Nonsense. What sort of "bad doin's"?

VILLAGER: 'Tain't me place to say, Miss. But if I was you I'd turn straight around this minute and go back to where I come from.

MARY BETH: *(Sadly)* Ah, would that I could. But you see, my father—a poor but genteel country parson—has died and left me penniless. I must go to Seven Chimneys to earn my living and support my bereaved mother and nine frail brothers and sisters.

VILLAGER: And what might your manner of work be, should I be so bold as to inquire?

MARY BETH: Though I was raised among the classics and speak five languages, I have only a college education. I must make my living teaching other people's children. I am without prospects of my own.

VILLAGER: A governess, eh?

MARY BETH: *(Simply)* Yes.

VILLAGER: Well, God knows those poor children, the Blessed Virgin protect them,*(Crosses herself)* need a good woman to look after them. Poor dears, to grow up in such a place.

MARY BETH: But what is wrong at Seven Chimneys?

VILLAGER: Oh, Miss, we daren't speak of such things in the village. But mark my words, you'll regret it. The devil's spawn, she is, that high-and-mighty lady. Unnatural things go on there.

MARY BETH: *(Pulls herself together bravely)* Kindly remember your place. I shall not be swayed by ignorance and superstition. I have been hired to care for those children, and care for them I shall. It is my duty ... and my financial necessity.

VILLAGER: *(Conspiratorially)* Payin' you a good salary, are they, Dearie?

MARY BETH:*(With dignity)* Perfectly adequate, thank you. Now I must hurry along. I am late, and there's a storm coming.

VILLAGER: Aye, and bad enough it is in sunlight. Well, I've said me piece and ye'll hear no more from me lips. 'Twas me Christian duty to warn ye, and warn ye I did. Whatever happens, they can't lay the fault at me doorstep.

NARRATOR: The wizened crone scuttled away, pulling her shawl tight around her and muttering to her fingertips. Mary Beth gazed after her thoughtfully. Then she remembered her father's admonition: "There is evil in all places, my child. Wherever you find it, cast it out." Fortified with resolution, she set her jaw and marched firmly through the gathering dusk, down the narrow path toward Seven Chimneys.

Deepening shadows fell like bony fingers across her way, and twilight congealed in oily pools as Mary Beth reached the end of her tortuous journey. The decaying manor house brooded over its past like an unrepentant sinner. Only the crumbling walls knew what evil, what abominations its towers and turrets had witnessed, what damned and restless souls still roamed its deep recesses. Gargoyles leered from the granite cornices, and though it had not rained in months, something dripped from green-encrusted copper gutters. Dark trees brooded above the house, while twisted vines curled with grasping tendrils over the walls. The unnatural dusk deepened almost to night. Mary Beth approached the heavy oaken door and lifted the ominous knocker, which bore the likeness of the head of Medusa.

Mary Beth recoils, lifts knocker.

It fell with a sound like thunder, that echoed through the halls and antechambers of the place, summoning who knows what demons and spirits of unspeakable evil. The door creaked open on long-neglected hinges, and before her stood a motherly, middle-aged woman, gray-haired and ample of bosom—the kindly housekeeper, Mrs. Graves. She eyed Mary Beth suspiciously.

MRS. GRAVES: Well?

MARY BETH: I am Mary Beth, the new governess.

MRS. GRAVES: You have identification?

MARY BETH: *(Rummaging through her knapsack)* I have a letter from Miss Cortlandt.

MRS. GRAVES: Miz Cortlandt. *(Snatches letter and scans it)*

MARY BETH: *(Humbled)* Of course. Forgive me.

MRS. GRAVES: Seems to be in order.*(Suddenly friendly)* Come in, dear. Let me take your things and make you a pot of tea. The mistress is down at the stables, breaking in the new filly.

NARRATOR: There was no turning back now. Her sturdy country

upbringing, sense of honor, and natural curiosity would not permit it. Mary Beth allowed herself to be drawn into the dank recesses of Seven Chimneys.

MRS. GRAVES: Now you just sit down here in the morning room and I'll send for the tea. Sally! *(Bellows)* Sally! Dear, dear, where is that girl? Never around when you need her.

NARRATOR: Sally, the faithful little servant girl, shuffled into the room. Though simply dressed, she appeared slovenly, sullen, and slightly adenoidal.

MRS. GRAVES: Tell Cook to bring tea, girl, and make it snappy.

SALLY: *(Stares with unabashed curiosity at Mary Beth)* Can't. Cook quit. Said she wouldn't spend another night under this roof.

MRS. GRAVES: Oh, dear. That's the third one this week. *(Smiles apologetically at Mary Beth)* So hard to get good help nowadays. Well, there's nothing for it but to do it myself. *(Exits)*

SALLY: *(Still staring)* You the new governess?

MARY BETH: *(Simply)* I am.

SALLY: Hope you stay longer than the last one. We been through five governesses in the past year.

MARY BETH: Oh, I hope the children aren't ... exceptional. I have no training in special education.

SALLY: Nah, it ain't the kids. They're okay, for kids. It's the mistress. Terrible temper she has. Moody, like. Stomping around the house in them boots, scratching the floor I work so hard to put a nice shine on. Won't let me use GloCoat, neither. You might have noticed when you come in.

NARRATOR: Cleverly sensing a well of information to be tapped, Mary Beth vowed to befriend the little servant girl.

MARY BETH: Yes, I did. It must have taken you hours to do such a lovely job.

SALLY: It did, indeed. And then <u>she</u> come in, tracking mud all over. No appreciation, no appreciation whatsoever. There's a lot of work keeping up a house like this, with no one to help me, and me trained as a <u>personal</u> maid. It's downright insulting. Now, if I could just use Mop 'n Glo ....

MARY BETH: Yes, yes, but the mistress.

SALLY: Ach, her ! Moody, moody, moody. Moping around the house, running off to the stables all the time. Won't talk to no one but them horses, smelly things. Gettin' drunk half the nights, yellin' at everyone. Oh, I suppose I shouldn't be too hard on her, what with the great tragedy in her life. But that don't give her the right to dirty up my floors.

MARY BETH: Tragedy?

SALLY: Just a year ago it was, her lover run away. Car went over a cliff. Killed outright. Coroner said it was an accident. But I heard from Bob, down to the junk yard, the brakes had been cut—sawed clean off. Now that don't look like no accident to me, no ma'am. Way I figure it, the mistress was jealous, and she ....

NARRATOR: Alas, just as it seemed the secret of Seven Chimneys was about to be revealed, the housekeeper returned, bearing a lavish but deeply tarnished tea service.

MRS. GRAVES: Sally! Stop this idle gossiping and go wheel in Granny Semple. *(To Mary Beth)* Now, you just ignore her, dear. She's not too bright, and she exaggerates.

NARRATOR: Suddenly an object propelled itself through the open door. Mary Beth caught her breath. It was a wheelchair, in which sat an ancient bundle of bones and human hair. It carried a cane and breathed with a death-like rattle. It appeared to sleep.

MRS. GRAVES: *(Catching the chair just short of disaster)* And this is Granny Semple.

MARY BETH: Simple?

MRS. GRAVES: A little. Age, you know. *(Shouts in Granny's ear)* HAVE WE POTTIED TODAY, GRANNY? *(Granny gives her the finger)* Dear, dear, she's always doing that. I suspect Huntington's Chorea.

MARY BETH: *(Disconcerted)* I think I should like to meet the children now, Mrs. Graves.

MRS. GRAVES: Unfortunately, the twins have gone to spend the week with their grandmother. But that will give you time to get used to Seven Chimneys ... learn your way around.

MARY BETH: Well, I suppose ....

MRS. GRAVES: Now, don't you worry about a thing, dear. And you're going to get along famously with the mistress. Why, she's a lovely, lovely ....

STEPHEN: *(Offstage)* Mrs. Graves! Mrs. Graves! Why isn't tea ready?

MRS. GRAVES: We're having it in the morning room, dear.

STEPHEN: We? Who's we? If that anemic butterfly Emmaline is here again, I'll break her neck. I told her to ....

NARRATOR: The moody mistress of Seven Chimneys strode into the room, stopping in mid-sentence at the sight of Mary Beth. Stephen was a tall, athletic woman in her mid-thirties. She was dressed for riding, in muddy boots and rough clothing, and slapped her riding crop against her boots menacingly. Despite her intimidating demeanor, there was about her eyes an inner sadness. Sternly, she pointed to Mary Beth.

STEPHEN: What's <u>that</u>?

MRS. GRAVES: Mary Beth, the new governess.

STEPHEN: Human Services Counselor. *(Circles around her appraisingly)* Looks kind of puny.

MARY BETH: *(Indignant)* I beg your pardon! I am not a piece of merchandise to be examined and commented upon. I was hired for my mind, not for my ....

STEPHEN: Feisty little number. You'll do. *(Turns on her heel)* Dinner's at seven. Be prompt.

NARRATOR: Eyes flashing, Mary Beth stared after the departing figure. She could feel the color rise to her cheeks. Never in her life had she been so insulted. Why, even the village urchins had better manners.

MARY BETH: I shan't be treated like this. Mrs. Graves, I hereby give my notice. Under the terms of our agreement, I am entitled to two weeks' wages.

MRS. GRAVES: Oh, dear, please give her a chance. The mistress doesn't mean to be rude. She's just ... shy.

MARY BETH: Shy, indeed. She's an uncouth, spoiled, unmannerly ....

MRS. GRAVES: *(Laying a motherly hand on Mary Beth's arm)* Of course, dear. And that's why it's so vital that you stay. To be a good influence on ... the twins.

MARY BETH: *(Going mushy)* Ah, yes, the children. How selfish I was not to think of them. All right, Mrs. Graves, I shall stay for one month. *(Aside)* But, believe me, before that month is over, Stephen Cortlandt and I shall have it out!

BLACKOUT

NARRATOR: Despite a sleepless, though uneventful night, Mary Beth tried to appear alert and cheerful for the next day's afternoon tea. But she could not shake the premonition that some unknown evil was growing, gaining strength, deep in a dark, unexplored corner of Seven Chimneys.

Storm clouds continued to gather over the gloom-filled mansion as the little family met in the morning room. Mary Beth sat demurely, legs crossed at the ankles, glancing now and then toward Stephen, who slouched in a corner of the couch and marred the fine polish of the coffee table with her dirt-encrusted boots. Everything appeared to be normal. Kindly Mrs. Graves poured tea and chatted gaily about the weather, while dear old Granny Semple dozed on her cane, waking from time to time to add lumps of sugar, by threes, to her tea. And yet, and yet ....

MRS. GRAVES: *(Relentlessly cheerful)* Surely the storm will break by nightfall. Have another tea cake, dear. So good for the petunias.

GRANNY: Marigolds.

MRS. GRAVES: Why, I was saying to Grace ... she's the gardener ... this morning, if we don't soon have rain I just don't know what's going to become of my poor petunias.

GRANNY: Marigolds.

STEPHEN: *(To Mary Beth)* You missed dinner and breakfast. Where were you?

MARY BETH: *(Haughtily)* I had a tray brought to my room.

STEPHEN: Extra work for the servants. I don't approve of that.

MARY BETH: *(Icily)* It won't happen again.

MRS. GRAVES: And the radishes. I don't know how the dear little radishes have survived so long without rain.

GRANNY: Silly damn fool.

MARY BETH: Miss Cortlandt ....

STEPHEN: *(Automatically)* Miz.

MARY BETH: Miz Cortlandt, I must report an intruder. Someone was prowling around outside my room last night.

Stephen and Mrs Graves glance at one another significantly.

MRS. GRAVES: It was your imagination, dear. These old houses are filled with strange noises. Why, I was saying to Colleen, the stable hand, only yesterday ....

A blood-curdling shriek fills the air.

MRS. GRAVES: Why, I didn't hear anything. Did you, Stephen?

GRANNY: *(Rousing herself)* Lillian. What have you done with Lillian?

MARY BETH: Who is Lillian?

MRS. GRAVES: Nobody, dear. A figment of dear old Granny's feeble imagination, poor old thing.

GRANNY: Lillian.

MRS. GRAVES: *(To Granny)* Now, Granny, you know Lillian's all gone bye-bye.

MARY BETH: Mrs. Graves, I am here as a governess ....

STEPHEN: Human Services Counselor.

MARY BETH: ... not a Home Health Aide.If you are hiding a Senior Citizen in the attic, expecting to spring her on me in addition to my other duties once I have become too attached to the twins to leave ... I shall consider it a serious breach of my contract.

STEPHEN: She has grit. I like that.

MARY BETH: *(Whirling on Stephen)* Now, see here ....

NARRATOR: The friendly scene was interrupted as Sally, wiping her nose on her sleeve, slouched into the room.

SALLY: Miss Emmaline has come to tea.

STEPHEN: How many times do I have to tell you, it's Miz Emmaline. *(Mutters)* Anemic butterfly.

NARRATOR: Like a shaft of sunlight dispelling the gloom, Emmaline swept through the doorway, accompanied, it seemed, by lilting music and the happy laughter of children at play. She was a sweet, feminine young woman of about twenty-five, dressed in flouncing skirt and puffed sleeves. Pirouetting about the room, she alighted at last near Stephen.

EMMALINE: *(Kissing the air near Stephen's face)* Hello, hello, all you lovely people. Isn't it a lovely day? I see I'm just in time for tea. How lovely. Two lumps.

NARRATOR: Stephen strode morosely to the breakfront and poured a stiff brandy, which she downed in a gulp.

MRS. GRAVES: Do sit down, dear, and let me pour you some tea.

EMMALINE: *(To Mary Beth)* You must be the new governess. The twins have talked of absolutely nothing else for weeks.

MARY BETH: *(With an accusing glance at Stephen)* I am most eager to meet them. I find their absence quite ... disconcerting.

MRS. GRAVES: The visit to their grandmother is a special treat, a last little vacation before they start the....

STEPHEN: *(Dully)* Miz.

MARY BETH: *(With a twinge of annoyance)* Miz Cortlandt. May I ask, why aren't they attending the public schools?

STEPHEN: I don't want my children taught by men.

MARY BETH: How sensible!

EMMALINE: Now, Stephen, you know they're not really your children. They were my sister's children. *(To Mary Beth)* Twins run in our family.

STEPHEN: She left them to me. They're my responsibility.

MARY BETH: I don't understand. They're your sister's children, but she left them to ....

EMMALINE: *(With distaste)* My sister and Stephen were ... lovers.

MARY BETH: *(Bewildered)* I see.

Another blood-curdling shriek.

GRANNY: Lillian.

Everyone else ignores it.

STEPHEN: I expect you to give my children a matriarchal education.

MARY BETH: I beg your pardon?

STEPHEN: Women's herstory, women's psychology, women's studies, women's calculus.

MARY BETH: Calculus?

STEPHEN: Women's auto repair. Women's first aid ....

MARY BETH: Surely they're too young for calculus.

EMMALINE: Nonsense. They're eighteen.

MARY BETH: Eighteen!

MRS. GRAVES: The zucchini have been suffering, too. Poor things, all limp and wilted. Yes, the rain will be good for them.

NARRATOR: Colleen, the stable hand, rudely dressed and—to Mary Beth's experienced eye—undoubtedly illiterate, materialized at the French windows. In one hand she held the reins of a handsome but vicious-looking mare. With the other she pulled a flask from her hip-pocket and took a large swig. Mary Beth shuddered as Stephen tossed off another brandy.

STEPHEN: I'll be in the stables.

NARRATOR: Flouting decorum, Stephen leapt through the windows and threw a casual arm around Colleen's shoulders. Mary Beth smoothed her skirt to hide her discomfort.

MRS. GRAVES: Nothing to be concerned about, dear. They're just friends. *(Calls)* Stephen, dear, before you go, there are some bills you have to look over. *(Exits)*

GRANNY: Marigolds.

MARY BETH: Oh, dear, I have the feeling Miss ... Miz Cortlandt doesn't approve of me.

EMMALINE: She's a very difficult person. Why, I told my sister a thousand times, "Don't get mixed up with a person like that." And look what happened. *(Sobs softly into her lace handkerchief)* Now she's dead, and my poor nieces are trapped here with that horrible woman.

MARY BETH: *(Comforting her)* Now, now, you're not to worry. I have no experience with Adult Children of Alcoholics, but I shall do everything in my power to keep her from influencing them further.

EMMALINE: Oh, thank you. I feel so much better, just knowing you're here. *(Smiles sweetly and sadly at Mary Beth)* I would go away and never see her again, but it's my duty to be with them as much as possible. I can't leave them alone with her.

MARY BETH: I understand completely.

EMMALINE: Mary Beth ... forgive my familiarity, but I sense you're someone I can trust. May I tell you a secret? *(Mary Beth nods, all ears)* I have no proof, but I have reason to believe that Stephen—killed my sister.

MARY BETH: The brakes were cut, clean off.

EMMALINE: However did you know?

MARY BETH: Village gossip.

EMMALINE: Yes, but alas, that's all it is for now. Gossip. But someday, somehow, I intend to bring that wretched woman to justice. It has become my mission in life. Mary Beth, may I ask a favor of you?

MARY BETH: Of course.

EMMALINE: But it must be our little secret. No one must know, not even Mrs. Graves. She's a dear old woman, but totally devoted to Stephen.

MARY BETH: *(With distaste)* Co-dependent.

EMMALINE: If you hear anything, see anything that might help me prove Stephen's guilt, you must tell me immediately.

MARY BETH: I shall.

EMMALINE: And another thing. You must be very, very careful. Anyone who has murdered once could....

MARY BETH: *(Shudders)* The brakes.

EMMALINE: Clean off. *(Gets up to go.)* Now, if you're ever in trouble, you come straight to me. I live, in a more modest house, right next door. You must consider me your very best friend.

MARY BETH: Thank you, Emmaline. I <u>have</u> been lonely here.

They embrace in parting as Stephen strides in.

STEPHEN: Are you still here?

EMMALINE: *(Dignified)* I am just leaving.

Granny gives her the finger as she exits.

STEPHEN: *(To Mary Beth)* What has she been saying to you?

MARY BETH: Nothing.

STEPHEN: Damn fool! If she weren't my accountant, I'd never let her in this house.

Another blood-curdling shriek

<u>BLACKOUT</u>

NARRATOR: At last, it seemed, life was returning to Seven Chimneys. Unaccustomed to inactivity, Mary Beth passed her days wandering the dark, empty halls, where the roots of the ancient oaks themselves violated the granite foundations of the crumbling house. But, try as she would, she could find no clue as to what had really happened on that fateful night a year ago. Downstairs, the Great Hall was readied to celebrate the twins' return. But even the flickering candles and colorful decorations could not obliterate the feeling of impending doom that hung forever over the brooding manse. The storm that had threatened for days seemed as though it would contain itself no longer. A faint breeze, smelling of salt marshes and decay, rustled the leaves of the moribund oaks. Thunder, like the rumble of a hundred heavy wagons, warned of the barely-leashed fury of what was to come.

Mary Beth was troubled as she prepared herself for the party. She knew she must appear cheerful, must give no hint of the fears that gnawed at her mind like the rats that scurried through the walls of that evil place.

Mary Beth is at her dressing table. Sally enters.

SALLY: Wadda ya' want?

MARY BETH: I seem to have misplaced my lipstick. Do you think there's any in the house?

SALLY: Bound to be. Miss Emmaline's sister, she always wore red.

MARY BETH: *(Automatically)* Miz. Please see if you can find it.

SALLY: Can't. Gotta set the table for the party. They make me do everything around here. 'Sides, the twins'll be here soon.

MARY BETH: But whatever shall I do? I want to look my best.

SALLY: Try right where you're sittin'. That's her dressing table.

MARY BETH: *(Recoils in horror)* Hers!!!!!!

SALLY: Yeah. You want anything else?

MARY BETH: *(Regaining her composure)* No, you may go.

NARRATOR: The little servant girl hurried away to fulfill her duties. Drawing courage about her like a cloak, Mary Beth forced herself to search through the dead woman's dressing table. Suddenly, to her amazement, her fingers touched an iron latch. It gave under the slight pressure, revealing ....

MARY BETH: Why, this drawer has a false bottom!

NARRATOR: Her curiosity piqued, she rummaged deeper and discovered a mouldering, dust-encrusted diary.

MARY BETH: *(Reading aloud)* "I hate her. She has betrayed me for that other woman. I have cut the brakes on her car. Tonight, when she goes to meet her, she will meet death instead. When she slows for the curve on the cliff road, I shall have my revenge." Stephen's journal! The proof! I must hide it until I can talk to Emmaline!

NARRATOR: Hurriedly she put it back, arranging the contents of the drawer to conceal the evidence of her terrifying discovery. Meanwhile, in the Great Hall, Stephen, in clean riding clothes, paced nervously. At last the time had come. Mary Beth, knowing her life was now in danger, prepared herself to meet her employer. But little did she realize that before the night was out she would have to call upon depths of courage she had never tapped before. Smiling bravely to cover her apprehension, Mary Beth entered the Great Hall.

Stephen looks up, gasps, and takes her hand.

STEPHEN: How lovely you are. *(Gallantly, she kisses Mary Beth's hand.)*

MARY BETH: *(Aside)* Be still, my heart! How can you beat so for a—a murderess?!

Emmaline makes a grand entrance.

EMMALINE: Good evening, all you lovely, lovely people. Isn't it a lovely party? And just look who I've brought!

Daisey, Maisie, and Hazey enter, do a terrible song-and-dance number.

MARY BETH: Good heavens!

EMMALINE: This is Mary Beth, your new governess. Mary Beth, Maisie, Daisey, and Hazey.

MARY BETH: *(In shock)* I'm pleased to meet you.

THE TWINS: Groovy!

Blood-curdling shriek offstage.

Great Aunt Lillian!

They do their number again.

EMMALINE: Aren't they charming? They're going on Star Search, aren't you, darlings?

THE TWINS: Yes, Aunt Emmaline.

EMMALINE: And now you must dash upstairs and get ready for the party. We want to look our very best, don't we?

THE TWINS: Yes, Aunt Emmaline

They exit, leaving Stephen looking as if she might throw up, and Mary Beth building up a head of steam.

MARY BETH: Miz Cortlandt, I must protest. My contract *(Pulls it from the bodice of her gown)* specifically states two twins, not three!

EMMALINE: *(Brushing her aside)* Here are your tax forms, Stephen. Sign right over my name and I'll mail them in the morning.

STEPHEN: Damn it, Emmaline, this is no time to ....

EMMALINE: *(Syrupy)* Now, Stephen, you know we've filed three extensions already. Just take a second and do it now.

STEPHEN: Oh, all right. I have to get my pen. *(Exits)*

MARY BETH: Emmaline, I found it! The proof!

EMMALINE: Oh?

MARY BETH: In my dressing table, a drawer with a false bottom. There was a diary in it. It must be Stephen's journal. She describes the whole thing, how she planned to kill your sister, the brakes, the curve on the cliff road. Emmaline, she was insane with jealousy!

EMMALINE: Give it to me immediately!

MARY BETH: I left it upstairs. After the party ....

EMMALINE: No, no. I must have it now. Your life is in danger.

STEPHEN: *(Returning with pen)* All right, let's get this over.

NARRATOR: Unconsciously, Mary Beth glanced down as Stephen bent to sign the form. Odd. Stephen's handwriting bore no resemblance to that in the diary. But ... she looked again ... Emmaline's did!

MARY BETH: *(In horror, clasps her hand over her mouth)* Emmaline! Oh, my God!

Blood-curdling shriek offstage.

NARRATOR: Pursued by Emmaline, Mary Beth rushed to her room. She leaned against the door for half a frantic heartbeat, then dashed to the dressing table and scrabbled through the drawer. She clutched the diary behind her back as Emmaline burst in. She knew! At last she knew the evil secret of Seven Chimneys. Emmaline attacked her viciously. They fought over the all-revealing book. Mary Beth felt herself begin to weaken. She must hold out. Her life, Stephen's life depended on ... Emmaline snatched up a pair of scissors.

EMMALINE: Give it to me.

MARY BETH: It was you! It was you all along! You killed your own sister!

EMMALINE: Yes, I killed her. I loved her and she left me for that woman. I planned it all. But it was Stephen who was supposed to die. Stephen was going to a softball game that night. But Stephen's homophobic Aunt Lillian locked herself in the closet and my sister...my dear, dear sister...drove to town for the locksmith. When she slowed—the curve on the cliff road ....

MARY BETH: Yes, yes, I know all about that.

EMMALINE: But I knew someday I'd find a way to make Stephen pay for taking her away from me. Now Stephen will be blamed for her death, and for yours, too.

MARY BETH: You're sick!

EMMALINE: *(Laughs crazily)* Maybe I am, but that won't help you now.

NARRATOR: The deranged woman's strength was too much for her. Mary Beth struggled, faltered .... The door exploded open as Stephen leapt into the room, followed by Mrs. Graves and Granny Semple. Granny Semple???

GRANNY: Hit her again, Stephen! Bust her nose! Sock her in the breadbasket!

NARRATOR: With a single deft karate chop, Stephen knocked Emmaline to the ground. Mary Beth and Stephen flew into each other's arms.

STEPHEN: Mrs. Graves, please call the police.

Mrs. Graves exits.

Darling, I thought the joy had gone from my life forever. I thought I would never love again. But when I saw you tonight. .

MARY BETH: I never should have doubted you, Stephen.I think, deep in my heart, I always knew you were innocent. It was Emmaline all along, the poor, demented soul.

STEPHEN: We'll send the children off to a chem-free, vegetarian, politically correct co-operative women's college. You'll never be desperately poor again.

MARY BETH: And you, dear Stephen, will never be lonely. We'll be here together, forever, at Seven Chimneys.

NARRATOR: At last it was over. Over the fallen body of their adversary, the lovers were united. The kindly housekeeper, her dreams come true, smiled benignly. And little Sally, free at last to pursue her true calling, brought forth her cherished bottle of Mop 'n Glo and set to work. As Stephen promised, the twins departed immediately to complete their education. Once again the halls of Seven Chimneys would echo with the sound of music and the singing of birds. The rats and the shadows were banished forever. And nevermore would it be said in the village ....

VILLAGER:*(Returning)* 'Tis an evil place, that 'un. Bad doin's.

Blood-curdling shriek offstage.

THE END

Hollandia '45

Introduction

Sometimes scattered ideas, thoughts, and feelings come together and arrange themselves in ways you never thought of. This happened to me with *Hollandia '45.*

While I was working on my mythical-Women's-Army play, I read everything I could get my hands on about the WAC, in the course of which I came across a weighty-looking volume in the *U.S.Army in World War II* series entitled *The Women's Army Corps,* by Mattie Treadwell. I could hardly believe it, but I was reading a crash-course in feminism. Change the context, and I could see my life passing before my eyes. (The only way you can get the book is through the Government Printing Office, and it's expensive, but I have a fantasy of hundreds of women suddenly ordering this book. It would make them crazy trying to figure out what we're up to.)

So I was thinking a lot about war, particularly W.W.II, and about the WACs, and movies like *Cry Havoc*, and women in uniforms and difficult places. And about New Guinea, where thousands of WACs and nurses were stationed during the closing months of the War, dying of boredom and frustration and malaria.

When I was a child, my grandmother had a good friend named Beatrice Bowman. "Auntie Bea," as I called her, was a retired Navy nurse and lived in a winterized cottage at Brown's Dam along the Conewago Creek a few miles from my home in Pennsylvania. She had a dog named Judy, had never been married, and shared my love of woods and camping and the outdoors. I never thought of her as "old," and she never treated me as "young." I loved her, as much as I loved anyone in my family, maybe more. Later, years after she had died, it occurred to me in one of those flashes of brilliant hindsight in which we see things that have been under our noses for decades, that Auntie Bea had probably been a lesbian. She had served for a while in the South Pacific, on a hospital ship, before the start of World War I, and liked to tell me stories and show me artifacts and pictures of those days.

I was thinking about Reality, a greatly overrated concept, which some people are fond of foisting upon persons who are powerless to resist, and which none of us is going to survive anyway. In particular, I was thinking about the current Mental Health fad called "Normalization." Normalization involves taking very elderly patients away from institutions and placing them in community homes, from which they are forced to attend jazz concerts, shopping malls, supermarkets, and other piquant tortures of everyday life. They are deprived of all objects of harmless fantasy and forced to live in the Real World—a great place to visit, if you could get any two people to agree on what it looks like.

WACs, Auntie Bea, and fantasy, three seemingly unrelated threads. Until they spiralled down together in my head and became *Hollandia '45*.

For the character of Marian, I needed a way to make her charming and somewhat endearing, but irritating. I decided to use my mother's speech patterns. Then there was the question of where to place the action of the play. Certain localities have strong regional or personal associations. The coast of Maine, for instance, has qualities which adhere to it and create associations in our minds. As does New York City. If you're going to place a New Yorker in Maine, it has to be a conscious choice, and one that serves a purpose in the script. And it had to be in a place where it would be a little strange (but not certifiably crazy) to live in a cottage, since I wanted Kit's behavior to be odd or not, depending on your point of view. Pennsylvania would have been all right, but it has too much personal history for me. So I settled on Maryland.

(A note of caution: this play can be a lot of fun to do, but it requires some pretty creative set-building. Putting a tent on stage is easier said than done. And beware of the Coke scene. Aspirin added to warm Coke may not make you high, but it makes the Coke spray all over the stage.)

One night after a performance of *Hollandia '45*, a woman approached me to say she had actually been a WAC in Hollandia in 1945, and that she was leaving the next week for a reunion with other woman who had been there. She said what she had seen on stage was "exactly what it was like"—the greatest compliment an author can receive.

While I was in Washington for the 1987 Gay Rights March, I took time to go to Arlington Cemetery, where Auntie Bea is buried. She is in the Nurses' Section, on a sloping hillside dotted with falling leaves, surrounded by the graves of women. It seemed right.

CHARACTERS

KIT FORTESCUE, a woman in her early 70's. She is retired from the Army Nurse Corps. During the course of the play, her age shifts between 35 and 70.

MARY CLEVELAND, Kit's lover, a WAC in the Signal Corps, WWII.

HAZEL BAINBRIDGE, an Army nurse, WWII.

EDITH RUSKIN, a WAC typist, WWII.

(Kit, Mary, Hazel, and Edith were stationed together in Hollandia, New Guinea, during the closing days of World War II.)

MARIAN JOHNSON, Kit's niece, in her 50's.

SET

There is one set, with the stage divided into two discrete sections: the tent, representing the Hollandia memories; and the porch of Kit's home.

The TENT is standard WWII Army issue, with two cots, footlockers, and a table made from orange crates. A kerosene lamp hangs from the ridge pole. On the table is a handmade chess set, with painted rocks for chessmen. Outside the tent, a hand-lettered sign reads "Hollandia, Jewel of the Pacific."

The PORCH belongs to a winterized summer cottage, furnished with well-worn chairs, a rocking chair, and a table. A hurricane lamp and fishing tackle are in evidence. All incidental objects and *bric-a-brac* are vintage pre-1945. There is an air of comfortable clutter about the place. Entrances lead to the yard and to the interior of the house.

PLACE: Along a stream in the hills of Maryland.

TIME: The present, a Saturday in June

ACT ONE

SCENE 1: A Saturday morning in June.

SCENE 2: A few minutes later.

ACT TWO

SCENE 1: That night.

SCENE 2: Early the next morning.

PROGRAM NOTE

Between January 1944 and the end of World War II, 5500 members of the Women's Army Corps served in the South Pacific. They were billeted in compounds surrounded by barbed wire, and marched to and from work under armed guard.They were not permitted to ride in jeeps or public transportation, or to attend recreational activities except in groups. The official explanation for these "protective" measures was that they were "in danger of being raped by Negro soldiers." The real reason was that their presence was resented by the men.

Each WAC arrived on New Guinea with one pair of woolen slacks and a light cotton shirt, even though the temperature was normally above 100 degrees, rain fell constantly, the humidity was unbearable, and the island was infested with malaria-carrying mosquitoes. They were refused men's uniforms because they were considered "unsightly for women." They were not provided with pajamas, bras, or sanitary napkins—because the men didn't use them—and were not allowed into R and R areas where they might purchase them. Eventually, most managed to scrounge some of the men's cast-off clothing.

A typical work day ran from 7 a.m. to 10 p.m., with time off in the heat of the day, seven days a week.When a woman was moved forward to Manila, the others were expected to pick up her work. They often worked double shifts, three days in a row. There were no replacements.

Malaria, jungle rot, skin rashes, and respiratory diseases were rampant. Many of the women doing censorship work developed headaches and anxiety attacks from reading obscene letters written by the soldiers. Their clothes never dried, and the heat kept them from sleeping. They were forced to submit to monthly pelvic examinations under primitive conditions. By the end of the war, the medical loss rate was 30%, due mostly to exhaustion, anxiety, and tropical diseases.

Very few WACs received promotions or commendations, as the Army feared the men would be jealous.

This play is dedicated to the memory of Josephine Beatrice Bowman, U.S. Navy Nurse Corps.

ACT ONE

SCENE 1: Early on a Saturday morning in June. The gray dawn of a rainy day. There is a sound of rain on the porch roof, which fades over to the sound of rain on canvas.

Mary, Edith, and Hazel are in the tent. They are dressed in bits and snatches of worn Army uniforms and civilian clothes. Edith and Hazel are seated at a homemade chessboard, playing. The chess pieces are odd lumps of an unidentifiable substance resembling rocks, shells, etc. Kit stands on the darkened porch holding a cup of tea. She is dressed in slacks, old shirt, and ragged sneakers. When she is in the present, she walks with a cane and the stiffness of old age. When entering the tent, she leaves her cane behind and moves with the ease of a 30 year old woman. For now, she is old, and stands watching the action in the tent like an actress awaiting an entrance cue. Mary extinguishes the lamp, bringing up the light in the tent. She watches the chess game.

EDITH: If they let us kill, would you?

MARY: No.

HAZEL: Sometimes I get mad enough to kill.

EDITH: I killed yesterday, in self-defense.

MARY: Who?

EDITH: I don't know, but it was in my soap dish. One of the girls in the typing pool is keeping a list of all the insects on New Guinea. She's found ten different kinds of mosquitoes.

MARY: I've met every one of them.

EDITH: Only the female bites, you know. It has something to do with sex.

HAZEL: Fabulous.

EDITH: She's already done the tropical diseases: beriberi, hookworm, malaria, dysentery, pellagra, dengue fever....

HAZEL: I've met every one of <u>them</u>.

EDITH: Dengue fever. Sounds like a popular song. What's it like?

HAZEL: Give me a break. I just got off duty.

EDITH: Do they have any dengue fever at the hospital?

HAZEL: Yes, they have dengue fever. And all the rest of them.

EDITH: There are four kinds of malaria: benign tertian, quartan, ovale tertian, and malignant.

HAZEL: <u>Edith</u>.

EDITH: When she finishes insects, she's going to do fungus.

HAZEL: Oh, good Lord.

MARY: Is that all you do over there?

EDITH: Yeah, it gets pretty dull.

MARY: Want to trade jobs?

EDITH: I can't work a radio.

MARY: That's okay, I can't type.

Mary and Edith laugh.

HAZEL: Five thousand WACs in the South Pacific, and I get stuck with Laurel and Hardy.

MARY: Come on, Hazel, you wouldn't part with us for the world.

HAZEL: Make me an offer.

EDITH: The symptoms of malaria are ....

HAZEL: KNOCK IT OFF!!

MARY: Gosh, Edith, maybe you should transfer to the Nursing Corps.

HAZEL: Keep her out of my hospital!

EDITH: Want to have some fun tonight? Let's blow up the U.S.O.

MARY: Can't. I have to work.

HAZEL: You just finished a shift.

MARY: We're short-handed.

HAZEL: You've been short-handed for seven months.

MARY: Yeah. You should have heard the pep talk we got from the new Sergeant this morning. "This is a war, ladies. Not afternoon tea. So let's cut the griping and get this job done." I'm twice his age, and been in this man's Army twice as long. I've suffered, kids, suffered for the War Effort, and here comes a little twerp fresh from the States.... You can still smell the dye on his olive drabs, and he outranks me.

EDITH: *(Sniffing her own shirt)* Nobody outranks me.

MARY: Maybe I'll radio MacArthur's headquarters and tell them Japan surrendered.

EDITH: Tell them Truman surrendered.

HAZEL: Tell them I surrendered.

EDITH: Let's stow away on a plane to Australia.

HAZEL: Australia's off limits to women.

MARY: Everything's off limits to women.

EDITH: Do you remember when we came through Australia?

MARY: Not very well.

EDITH: Neither do I. *(Sighs)* This war is taking too long.

MARY: The Army grinds exceeding slow. And exceeding small.

HAZEL: I thought that was God.

MARY: The Army is God. If you don't believe me, ask Sergeant What's-His-Name.

EDITH: I think I have jungle rot.

HAZEL: Edith ....

EDITH: Can you get jungle rot from boredom?

HAZEL: Probably.

MARY: I want to go home.

HAZEL: Through six thousand miles of sharks, submarines, and deranged *kamikazes* ?

EDITH: I can name every kind of fighter plane. Both sides.

HAZEL: Don't.

MARY: *(Looking out the tent door)* Darn it, hasn't the Medical Service ever heard of schedules?

HAZEL: Relax, she'll be here.

MARY: This war needs unions. Refuse to maim or kill except between nine and five.

HAZEL: Bolshevik.

MARY: Do you know they have rules about wars? They all sit down and decide on the rules. If they can agree on the rules, why can't they agree not to fight the darn war. Does that make any sense? I mean, who's crazy here? Us or them?

HAZEL: Watch it, kid. You can get thrown out for thinking.

EDITH: Know what gets me? Back home they have a War College. A War College. They go to school to learn how to kill.

HAZEL: Some do. Some come by it naturally.

EDITH: Well, at least they get uniforms. Ours look like something out of a rag bag.

HAZEL: Killing doesn't get you a uniform. You need that extra little appendage.

EDITH: Hazel! I haven't played wife in so long I've forgotten what they use it for. Ask your Major, will you?

HAZEL: Ask him yourself. *(Quickly)* I take that back.

EDITH: Come on, I wouldn't bird-dog a pal. Not at my age. Back home they give a girl nylons when they want to make a pass. Hold out for that gold band, buddy.

HAZEL: What would I do with nylons out here?

EDITH: I don't know, but I sure know what I'd do with a bra. *(Looks down at her breasts)* By the time I get home, I'll have to tote these around in a bushel basket.

HAZEL: Oh, stop griping.

EDITH: They hurt.

HAZEL: I'm sorry.

MARY: Darn, I wish I could put a cap on my nerves.

HAZEL: Read a magazine.

MARY: I've read the magazine.

HAZEL: There's the Signal Corps for you. Make a girl a specialist, and she wants new magazines every month.

MARY: I bought that Modern Screen in San Francisco. It's probably a collectors' item now.

HAZEL: Well, light somewhere, will you?

MARY: You may outrank me, Hazel, but that doesn't mean you can order me around.

HAZEL: *(With a laugh)* I think it does.

EDITH: Want me to name all the movie stars in the U.S.O.?

HAZEL: Oh, dear God, transfer me to Okinawa.

EDITH: They're invading Okinawa.

HAZEL: I know they're invading Okinawa. They've been invading Okinawa for six weeks.

MARY: They won't let you near the front. Remember, all WACs are whores and sluts.

HAZEL: Not the Nursing Corps.

MARY: The Angels of Mercy.

EDITH: Yeah? How come they live in the mud with us?

HAZEL: To set a higher moral tone.

MARY: Now I know why Kit's giving me a hard time. It's her high moral tone.

EDITH: Is she still holding out on you?

MARY: I think she's saving herself for something better to come along.

HAZEL: Not a chance.

MARY: Sometimes I wonder.

HAZEL: She's afraid it'll get out. She doesn't want to walk into the latrine and have the other girls run out screaming.

EDITH: Hey, if it'll buy me a little privacy in the privy, start a rumor about me.

Kit enters.

KIT: Morning, soldiers.

HAZEL: How goes the war, Kit?

KIT: Great. Head wounds are up, tonsillectomies are down, and we're losing the battle against jungle rot. *(To Mary)* Hi, Sparks. Any news from the front?

MARY: We're invading Okinawa.

HAZEL: Do they need me at the hospital?

KIT: Not that I know of.

HAZEL: You're late. I thought they might have brought in a new shipment of parts.

KIT: I stopped off to feed the chickens.

HAZEL: Why don't you just turn them loose? They haven't laid in seven months.

EDITH: Who has?

KIT: Why, Edith, you're a married woman!

EDITH: For all the good that does me. Hazel, old buddy, if you ever land that surgeon of yours, stay out of wars.

HAZEL: I wouldn't be in this one if I hadn't gotten carried away. The recruitment posters promised romance and adventure. *(They all laugh)* There wasn't much to see in Wilkes-Barre but coal and slag.

EDITH: They promised us we'd win the war together, side by side, fighting to make the world safe for Democracy. Six weeks later he was in France and I was on my way here. He'd better be wearing that darned wedding ring.

KIT: I thought I saw you down on the beach last night. With a Marine.

EDITH: Must have been some other girl. All clerk-typists look alike. Especially without brassieres.

HAZEL: Can't you think of anything but your foundation garments?

EDITH: I suppose you like khaki drawers.

HAZEL: Love 'em. They make me feel so G.D. Army.

KIT: I'm in the Army? I thought I joined the Girl Scouts. And all this time I've been slaving on my Homemaker's badge.

MARY: From the looks of this tent, you'll never make it.

KIT: That's all Hazel's stuff.

HAZEL: It is not. I keep my half by the book.

KIT: When Hazel dies, they're going to bury her with Emily Post in one hand, and an Army Training Manual in the other. *(Pulls a lemon from her pocket)* Anyone want a lemon?

HAZEL: I had a lemon back in Pennsy. It was a Ford.

EDITH: Lemons are good for scurvy.

HAZEL: Edith, if you don't shut up about disease ....

MARY: Where'd you get it?

KIT: I happened to be strolling by the Officers' Mess ....

MARY: You've lost your morals. War's turned you into a crook.

KIT: We live in desperate times.

MARY: *(Sighs)* I know.

EDITH: Mary wants to go home.

KIT: Home? They're suffering back there. Gas rationing, sugar rationing, coffee rationing, meatless Tuesdays ....

HAZEL: That's the charm of this place. We don't have anything to give up.

KIT: Army life. Luxury and self-indulgence from sun-up to sundown, and all points in between.

HAZEL: How can any human being work all night and be so cheerful?

KIT: I'm not human.

MARY: I've been trying to make time with a robot.

KIT: Mary.

EDITH: I'm hungry.

HAZEL: Don't worry, it's a sign of life. *(To Kit)* The U.S.O.'s in town.

KIT: *(Rubbing her hands gleefully)* Hot spit!

MARY: What do you care? You never go to the shows.

HAZEL: Not since Vera Lynn refused to dance with you.

KIT: I love the U.S.O.

EDITH: You rob them blind.

KIT: They have, we need. That's the Democracy we're making the world safe for.

HAZEL: That isn't Democracy, it's Communism.

EDITH: I'm hungry.

HAZEL: I thought you swore off Army food.

EDITH: I can't live on your cookies from home. The last batch was oatmeal raisin.

HAZEL: You told me you liked oatmeal raisin.

EDITH: The raisins were moving. *(Innocently)* Gee, didn't you notice?

HAZEL: One of these days, Edith Ruskin, I'm going to strangle you in your sleep.

EDITH: Coming? Gosh, I hope it's Spam and canned peaches. I haven't had Spam and canned peaches since yesterday. Hey, Mary, what's Morse code for Spam?

Hazel grabs Edith by the scruff of the neck and drags her out. Kit collapses on a cot.

MARY: Rough night?

KIT: Rough enough.

MARY: Why the big act?

KIT: Trying to keep up morale. Mine.

MARY: Want me to rub your back?

KIT: *(Jumping up)* No, thanks.

MARY: Kit.

KIT: *(Quickly)* Got your mail. *(Pulls out a post card)* Boise.

MARY: My mother-in-law?

KIT: Yep.

MARY: You read it. Tell me if there's anything new.

KIT: *(Scanning the card)* She wants you to come home and "resume your rightful place in the community."

MARY: Whatever that is. Bill joined the Army to get away from me, and I joined to get away from his mother. Running was all we had in common.

KIT: You're not a runner.

MARY: You do enough running for both of us.

KIT: *(Nervously changing the subject)* Why'd you marry him, anyway?

MARY: We were too young to know the difference between love and a quick grope in the back seat of a Studebaker.

KIT: Why didn't you have children?

MARY: Because, contrary to what your mother might have told you, you can't get pregnant from a toilet seat.

KIT: She didn't tell me. She wouldn't say the word.

MARY: Pregnant? Or toilet seat?

KIT: Neither. Mother was a proper lady. I come from a long line of proper ladies.

MARY: I can tell.

KIT: Didn't you ever ... you know ... with him?

MARY: Not after we sold the Studebaker. You're full of questions today.

KIT: I guess so.

MARY: I wonder what they'd say back in Boise if they knew I'd fallen head over heels for an Army nurse.

KIT: Probably wonder where you met a male nurse. What will you do after the war?

MARY: That depends on you, Kit. *(Pause, gently)* This gives you the creeps, doesn't it?

KIT: Sometimes, a little.

MARY: Well, maybe the next war will make the world safe for love. We have to take what we want, Kit. Nobody's giving us any handouts.

KIT: I know.

MARY: One of these nights I'm going to hide out behind the latrine, and when you come out of the shower...BANG! Right in front of God and the entire Women's Army Corps.

KIT: You wouldn't!

MARY: If you don't loosen up, I won't be responsible for my actions.

KIT: I'm sorry, Mary. It's just ... I've never ....

MARY: Good God, woman. Back home even the cows do it.

KIT: Not in Maryland.

MARY: Sure, they do. You're so well-bred you probably look the other way.

KIT: I do not. *(Sheepishly)* Yeah, I do. Anyway, what makes you so sure I want ....

MARY: You talk in your sleep. Hazel told me.

KIT: *(Embarrassed)* Mind stepping outside for a minute while I slit my wrists?

MARY: Oh, sit down. And take your hands out of your pockets.

KIT: What for?

MARY: I'm not going to compromise you. I'm going to rub your shoulders.

Apprehensively, Kit obeys. Mary rubs her shoulders for a moment. Kit stiffens.

What's wrong?

KIT: World War III just erupted in my stomach.

Kit reaches up and touches Mary's hand. Mary turns her around to face her. They start to kiss.

MARY: *(Pulling back)* Look out!

KIT: What did I do?

MARY: *(Brushes at Kit's back)* Bug!

KIT: What kind of bug?

MARY: *(Chasing the bug)* Tyrannosaurus Rex! Got it.

KIT: Mary.

MARY: What?

KIT: Do you always kiss with your eyes open?

Mary hits her playfully. Kit grabs Mary, they tussle a little, ending up on the cot. They are about to kiss when Marian's voice is heard offstage.

MARIAN: Kit. Yoo-hoo, Kit!

Marian enters. She is in her mid-fifties, dressed in a garish, flowered dress and sling-back pumps, plastic raincoat and rain bonnet. She carries a handbag and a large paper sack.

Kit!

Notices she is dripping on the floor, takes off her coat and bonnet, shakes them out, rummages in her handbag, finds a Kleenex, and tries to wipe the water from the floor. Shakes her head over the tracked mud (not her own) on the porch.

Darn.

Giving up trying to clean up, she takes a small table lamp from the paper bag, sets the kerosene lamp aside with a gesture of distaste, replaces it with the table lamp, and looks around for a light socket.

Kit enters.

KIT: Well, Marian. As usual your timing is flawless.

MARIAN: Oh, were you in the bathroom?

KIT: No.

MARIAN: I've made a terrible mess here. But it's always something, isn't it? We no sooner finish coping with slush, and the mud is upon us. Where's your sponge mop?

KIT: Why didn't you call first?

MARIAN: It's impossible to get you on the phone. You're always out fishing.

KIT: Not at night.

MARIAN: Well, I wouldn't want to wake you.

KIT: I never go to bed before midnight.

MARIAN: Oh, dear. Insomnia?

KIT: Antiquity.

MARIAN: Just like Mother, poor thing. Her light was on at all hours. It must run in the family.

KIT: It must. *(Marian wipes furiously at the floor with her Kleenex)* Leave it alone, Marian. It'll dry.

MARIAN: Then you'll never get it up.

KIT: I can plant tomatos.

MARIAN: You should have a cleaning lady.

KIT: I don't need a cleaning lady.

MARIAN: Nonsense, your windows look like an abandoned warehouse.

KIT: They're old, not dirty.

MARIAN: Then you should have them replaced.

KIT: I like them the way they are.

MARIAN: Of course you don't. I'll call around and find someone to do it first thing Monday morning.

KIT: Marian ....

MARIAN: You're worried about the money, aren't you? They can bill me. It won't cost you a thing. *(As Kit starts to protest)* Now don't be silly and proud. I know how hard it is to manage on a pension. I watch television.

KIT: And vote Republican.

MARIAN: I won't have my favorite Aunt ....

KIT: Your only Aunt.

MARIAN: ... living in shabby surroundings. Not as long as there's breath in my body. Where's your mop?

KIT: Leave my dirt alone.

MARIAN: Oh, Kit, don't be childish.

KIT: Cleanliness reminds me of death.

MARIAN: Dirt causes death. Disease and death.

KIT: Marian, what are you doing here?

MARIAN: I haven't seen you in ages.

KIT: It's been a week.

MARIAN: And since you're too stubborn to call ... Well, how am I supposed to know if you need anything?

KIT: You don't give me time to need anything. Marian, I really don't like these spot inspections.

MARIAN: You don't mean that, you're in a bad mood. Did you have an uncomfortable night?

KIT: I'm having an uncomfortable morning.

MARIAN: Poor thing, it must be the dampness. This house positively exhales dampness. I don't know how you stand it. *(Pause)* Would you like me to leave?

KIT: No, but I do wish you'd learn to mind your own business.

MARIAN: I'm awful, aren't I?

KIT: Not awful, but pretty bad.

MARIAN: I don't know what gets into me. Some mornings I wake up so frightened ... do you suppose it's menopause?

KIT: I think you have too much time on your hands.

MARIAN: I haven't been right since Mother died.

KIT: It'll pass. Give yourself a while. If I know my sister, you never had to think about how to spend your spare time while she was alive.

MARIAN: *(Sighs)* She needed so much care at the end.

KIT: She demanded so much attention from the beginning.

MARIAN: You never got along with her, did you?

KIT: We didn't have much in common.

MARIAN: She always said you'd never come back here.

KIT: Well, she was wrong, wasn't she?

MARIAN: She said you wouldn't dare.

KIT: Why?

MARIAN: Because of ... how you spent your life.

KIT: Really?

MARIAN: She said a woman only worked for a living if she couldn't snag a husband.

KIT: *(Laughs)* Helen certainly saw things from her own point-of-view. It never occurred to her that I might simply like the way I lived.

MARIAN: Well, you must admit it's a little hard to understand.

KIT: I've never had trouble understanding it. Though, to be perfectly fair, I didn't make much of an effort to understand her, either.

MARIAN: You worried her.

KIT: Oh, I doubt that. But I will admit I annoyed her. It was one of the few things that made visiting worth while.

MARIAN: I always wanted a sister.

KIT: You could have had mine.

MARIAN: I did. Kit, why didn't they have other children? Was there some problem?

KIT: Helen couldn't stand the competition. When you were a baby and people made a fuss over you, she bristled like a hairbrush.

MARIAN: I have terrible dreams about her. I should have done more.

KIT: Helen didn't die of neglect, she died of old age. All the doing in the world wouldn't have changed that.

MARIAN: You're not going to die, are you, Kit? I couldn't bear it.

KIT: Not in the foreseeable future.

MARIAN: You know what they say. When people retire ....

KIT: I survived three wars. I think I can handle retirement.

MARIAN: I've always envied your moral fiber.

KIT: You make me sound like whole wheat bread.

MARIAN: You were the strong one. Mother always said so.

KIT: Don't try to put a nice face on it. "Pigheaded" was the expression she used.

MARIAN: Well, it's the same thing. *(Gets the lamp)* What do you think of this?

KIT: Charming, in a boudoir sort of way.

MARIAN: It's perfect for this table. *(Looks around for the outlet)*

KIT: Marian ....

MARIAN: There it is! *(Tries to plug in the lamp. The cord is too short.)* Honestly, I don't know what people use for brains nowadays. They charge an arm and a leg for a lamp, and put a cord on it that barely reaches the floor. Where do you keep your extensions?

KIT: I know you mean well, Marian, but ....

MARIAN: *(Looking at her lamp)* I wonder if this was intended for a motel.

KIT: You keep the lamp.

MARIAN: Have they shut off your electricity? The public utilities have no compassion for the elderly. I'll have Chet give them a call. A man can get things done.

KIT: The electricity is in perfect health. I prefer the kerosene lamp.

MARIAN: And before you know it you'll go stumbling around in the dark and smash your other hip. When old people smash a hip, it's all downhill from there.

KIT: Good God.

MARIAN: The last time I was here, the minute I got home I said to Chet, "Kit has those smelly kerosene lamps all over the house. She's going to poison herself." If you don't believe me, ask him.

KIT: I believe you. And what did he say to that?

MARIAN: Oh, he mumbled something or other, you know him. *(Holds up the lamp)* Well, if you won't have it on the porch, where should I put it?

KIT: Don't tempt me.

MARIAN: What? *(Gets the joke, laughs)* You dirty old lady.

KIT: Can I get you something? Coffee?

MARIAN: Let's visit for a while first. *(Fans herself)* It's delightfully cool here. I don't know when we've had such a hot spring. If this is any indication, the summer will be an abortion. I envy you.

KIT: It's the breeze off the stream, and the trees.

MARIAN: I'm not too crazy about trees, myself. They're always dropping things. Leaves, twigs ....

KIT: Bird plop.

MARIAN: That, too. Do you know what you should do?

KIT: Tell me.

MARIAN: Have the Fourth of July picnic here, the way you used to.

KIT: Oh, Marian.

MARIAN: Why not?

KIT: For one thing, there isn't much family left.

MARIAN: *(Sighs)* I suppose not.

KIT: We have a tendency to die off. It's probably hereditary.

MARIAN: I have such fond memories of those picnics. It broke my heart when you closed the place. The Fourth of July isn't the same any more.

KIT: I hope not. You spent the entire day under the kitchen table.

MARIAN: I never.

KIT: You did. You were afraid of the Baptist Aunties from upstate New York.

MARIAN: *(With a laugh)* Weren't they terrible?

KIT: They went after sin faster than a coon hound on a fresh scent. I'll bet they knew more about sin than God Himself. They'd sit out there under that Norway maple, eating peppermint drops and watching for the rest of us to transgress, while the men sneaked behind the outhouse for a drink.

MARIAN: My father never sneaked.

KIT: John was the worst of the lot. He'd parade around here giving orders like Captain Bligh on the bridge of the Bounty, and the minute the old ladies' Model A pulled up, it was all "Yes, Ma'am" and "No, Ma'am."

MARIAN: He was only being polite.

KIT: The whole family was afraid of Baptists, even the in-laws. I don't know why we kept inviting them.

MARIAN: Of course you had to invite them.

KIT: They'd have come, anyway. At least the War did one thing for me. It cured me of my fear of Baptists. And everyone else. I went out to New Guinea timid, and came back mad. Love and death do that, I suppose.

MARIAN: Really, Kit, I wish you wouldn't talk like that.

KIT: What offends you? Love? Or death?

MARIAN: War.

KIT: It offends me, too.

MARIAN: Then put it out of your mind. It's over and done with.

KIT: What were Korea and Vietnam? Echoes?

MARIAN: You're obsessive on the subject. You plunk that rotten old tent right in the middle of your lovely yard—God only knows why. Army blankets on your beds, old pictures ripped out of Life magazine on the walls, every available space littered with dime store rubbish. Your house looks like a garage sale.

KIT: You know, Marian, you can be very rude.

MARIAN: How can I be rude to you? You're family.

KIT: There's a subtlety here that eludes me.

MARIAN: Families can speak their minds. Niceness is for strangers, and guests.

KIT: I see. Excuse me.

MARIAN: Well, it isn't your fault. You've been away so long you probably don't know any better.

KIT: I probably don't. Thank you for clearing that up.

MARIAN: You're welcome. *(It occurs to her something's not right)* Kit, are you laughing at me?

KIT: I suppose I am. I apologize.

MARIAN: You think I'm stupid.

KIT: No.

MARIAN: Everyone else does.

KIT: Marian, it would take an Einstein to follow your twists and turns.

MARIAN: Why, thank you.

KIT: You're welcome.

MARIAN: Now, as long as I'm here, why don't I help you clear this place out?

KIT: Marian!

MARIAN: We'll get some nice chintz curtains for the windows. And chenille bedspreads. They're quaint and old-fashioned.

KIT: Quaint and old-fashioned?

MARIAN: I'm not calling <u>you</u> old-fashioned. But you like old-fashioned things, and they might as well be in good taste.

KIT: Chenille bedspreads are in good taste? They have them in rundown motels in small towns in Ohio.

MARIAN: When were you ever in Ohio. *(With an edge)* Excuse me, I forgot. You've been everywhere with your beloved Army.

KIT: There's nothing beloved about the Army.

MARIAN: You could have fooled me.

KIT: Marian, I ... oh, never mind. You wouldn't understand.

MARIAN: I suppose not, given my limited intelligence.

KIT: *(Frustrated)* I'm not criticizing you! Honest to God, if someone breaks wind, you think they're criticizing you!

MARIAN: Well, I'm delighted to hear I'm not being criticized.

KIT: The Army wasn't a nice place. As corporations go, its products left something to be desired. *(Marian looks bewildered)*

War isn't culturally enriching. I've always felt guilty for being part of that.

MARIAN: No one forced you to stay.

KIT: I did try to leave, several times. But there were things we had been through, those of us who had served in the wars, that people on the outside could never understand.Things they didn't want to hear about. We shared a language, an experience. I was lonely without it.

MARIAN: Well, you're out now.

KIT: With some regrets.

MARIAN: If you're going to retire, retire. There's nothing worse than someone who hangs on.

KIT: I can't erase my whole life, Marian. I don't have the time, or the strength, to start a new one. So I surround myself with memories. And, as the shadows creep toward me, those memories take on a special glow.

MARIAN: I think that's morbid and peculiar.

KIT: It's a harmless pastime. People expect the elderly to be morbid and peculiar. It's probably the first normal thing I've ever done.

MARIAN: It must be terrible to be old.

KIT: Not so terrible. It didn't happen overnight.

MARIAN: Mother hated being old.

KIT: Well, you see, it cramped her style.

MARIAN: I worry about you.

KIT: There's no need.

MARIAN: This ramshackle place ....

KIT: I'll be gone long before the roof caves in.

MARIAN: But it's stood empty for years. A house that stands empty for years is never the same.

KIT: Twenty-four hours of your presence, Marian, makes up for centuries of disuse.

MARIAN: Are you insulting me?

KIT: How can I insult you? You're family.

MARIAN: The only family you have.

KIT: That's a fact.

MARIAN: *(Firmly)* Kit, I think you should move into town.

KIT: Me?

MARIAN: We have plenty of space. We'll fix up Mother's old room for you.

KIT: I never knew you had a sense of humor.

MARIAN: You don't have anyone here.

KIT: I have neighbors.

MARIAN: Hillbillies.

KIT: Marian, have you heard a single word I've said?

MARIAN: You have memories. Memories are portable. Bring them along.

KIT: *(Tired of arguing)* Go make coffee.

Marian exits to kitchen, carrying on the ensuing conversation as she bangs cupboard doors offstage.

MARIAN: If you came to live with us, you wouldn't have to be afraid.

KIT: I'm not afraid now.

MARIAN: You should be.

KIT: Thank you, dear niece, for that comforting thought.

MARIAN: I can't find the coffee.

KIT: Over the stove.

MARIAN: I've got it. This can't be it. *(Enters with a nearly empty jar of instant coffee.)* Is this it?

KIT: That's it.

MARIAN: It's nearly empty.

KIT: It'll do for now.

MARIAN: I'll borrow some from the neighbors.

KIT: They don't drink coffee. It's a caffeine-free, salt-free, sugar-free, chemical-free vegetarian hillbilly household.

MARIAN: How in the world do they live?

KIT: Moonshine and acorns.

MARIAN: I suppose I'll have to drive down to the store, then.

KIT: You take the coffee. I'll be fine with tea.

MARIAN: We still need coffee for the morning. *(Kit looks at her)* Oh. Well, I thought I'd stay the night, if you don't mind. Chet's out of town.

KIT: Afraid to be alone?

MARIAN: It's such a big house. With the children gone, and now Mother ... It ... makes funny noises. No, not really noises. Silences. The silences that come at the end of noises. Isn't that silly?

KIT: You're welcome to stay.

MARIAN: Well, I'd better get going. We could have torrential rains later. *(Hurries into her raincoat and bonnet, talking nonstop)* I might as well pick up a few things for dinner. I barged right in, it's not as though you have to feed me, too. Suppose I make us some nice popovers for breakfast. And for tonight ... a cute little roast with browned new potatoes and tiny peas. You must have peas in your garden. Or is it too late for peas?

KIT: I have peas. Not tiny peas, monstrous, mind-boggling peas. And the store doesn't have cute little roasts. Or darling little steaks. They have an ingenuous little pork chop from time to time, but rarely.

MARIAN: What kind of a grocery store is that?

KIT: The kind that's never open when you need it, and never has what you want. A convenience store.

MARIAN: What in the world do you eat?

KIT: Adorable little tuna fish, mostly. I had a precious little omelet last week.

MARIAN: Well, there's precious little in your refrigerator now. You're making fun of me again.

KIT: I'm sorry, Marian. But sometimes I can't resist.

MARIAN: Oh, go ahead. Chet and the boys do it all the time.

KIT: Then I'm doubly sorry. Do you ever stop to realize you married a man exactly like your father?

MARIAN: I did, didn't I? Think what a heyday a psychoanalyst would have with that?

KIT: John treated his hunting dogs better than he treated you.

MARIAN: Well, Chet doesn't keep dogs, thank God. But he does hunt pheasant. I swear, Kit, every time he comes striding in the kitchen door, reeking of bourbon, and tosses those dear, beautiful, dead birds in the sink, I could ... break down and cry. *(Turns to leave)*

KIT: Marian? *(Marian turns back)* This is a very nice lamp. Thank you for your kindness.

MARIAN: Do you really like it? It was Mother's, you know.

KIT: No, I didn't know.

MARIAN: She kept it on that little table beside her bed. The last thing I'd do every night was give her a kiss and turn it out. Every night.

KIT: Then I'll put it beside my bed, and think of you.

Marian exits.

BLACKOUT

SCENE 2: A few minutes later. Lights up in the tent.

Hazel and Edith are playing chess. Mary is reading an old magazine.

Kit enters carrying four Cokes.

KIT: Who's winning?

EDITH: Three guesses.

KIT: *(Looks at the board)* Take her coral with your lava.

HAZEL: *(As Edith moves)* That isn't fair, Kit. *(Moves)*

KIT: *(To Edith)* Now block her shale with your ... *(Picks up a piece)* What is this thing?

EDITH: Petrified brownie.

KIT: Looks more like fruitcake.

HAZEL: Kit ....

EDITH: Really? *(Studies it)* I've been playing it as a brownie.

KIT: What's that green stuff?

HAZEL: Will you put it down?

EDITH: *(Still studying the piece)* I don't know. Mold?

KIT: Hazel got those brownies in January. They should be past mold.

EDITH: Yeah, you're right.

HAZEL: For crying out loud.

EDITH: It is fruitcake. *(To Hazel)*Cheater!

HAZEL: We've been playing it as brownie, so it's brownie.

EDITH: Let me see your sand dollar. *(Grabs it)* Congo square!

HAZEL: Congo squares are square.

EDITH: You filed off the corners.

HAZEL: With what???

EDITH: Yeah, with what? Hazel, do you have a nail file?

HAZEL: Of course I don't have a nail file. There isn't a nail file in Hollandia.

MARY: Will you two knock it off?

KIT: Anyone want to run up to Iwo Jima and watch the moon rise over Mount Suribachi?

MARY: I'm trying to read.

KIT: Photoplay? They going to quiz you on it?

MARY: By the time I get home I won't remember how to read. I'll have to communicate in Morse code. Dit-dit-dit, dit-dit-dit-dit, dit-dit, dah.

HAZEL: What was that?

KIT: I don't know, but I think it was obscene.

EDITH: I had an IQ of 120 when I left the States. It's probably about 72 now.

HAZEL: I thought that was your bust size.

EDITH: How would I know? I haven't seen the inside of a bra in eight months.

MARY: Seven months.

EDITH: That was last month.

MARY: It was?

EDITH: We've been here eight months.

MARY: I'm losing track of time.

HAZEL: Doesn't surprise me. How can we tell one day from another?

EDITH: I hate this place.

KIT: Have a Coke.

HAZEL: Who'd you rob this time?

KIT: U.S.O.

HAZEL: Again?

KIT: If they're going to leave this stuff hanging around... *(Passes out the Cokes)* A sailor told me if you put aspirin in Coke it'll make you high.

HAZEL: Sailors are crazy.

MARY: What do we have to lose? Where's your aspirin?

KIT:I don't know. Around somewhere.

Mary paws through Kit's things looking for the aspirin.

HAZEL: *(To Kit)* What are you going to do when they ship out?

Go into withdrawal?

KIT: Back to Spam and canned peaches, I guess.

MARY: *(Tossing things out of Kit's footlocker)* I thought nurses were supposed to be compulsive.

KIT: Go easy on that stuff. It has to last me the duration. *(Opening her Coke)* Anybody going to the show?

MARY: Not me. I'm not in the mood for Bob "Ain't Dying Fun?" Hope.

HAZEL: I'm on duty.

EDITH: Tough break.

KIT: Not really. So is Clark Guidry.

HAZEL: Coincidence.

KIT: Yeah, <u>he</u> made up the duty roster.

EDITH: I think I'll pass it up. All I do at those shows is covet. I covet their make-up. I covet their clothes. I even covet their nail polish.

HAZEL: I have nail polish.

EDITH: Where?

HAZEL: A tiny speck, right there.

KIT: *(Peering at Hazel's nail)* That isn't nail polish, it's blood.

HAZEL: Oh, must be from that leg amputation.

MARY: *(Flinging something to the floor)* Will you cut it out? If I have to hear one more word about gore, I'll lose my mind.

KIT: Something bothering you. Mary?

MARY: There's a war on.

HAZEL: Didn't your mother ever tell you not to listen to rumors?

MARY: I didn't have a mother. We couldn't afford it.

HAZEL: I think we have a small morale problem here.

MARY: *(Flaring up)* Morale problem! We sit here on this garbage scow of an island with nothing to do but count the dead and observe the life cycle of mildew, and you say we have "a small morale problem!" *(A shocked silence)* I'm sorry. It's the noise and static in my head, day after day. And now the guns all night ....

KIT: What guns?

MARY: Artillery practice, I guess. *(Finds the aspirin)* Do you always keep aspirin in your socks?

KIT: Those are Hazel's socks. Mary, I haven't heard any ....

HAZEL: What are <u>my</u> socks doing in <u>your</u> footlocker?

KIT: I thought they were mine.

HAZEL: My socks don't fit you.

KIT: They don't fit you, either. Mary ....

HAZEL: They don't fit me better than they don't fit you.

MARY: *(Drops aspirin into her Coke)* Here goes nothing. *(Drinks)* Nothing.

HAZEL: I told you sailors were crazy.

KIT: Mary, what guns?

MARY: I don't know what guns. Guns.

HAZEL: They wouldn't invade Hollandia again, would they?

EDITH: What for? There's nothing left on New Guinea that's worth anything.

HAZEL: Now we know where <u>we</u> stand.

MARY: I'd have heard about it. I haven't missed a single golden moment of this war. Where's Tinian?

EDITH: Tinian? Sounds like something you get between your toes.

KIT: North. What about it?

MARY: It's all very hush-hush, but it sure has the Air Force aroused.

KIT: It's too far away for us to hear it.

HAZEL: Maybe you heard Edith blowing up the U.S.O.

EDITH: *(Fighting with the bottle opener)* I'd <u>like</u> to blow up the U.S.O. It's a walking drug store, and we can't even get soap.

KIT: I'll see what I can do while they're performing their little dimples off.

EDITH: It isn't fair.

KIT: It's for the press. You don't want the folks back home to think this is an ugly war.

EDITH: *(The bottle opener slips, breaking a nail. She throws it across the tent)* This <u>is</u> an ugly war.

HAZEL: For Heaven's sake, it'll grow back.

EDITH: I'm tired of being dirty. I'm afraid to look in the mirror.

HAZEL: Well, we don't have mirrors.

MARY: Don't, Hazel.

KIT: It's getting us all down, Edith.

EDITH: Aren't we ever going home?

KIT: Sure, kid. As soon as the world's safe for Democracy.

EDITH: I don't care about Democracy. I want to wash my hair. I want to look nice. I want to smell good. I'm nothing but a <u>lump</u>.

HAZEL: Oh, grow up.

MARY: Hazel, lay off.

KIT: Terrific! Let's pick on each other.

HAZEL: At least <u>you</u> know who you're going home to.

EDITH: Aw, Hazel, honey, I'm sorry. You've got it bad, huh?

HAZEL: Yeah, I've got it bad.

EDITH: If he doesn't want you, he's a horse's behind. Who wants to go through life hitched to a horse's behind?

KIT: Not me. I certainly don't want to do that.

HAZEL: It gets the spring plowing done.

EDITH: Trouble is, once you've got a man, how do you keep him?

When you're getting uglier by the week and he's lying in a hospital in Belgium surrounded by cute young nurses like Kit?

HAZEL: If they're all like Kit, I don't think they'll be looking his way.

MARY: Men! Who needs them?

EDITH: Middle-aged women with grandchildren, stretch marks, no money, and only a high school education, that's who needs them.

KIT: I'll bet he's not too pretty himself right now.

EDITH: Men don't have to be. Besides, I love the old stallion.

HAZEL: Judging from his letters, you don't have much to worry about. Torrid stuff.

EDITH: He wrote those letters to a photograph.

KIT: You have letters? *Dirty* letters?

HAZEL: I don't know how they got past the censors.

KIT: Can I see one? Just one?

EDITH: You sure have changed *your* tune.

HAZEL: Ah, young love. Ain't it wonderful?

EDITH: Unless my memory deceives me, it was awful. Does he, doesn't he? Will he, won't he? I guess there are advantages to middle age. All *I* have to worry about is ... does he, doesn't he?

HAZEL: Will he, won't he?

EDITH: *Can* he?

KIT: I thought you lost interest when you got older.

EDITH: Who told you that?

HAZEL: Why Edith, I believe you're horny.

EDITH: I *know* I'm horny. I'm so horny I'd be climbing the walls, if we had any walls.

HAZEL: Me, too. Do you think it's the climate?

EDITH: It sure isn't the Spam.

HAZEL: We'd better knock it off. We're embarrassing the children. *(Looks at the Coke)* This stuff really <u>does</u> make you high.

MARY: There! Did you hear it?

KIT: What?

MARY: Guns.

KIT: There aren't any guns, Mary.

MARY: I <u>heard</u> them.

HAZEL: You're tired.

MARY: We're all tired.

HAZEL: Well, be careful. Half the WACs on this island are walking around with malaria.

MARY: *(Irritable)* Why not? They work us sixteen hours a day in hundred-degree heat. Keep us on short rations of food I wouldn't give to a pig. Dress us in clothes the men can't wear. The mosquitoes breed on our tooth brushes, and my shoes haven't been dry since I left Idaho.

EDITH: She doesn't sleep, either. *(Mary glares at her)* Well, you don't.

HAZEL: Are you taking your atabrine?

MARY: I've swallowed so much atabrine I could hide in the jungle and pass for moss. Leave me alone.

HAZEL: I'm ranking medical officer in this crowd. It's my job to make sure you take care of yourself.

MARY: *(Bitter)* Good girl, Hazel. Protect the Army's investment.

KIT: You know Hazel's not like that.

MARY: I'm sorry. I'm not myself.

HAZEL: It's okay, Sparks. Who is? Go take a nap. Now.

MARY: I'm on duty in ten minutes.

KIT: You just got <u>off</u> duty.

MARY: Double shifts.

KIT: They can't do that.

MARY: Tell it to the Marines.

Mary strides out of the tent. Kit follows.

KIT: Mary ....

MARY: Don't start in on me, Kit.

KIT: Hey. *(Embraces her)* Take it easy, will you?

MARY: I'm all nerves, Kit. What's happening to me?

KIT: Too much sun and rich food?

MARY: Please don't joke. I'm frightened.

KIT: So am I. You feel a little feverish.

MARY: I can't be. I'm cold. *(They look at each other)* It's lack of sleep, that's all.

KIT: Sure.

MARY: I'm adjusting to jungle living. Turning into a reptile.

KIT: Sure.

MARY: I have to go. See you tonight?

KIT: I'm on the night shift.

MARY: This is an inhuman war.

Mary exits. Kit returns to the tent.

EDITH: I don't like it.

HAZEL: Neither do I.

EDITH: Do you think she's sick?

HAZEL: Maybe.

KIT: She's sick.

HAZEL: Don't jump to conclusions.

KIT: Why not? It's the only approved form of exercise around here.

HAZEL: She's working too hard, that's for sure.

KIT: Those replacements better show up before the whole thing falls apart.

EDITH: There aren't any replacements.

KIT: What?

EDITH: The request went out months ago. It was denied.

KIT: You mean we're it? For the duration ?

EDITH: I'm afraid so.

KIT: Christ!

HAZEL: Easy, Kit.

KIT: What the hell are we doing in this mess?

HAZEL: You wanted to comfort the afflicted.

KIT: Next time I'll stay home and afflict the comfortable.

EDITH: Maybe there won't be a next time.

KIT: There'll be a next time.

EDITH: I don't think she looks so bad.

KIT: She looks terrible.

EDITH: No worse than your chickens.

KIT: The chickens are dying.

A stunned silence.

EDITH: Listen, some of the girls are being transferred to Manila. They say things are better there.

KIT: Manila's a hell hole.

EDITH: They sleep in real buildings. They work real hours. The sun even comes out once in a while.

KIT: Are they sending Signal Corps?

EDITH: It can be arranged.

HAZEL: How?

EDITH: I'll forge the papers. What do you say?

HAZEL: Forget it! You may think you're only one termite in the woodpile, but step out of line and you'll find yourself in a very bright spotlight.

EDITH: I don't care.

HAZEL: It's not just you. If they come sniffing around, and find out what Kit and Mary are up to ... We're Court Martial material, kid.

EDITH: Then we're stuck.

HAZEL: Like rats in a trap.

Kit starts out.

Where are you going?

KIT: For a walk. What is it we're making the world safe for?

EDITH: Life, liberty, and the pursuit of happiness.

KIT: Somebody lied.

Kit exits.

BLACKOUT

END OF ACT I

ACT TWO

SCENE 1: That night. Marian's lamp is lit on the porch table. There is a little moonlight, and the night sounds of insects.

Marian is setting up a game of scrabble.

In the tent, Hazel and Edith are playing their endless game of chess. Mary is asleep under a blanket.

Kit enters from the kitchen, a dish towel over her shoulder.

MARIAN: Finished?

KIT: Finished.

MARIAN: I wish you'd let me do it.

KIT: What's a little more KP in my life?

MARIAN: I don't want you to injure yourself.

KIT: Injure myself?

MARIAN: You might slip on the wet floor.

KIT: I only washed the dishes. I didn't climb in with them.

MARIAN: Well, you can't be too careful. *(Continues setting up the game board, blithering along neurotically)* I never know what to expect when I come here. I have a terrible apprehension that one day I'll find you curled up in a corner drooling.

KIT: One more crack like that and I'll toss you to the Gray Panthers.

MARIAN: Do you want to play, or not?

KIT: Yes, I want to play, unless you'd rather sit here and watch me deteriorate.

MARIAN: Don't be silly. You draw first.

HAZEL: Check.

EDITH: Rats. *(Moves a piece as Hazel reaches over and adjusts Mary's blanket)* Is she asleep?

HAZEL: I think so.

EDITH: How can she even look at a blanket in this heat?

MARY: *(Looks up)* Kit?

HAZEL: *(Gently)* Go back to sleep.

MARY: Where is she?

HAZEL: She'll be along.

MARY: Are you sure?

HAZEL: I'm sure.

MARY: Wake me when she comes?

HAZEL: Since when did Kit enter quietly?

MARIAN: *(Making a word)* How do you like <u>them</u> apples?

KIT: I'm impressed.

MARIAN: *(As she counts up her score)* Chet won't play Scrabble with me. He says it's no challenge.

KIT: Let's give him a lobotomy.

MARIAN: Let's. Mother was crazy about Chet.

KIT: Of course she was. He's male.

MARIAN: And a gentleman.

KIT: Except when he's killing birds, and making fun of his wife.

MARIAN: Well, nobody's perfect.

KIT: I hope Helen never heard you say that. She thought she was.

MARIAN: She was very beautiful.

KIT: I'll grant you that.

MARIAN: That was why she hated it so, I guess.

KIT: Being beautiful?

MARIAN: Growing old. She said it was a nightmare.

KIT: I think it's unfair to say things like that. It frightens the young and gives a false impression.

MARIAN: It isn't a nightmare?

KIT: Heavens, no. It is a surprise. We spend so much of our lives young, old is always what we aren't yet. Of course, there are a lot of things I can't do any more. But, by and large, I'm horrified I ever did them. The worst of it is the way people treat you. They speak very simply, as if you've lost the capacity for abstract thought.

MARIAN: Don't you worry about dying?

KIT: Not as much as you do.

MARIAN: What about afterward?

KIT: I think we go on living as long as we're remembered with affection.

MARIAN: Then my immortality will be brief.

KIT: Why, Marian, are you fishing?

MARIAN: Mother didn't believe in life after death.

KIT: Your mother hardly believed in life before death. It was something she had to put up with between cocktail parties.

MARIAN: The last few years, she seemed to be waiting to die.

KIT: Marian, aren't you well?

MARIAN: I have high blood pressure.

KIT: You always had high blood pressure. Probably had it *in utero.*

MARIAN: The doctor says I have to stop worrying.

KIT: Wonderful. Now if you run out of things to worry about, you can worry about worrying. It won't kill you, if you quit smoking and watch your diet.

MARIAN: It's impossible to watch your diet in a house full of men. Maybe I should take my meals with your neighbors.

KIT: I don't recommend it. They have small children. Small children and Granola are a vile combination.

MARIAN: You don't like children, do you?

KIT: Only for brief, meaningful, and mutually rewarding encounters.

MARIAN: That must be why you never married. Mother loved children.

KIT: She did not.

MARIAN: Did you like my boys?

KIT: Your boys were horrors.

MARIAN: They still are.

HAZEL: *(Looks over at Mary sleeping)* I never noticed how young she is.

EDITH: Twenty-five.

HAZEL: Too young for this. We're all too young for this.

EDITH: Hazel, do you think we'll ever feel safe again?

KIT: *(As Marian is pondering her next play)* Poor Hazel. All the way home, she planned her wedding. The first thing Clark Guidry did when we docked was introduce her to his wife.

MARIAN: She died, didn't she?

KIT: They all did.

MARIAN: So you're the last of the bunch.

KIT: Someone had to be, I guess.

MARIAN: You could have had a mass suicide.

KIT: Now, why didn't I think of that?

MARIAN: *(As she counts up her score)* I'm not too crazy about all that closeness. It feels sticky. Women aren't dependable.

KIT: Who told you that one?

MARIAN: Mother.

KIT: I don't know why I asked.

MARIAN: With men, you always know where you stand.

KIT: If that's where you want to stand.

MARIAN: Women are so messy.

KIT: Not Hazel. She was compulsive.

MARIAN: Emotionally messy.

KIT: Marian, if you don't like women, how can you like yourself?

MARIAN: I never said I did. "Family," she used to say. "The only people you can really count on are your family. Blood is thicker than water." *(Looks at the word Kit has made)* Kit! A triple word! And you used the X. Whatever made you think of noxious?

KIT: I can't imagine.

MARIAN: Well, that wipes out my lead. Now, don't talk to me. I have to be clever.

EDITH: Do you ever want to walk away from all this?

HAZEL: Right into a dishonorable discharge? No, thanks. It's going be be hard enough to find work.

EDITH: We might as well be in prison.

HAZEL: Food's probably better in prison.

EDITH: I could stand it if I knew when it'd be over.

HAZEL: You'll drive yourself nuts with that kind of thinking. Try to look at this as ... home.

EDITH: You're demented.

MARY: *(Half asleep)* No ... don't ....

HAZEL: Mary?

MARY: <u>Don't</u> ....

HAZEL: *(Goes to her)* Wake up, Mary. *(Pulls her to a sitting position)* Mary. Mary Cleveland. Look at me. *(Mary looks around in a daze)* Look at me, Mary. Come on, come on, focus. Focus, damn it!

MARY: *(In a panic)* Can't ... get ... back ....

HAZEL: Touch your arms. Feel. Stay with me. Feel your hands, your face. Now get up, move around. *(Mary does)* Better?

MARY: I thought I was dying.

HAZEL: It'll pass.

MARY: I couldn't get back. What'll happen if I can't get....

HAZEL: You can bring yourself back. Walk it off. *(Mary still looks distraught)* It'll be okay, Sparks. I promise.

Mary exits.

Edith, when Kit gets here, let Mary tell her.

EDITH: Sure.

HAZEL: *(Edith is looking after Mary)* Your move.

MARIAN: You're not paying attention.

KIT: Sorry.

MARIAN: How do you bear this silence? I know I won't sleep a wink. I'll lie there and listen to the roaches cantering across the kitchen floor.

KIT: There are no roaches in my kitchen.

MARIAN: How do you know? They don't come out in the daytime. This place should have been torn down ages ago.

KIT: Because you're afraid of silence?

MARIAN: It reeks of decay.

KIT: *(A little irritated)* You're having an olfactory hallucination. Probably a brain tumor.

MARIAN: Mother had hallucinations. They say crazy people get worse during the full moon. Of course, it isn't very scientific.

KIT: Well, science hasn't done much for me lately.

MARIAN: They put men on the moon.

KIT: And they hit golf balls. Your turn.

MARIAN: You're too quick for me.

KIT: Millions of years of evolution, for what? To hit golf balls on the moon. We should have stayed in the primordial muck.

MARIAN: I'm not going to worry about it.

EDITH: Mary didn't eat lunch.

HAZEL: Did you?

EDITH: Of course not. It was disgusting.

MARIAN: Let's see you beat that.

KIT: Very nice.

MARIAN: *(As she counts her score)* Kit, does life ever frighten you?

KIT: Constantly.

MARIAN: But are you ever ... deep down, in the marrow of your bones, frightened?

KIT: I have been. What do you say we call it a night?

MARIAN: I'll never get to sleep. I'm afraid I won't wake up.

KIT: *(Exasperated)* You're afraid to live, you're afraid to die. There isn't any middle ground, you know.

MARIAN: Some people are in comas for years.

KIT: Well, try that.

MARIAN: I can't imagine anything worse.

KIT: Marian, did anyone ever tell you you're a little neurotic?

MARIAN: It's my claim to fame.

KIT: Life is long, and fame is fleeting.

MARIAN: Now you're impatient with me.

KIT: My dear niece, you are exhausting.

MARIAN: *(Pouting)* We might as well go to bed, then.

Kit:*(As Marian starts to clean up)* Leave that. We can do it in the morning.

MARIAN: It won't take a minute.

KIT: Leave it. I have the roaches trained.

MARIAN: Do you want to use the bathroom first?

KIT: You go ahead. I'll take a walk.

MARIAN: You shouldn't stumble about in the dark with that bad hip.

KIT: I won't stumble.

MARIAN: You might.

KIT: I do it every night.

MARIAN: Well, all right, then. I'll lock up.

KIT: I never lock up.

MARIAN: You should.

KIT: *(Wearily)* Then lock up.

MARIAN: Popovers for breakfast?

KIT: That would be fine.

MARIAN: I forgot to get eggs. I'll go to the store first thing.

KIT: Don't bother.

MARIAN: It's no bother. Don't prowl all night.

KIT: Marian, if I wanted a dog, I'd get a dog. Good night.

MARIAN: There's a little something for you in that bag. Don't forget a flashlight.

Marian gives Kit a quick kiss on the cheek, which Kit tolerates.

Marian exits.

Kit peers into the bag, draws out a dress, very dull and old ladyish. Holds it up against herself, looks down, and laughs.

KIT: God love you, Helen, no wonder you died.

She returns the dress to the bag and goes to the tent.

Pack up your troubles, kids. The invasion of Japan has begun.

HAZEL: Glory be! We're invading a place I've heard of.

KIT: It's finally winding down.

EDITH: The country won't be the same without the war.

HAZEL: Don't break out the champagne. It took them twelve weeks to take Okinawa.

KIT: Where's Mary?

EDITH: Out for a stroll.

KIT: Anything new with her?

HAZEL: Not that we've heard.

KIT: *(Pulls a bra from her pocket)* Can anyone give this a good home?

EDITH: A brassiere? A real brassiere?

KIT: Looks about your size. Not that I've been peeking.

HAZEL: All right, who was it this time?

KIT: WAC Officers' laundry.

HAZEL: Those are our people.

EDITH: If a guy gives you nylons, he gets to make a pass. What's a brassiere worth?

KIT: *(Embarrassed)* For crying out loud.

EDITH: Name it, I'm yours.

KIT: Just try it on, will you?

HAZEL: Let's see what you've been bragging about.

EDITH: Hold onto your hats!

Edith exits.

HAZEL: That was a very nice thing to do, Kit. You look bushed.

KIT: Yeah. I thought Mary'd be here.

HAZEL: She will be.

KIT: Hazel, is she all right?

HAZEL: Sure.

KIT: Something's wrong.

HAZEL: Relax.

KIT: Tell me!

HAZEL: It won't help for you to carry on.

Mary enters with her laundry bag. Seeing Kit, she forces a light tone.

MARY: I was going to wash out a few unmentionables, but the line's a mile deep at the washtubs.

HAZEL: Hang it on a bush. The rain'll wash it.

MARY: Well, at least I don't have to wrestle with a soggy girdle. That's one advantage to wartime.

KIT: Hello, Mary.

MARY: Oh, hi, Kit. Rough day?

KIT: The usual.

MARY: I'm sorry to hear that.

KIT: How are you?

MARY: Not bad. How about you?

KIT: Fine.

HAZEL: I don't believe you've met. Kit, this is Corporal Mary Cleveland. Mary, Lieutenant Kit Fortescue. Kit's from Maryland—where the crabs come from.

KIT: All right, Hazel.

HAZEL: Kit says they're hitting Japan.

MARY: I know. I heard it on the squawk box.

KIT: How does it look?

MARY: With luck, we'll be out of here by the time we're ninety.

KIT: Home for Christmas.

MARY: They didn't say which Christmas.

Edith enters, strikes a pose.

KIT: Hubba-hubba.

HAZEL: That's what I call standing at attention.

MARY: Step aside, Jane Russell.

EDITH: *(Hugs Kit)* Kit, I love you.

MARY: *(Teasing)* Now, just a darn minute....

HAZEL: Come on, kid, let's show you off to the other girls. They're going to be green with envy.

MARY: They're already green with atabrine.

Hazel and Edith leave. An uncomfortable silence. Mary doesn't know how to start. Kit suspects what's coming, doesn't want to hear it.

I was over at the hospital today.

KIT: Hope Clark Guidry didn't make a pass at you.

MARY: I didn't see Clark ....

KIT: *(Quickly, picking up a chess piece)* How can they tell who wins with these things?

MARY: I didn't see Clark Guidry.

KIT: It's a real Garden of Eden, isn't it? No matter how much creosote they use, it smells of blood. I smell of blood. For the rest of my life, I'll smell of blood.

MARY: Kit ....

KIT: You'd think they'd be through with war. You'd think they'd have had enough of fear and pain. I'd had enough after four days.

MARY: Kit ....

KIT: As soon as they put that uniform back on, a little light comes into their eyes, and the muscles at the corners of their mouths start to work. And you know they're hungry for it.

MARY: Kit, listen to me.

KIT: When it's over they'll go home and sit in bars and show their scars like medals.

MARY: You have to hear this!

KIT: Please don't ....

MARY: Yes! Saying it won't make it real, Kit. It's already real. I have malaria. *(Silence. Kit looks at the floor)* It's an ugly word, isn't it?

KIT: How ... bad?

MARY: Bad enough.

KIT: Will they send you home?

MARY: Not a prayer. I'm needed for the war effort.

Helpless, Kit takes her hand, still staring at the floor.

It explains a lot, but it doesn't explain the guns.

KIT: Doesn't it?

MARY: Yes, it does.

Marian enters the porch.

MARIAN: Kit, are you out there?

Kit doesn't hear her. Marian lights a cigarette, sits down.

MARY: Please say something, Kit.

KIT: *(Explodes)* I HATE THIS GODDAMN WAR !!

MARIAN: *(Hearing)* Oh, dear God in Heaven.

BLACKOUT

SCENE 2: The next morning, early.

Marian creeps out into the yard, goes to the tent and removes blankets, chessboard, lantern,and Mary's laundry bag. She places them at the edge of the porch, and creeps back into the house.

Kit enters, takes a few wake-up breaths.

Marian enters.

KIT: You're up early.

MARIAN: I couldn't sleep. Rustlings and patterings overhead all night. When I finally drifted off for a few minutes, there was the most horrible screaming. I know someone was being murdered.

KIT: You checked, of course.

MARIAN: I took a peek out the window. You don't think I'd go out in the dark with some maniac running loose.

KIT: Your maniac was a pair of screech owls.

MARIAN: It was hideous. I don't know how you stand it.

KIT: They're usually the picture of decorum. I set them off when I walked too near the tree.

MARIAN: In the dead of night?

KIT: I'm not afraid of the dark.

MARIAN: God only knows who might be lurking out there.

KIT: Owls are very effective against lurkers.

MARIAN: I suppose. *(Briskly)* Well, what would you like to do today?

KIT: Whatever pleases you. *(Quickly)* I take that back. Who knows what you might come up with.

MARIAN: I could drive you to church.

KIT: I haven't been to church in so long, I wouldn't know how to behave.

MARIAN: You should have told me. You'd think the least those hillbillies could do is give an old lady a lift to church.

KIT: We all meet in the clearing and perform obscene rituals.

MARIAN: I wish you wouldn't talk like that.

KIT: God and I had a falling out some years ago. I'm not going down on my knees to a deity that sits around picking his nose while the rest of us claw each other to death.

MARIAN: Nobody kneels in church any more, only the Catholics.

KIT: That's a relief.

MARIAN: You don't go to town, you don't go to church, you don't go anywhere.

KIT: I moved twenty-seven times in my life. I think I'll stay home today.

MARIAN: I might as well make breakfast.

KIT: Aren't we out of eggs?

MARIAN: I've been to the store. They open at six.

KIT: *(As Marian exits)* Give me a shout when you're ready. I'm going to tackle the weeds.

MARIAN: *(Offstage)* Before breakfast?

KIT: It's a jungle out there. *(Starts to leave—notices the things piled on the porch)* Marian, what is this?

MARIAN: *(Entering)* What? Just some old junk. I cleaned out the tent for you.

KIT: You did <u>what</u>?

MARIAN: I'll drop it off at the dump on my way to town.

KIT: *(Explodes)* Damn it, Marian, keep your nose out of my business!

Kit tries to carry the things back to the tent, but can't handle them all in one trip. Frustrated, she tosses the laundry bag down and hobbles to the tent with the blankets.

MARIAN: I don't know what you want those disgusting old

things for. Those blankets are riddled with holes, God knows what's living in them. You could get a horrible disease. *(As Kit picks up the lantern)* What if that tipped over? You'd be burned to a crisp. *(Picks up the laundry bag)* And what in the name of all that's Holy is this?

KIT: *(Grabs it)* Take your hand off that.

MARIAN: It's packed with dirty clothes.

KIT: It belongs to Mary. *(Trying to keep her balance, she carries the laundry bag and chessboard back to the tent)*

MARIAN: Do you mean to tell me you've been carting that pile of rags around all these years?

KIT: I made it.

MARIAN: Oh, Kit, that's insane.

KIT: It's all I have. *(Starts trying to make the beds)*

MARIAN: I heard you out here last night, talking to shadows. Do you know what happens to people who talk to shadows? Pretty soon they don't know what's real and what isn't. And when that happens, they come and put you away. Do you hear me, Kit? They come and put you away.

KIT: *(Faces her)* Get out of my house, Marian.

MARIAN: Is that what you want, to be put away?

KIT: GET OUT!

Marian exits. Kit turns back to the tent, trying frantically to make up the cots. Frustrated at her clumsiness, she angrily kicks the laundry bag.

Damn it!

Shocked, she retrieves the bag, sits on a cot, and wraps her arms around it.

I'm sorry, Mary. I'm so sorry.

Puts her head down on the laundry bag and cries.

Hazel enters.

HAZEL: Who ransacked the tent?

KIT: I threw a fit.

HAZEL: I wish you'd thrown it on <u>your</u> side.

KIT: I can't take much more, Hazel.

HAZEL: I know. *(Teasing gently)* Developing a laundry fetish?

KIT: I see more of her laundry than I see of her.

HAZEL: It's going to get worse. They lost another girl today. Back to 24 hour shifts.

KIT: She can't handle that.

HAZEL: The Army says she can.

KIT: We have to <u>do</u> something.

HAZEL: Kit, you've done everything you can. Mary's done everything she can. I've tried, Clark's tried. We all get the same answer ... as long as she can work, they won't make an exception. The only thing we can do is pray.

KIT: To what? For what?

HAZEL: *(Trying to reassure her)* Malaria isn't always fatal.

KIT: Not unless you're stuck on a rain-soaked island in the South Pacific. Not unless you work 24 hours a day and never rest. Not unless you go to bed in wet clothes and get up in wet clothes. Not unless you hear guns that aren't there.

HAZEL: Don't, Kit.

KIT: There's no way to stop this war. It has its own life now. It feeds on beauty. It seeks out gentleness and crushes it, and picks its teeth with broken bones. And now it's coming for Mary. It's coming for Mary, and I love her.

Kit breaks down. Hazel holds her.

HAZEL: They move another bunch up every day. Her orders could come through tomorrow. When she gets to Manila, they'll take care of her. Look, buddy, I'm not much good at speeches, and I'm not the world's warmest gal. But I do love the two of you. So if you ever need me ... well, send up a flare, will you?

KIT: Hazel, why do I have to love so hard?

HAZEL: I guess it's your nature.

Mary enters.

MARY: The way this place is clearing out, Hollandia's going to be a ghost town.

HAZEL: Everybody's headed north.

MARY: Kinda gives you the creeps. *(To Kit)* You look like the Wrath of God.

HAZEL: Morale problem.

MARY: Cheer up. It can't last forever.

KIT: It already has.

HAZEL: I hear they upped your quinine.

MARY: Yeah. Malaria has its bright side. Quinine kills the taste of Spam. Wish it killed the texture.

HAZEL: I thought you were working a double shift today.

MARY: Lunch break. I get to spend a whole half hour with my girl.

HAZEL: I think I hear my mother calling.

Hazel exits.

KIT: Hazel's a good woman.

MARY: Am I doing this to you?

KIT: No, I'm on my morbid break.

MARY: I'm really sorry, Kit.

KIT: For God's sake, it isn't your fault. When this is over, I'm going to dedicate my life to removing every mosquito from the face of the earth.

MARY: Kit, have you thought much about what's going to happen when we get home?

KIT: Every chance I get.

MARY: It won't be easy. New Guinea's more than an island. It's outside of time, outside of the order of things. They won't welcome what we've become.

KIT: I don't care.

MARY: Listen to me. I've known other women like us.

KIT: We'll have a lifetime together.

MARY: A lifetime of fear.

KIT: Christmas together. Vacations together.

MARY: We'll have to hide the way we feel. We'll always be a little afraid of someone finding out.

KIT: We'll hold hands in the movies, and spend hours lost in the five and dime.

MARY: We won't know who to trust. Even with our closest friends, we'll have to be careful.

KIT: You'll put your arms around me while I'm cooking, and I'll pretend to be annoyed.

MARY: We can't touch in public.

KIT: We'll have arguments, and make up.

MARY: When we travel, we'll have to ask for a room with twin beds.

KIT: If you wake in the night, I'll be there.

MARY: You have to know what you're getting into.

KIT: Mary, I'm _in_ it. I'll do what has to be done.

MARY: There will be times when you hate it.

KIT: I _love_ you.

MARY: Maybe you'll even hate that. Maybe you'll hate me. Maybe you'll hate yourself. I couldn't bear that, Kit.

KIT: Are you telling me to get lost?

MARY: No. God, no. But if the time ever comes that you want to leave ... well, no hard feelings.

KIT: I'm no dewy-eyed bobby-soxer who believes life is what you see on the silver screen. I know life is what happens after the lights go on and the audience files out. My dear, ridiculous Mary.

Edith enters, depressed.

Morbidity's reaching epidemic proportions around here today.

EDITH: We're shipping out.

KIT: Home?

EDITH: Manila.

KIT: All of us?

EDITH: No.

KIT: *(Fearfully)* Who stays?

EDITH: *(Pause)* Mary.

They look at Mary. Mary turns away.

KIT: They can't toss you on their damn fire like a stick of wood.

MARY: That's where you're wrong, Kit. They can do anything they like.

Mary rushes off. Kit walks wearily to the porch, sits on steps, head in hands. Marian enters, approaches Kit tentatively.

MARIAN: Kit?

KIT: I told you to get out.

MARIAN: *(Holding out a pack of cupcakes)* I want to apologize.

KIT: What's that?

MARIAN: Peace offering.

KIT: You put a crack in our friendship the size of the Grand Canyon. You can't mend it with junk food.

MARIAN: Please take it.

KIT: Why do you have to look so pathetic? *(Takes it)*

MARIAN: Forgive me?

KIT: It'll take time.

MARIAN: I did what I thought was best for you.

KIT: What you think is best for me is seldom what I want.

MARIAN: People don't always know what's best for them.

KIT: I'm not going to argue with you. You can mind your manners, or you can leave. The decision is yours. If you want to be on good terms with me, don't come here and rearrange my life. I know you mean well ... you do mean well, don't you?

MARIAN: Of course I do.

KIT: Then understand one thing. My memories are very dear to me. They're all I have left.

MARIAN: You have your family.

KIT: "Family" has never been the center of my world.

MARIAN: It could be a great comfort to you.

KIT: Marian, for fifty years I've been surrounded by violence and death. I've loved, and been loved, and had that love taken from me. I've served in three wars ....

MARIAN: No one forced you.

KIT: I wanted to help in the way I knew best. Ultimately, I believe it made very little difference, but it was what I wanted to do.

MARIAN: Put all that out of your mind.

KIT: That would be an act of unspeakable immorality. But I think I've earned the right to be left in peace.

MARIAN: To talk to shadows.

KIT: To talk to shadows, or weave baskets, or cut out paper dolls. Whatever gives me pleasure.

MARIAN: What I heard last night didn't sound like pleasure.

KIT: I don't expect you to understand that.

MARIAN: Of course not. I haven't been lucky enough to be in a war.

KIT: Marian, you are a very foolish woman.

MARIAN: *(Gesturing toward the tent)* That gives you pleasure, and you call me foolish.

KIT: My life ... my life has been one of light and shadow, so intricately entwined that, if I were to try to separate one from the other, the whole fabric would fall apart in my hands.

MARIAN: Those people are dead.

KIT: They're very alive to me.

MARIAN: You talk to dead people!

KIT: Sometimes it's easier than talking to the living.

MARIAN: I've always suspected you don't like me.

KIT: *(Wearily)* Oh, Marian, I've hardly known you.

MARIAN: You never took the time.

KIT: I've met many people over the years, people with whom I could have shared moments of great delight. There wasn't time to know them all.

MARIAN: There's time now.

KIT: But no more room in my heart.

MARIAN: That's cruel.

KIT: I'm sorry.

MARIAN: You only have room for dead people.

KIT: Are you jealous of my poor phantoms?

MARIAN: Your "poor phantoms" mean more to you than your living family. You've been back here three years, and all you've done in that time is deteriorate.

KIT: Well, that's what I came home for, to deteriorate.

MARIAN: Like an old dog dragging itself off into the woods to die.

KIT: What would you have me do?

MARIAN: Involve yourself with your family.

KIT: I did as much of that as the traffic would bear. Any more involvement with me would have shortened Helen's life.

MARIAN: What am I, invisible?

KIT: Marian, what do you want from me?

MARIAN: I want us to be a family.

KIT: Chet and the children are your family.

MARIAN: That isn't enough. I want us to be close, and loving. I want us to be a ... a safe harbor.

KIT: *(With a laugh)* How many families do you know like that?

MARIAN: We could have been, if you hadn't gone away.

KIT: I don't think so.

MARIAN: In the old days, when we drove up you'd be standing on the back porch. As soon as you saw me, you'd throw out your arms and shout, "There's my girl! There's my Marooch!"

KIT: Marian ....

MARIAN: We'd sit on the swing and you'd make up stories for me. You'd let me help you cook, and set the table. You always put my chair next to yours.

KIT: I did those things because you were the only child among all those adults. Because your father was too busy talking about his Irish setters to notice you, and your mother couldn't stop flirting with the second cousins from North Carolina long enough to wipe your nose. I felt sorry for you.

MARIAN: You loved me.

KIT: I suppose I loved you, in a way. Please, don't make me say these things.

MARIAN: I need you. I'm lonely. I lie in bed at night, as close to the edge as I can get, trying not to touch that stranger I married.

KIT: There's nothing left inside me, Marian. I have nothing left to give you.

MARIAN: Some days I'm afraid to leave the house. I sit in my living room for hours, watching the cars go by on the street, waiting, waiting for it all to fall apart.

KIT: Marian, don't.

MARIAN: It's been like this since Mother died. I had someone to care for, and now she's gone. I reach out for her, like a blind person groping for a wall, but there's ... no one there.

Moved, Kit reaches out to touch her. Mary appears at the

entrance to the tent. Hazel and Edith enter, carrying duffel bags.

HAZEL: Kit, it's time. The plane's leaving.

Kit looks toward them, hesitates, looks back at Marian.

KIT: Marian, I can't.

MARIAN: Do you want me to get down on my knees and beg? All right, I'm begging. Love me, Kit. Please love me.

MARY: Don't go.

EDITH: Come on.

MARIAN: Love me, Kit.

KIT: Marian, I'm not Helen. I can't take her place.

MARIAN: *(Angry)* You're exactly like her. The world revolves around you. The moon and stars rise in your personal Heaven.

HAZEL: Kit.

MARY: Don't leave me. I'm afraid.

MARIAN: When I was a child I'd come to her, asking her to read me a story, wanting to tell her my day. And she'd say, "Run along, darling. Play with your little friends." She never even noticed I didn't have any "little friends."

MARY: Kit.

MARIAN: When I was sick she shut me away and let the housekeeper take care of me. Because sickness depressed her. She never touched my babies. Babies are messy. On my wedding day she didn't help me dress.

EDITH: They're loading.

MARIAN: She was too busy entertaining her guests.

MARY: Five minutes. Give us five minutes to say goodbye.

EDITH: You have to come now, Kit.

MARIAN: She was the center of attention. She got all the applause. When she came to live with us she brought all her old party dresses. Trunks of party dresses for an old woman.

KIT: I don't want to leave you, Mary.

MARIAN: Every day she dragged them out and made me look at them. "I wore this little organdy to my first tea dance. Isn't it pretty, Marian? See how perfectly the China blue sash matches my eyes?"

HAZEL: Kit!

MARIAN: "I was the Belle of the Ball. Everyone said so. 'Why, Helen, you're the Belle of the Ball.'"

MARY: Let me hold you one more time. Just one more time, Kit.

MARIAN: One day, as I was putting away one of those dresses, my foot caught the hem and tore it. She sat on the edge of her bed and cried. My mother, who never shed a tear for me, sat on the edge of her bed and cried over a torn dress.

KIT: Mary, forgive me.

MARIAN: The doctor said it was her age, her mind was going. He gave her something to calm her nerves. Then I knew what to do.

KIT: *(To Mary)* I thought we had a lifetime.

MARIAN: Every so often I'd take out one of those dresses and rip it to shreds. Right in front of her. I told them she did it. She was a senile old woman. She tried to say it was me, and we gave her more drugs.

EDITH: Kit, we have to go.

KIT: Mary!

MARIAN: Every night, when I bent down to kiss her, I'd whisper in her ear, "Which one will it be tomorrow, Mama?"

KIT: We'll be together, Mary. I promise. All of us.

MARIAN: I destroyed them all. The organdy, the wine satin, the dusty rose lace.

MARY: I'm afraid.

MARIAN: While she sat there, her hands trembling, tears leaking from the corners of her China blue eyes.

HAZEL: Kit! Come with us now!

MARIAN: It took a very long time. A very long time.

KIT: All right, I'm coming.

Kit starts off. Marian grabs her.

MARIAN: I tore up her memories, Kit. I'm very good at tearing up memories.

MARY: You had left Manila by the time they took me there. The moon was full the night I died. If I turned my head, I could see Corregidor, dark and silent, reflected in a pool of moonlight. I was too tired to cry. The only thing I wanted, the only thing I ever wanted was you.

MARIAN: Are you listening to me? I'll rip your memories to pieces.

KIT: God damn you, Marian, GET OFF MY PROPERTY!

MARIAN: I'll be back.

KIT: Not without a court order.

MARIAN: It's on the way.

KIT: I'll fight you, Marian.

MARIAN: Ah, but who'll speak for you, Kit? All your friends are dead.

KIT: I'll fight your courts and your doctors. I'll fight your love and your need. And when I can't fight any more, I'll die. But I won't lose her again. Do you hear me, Marian? *(Goes to Mary, embraces her)* I won't lose her again.

BLACK OUT

THE END

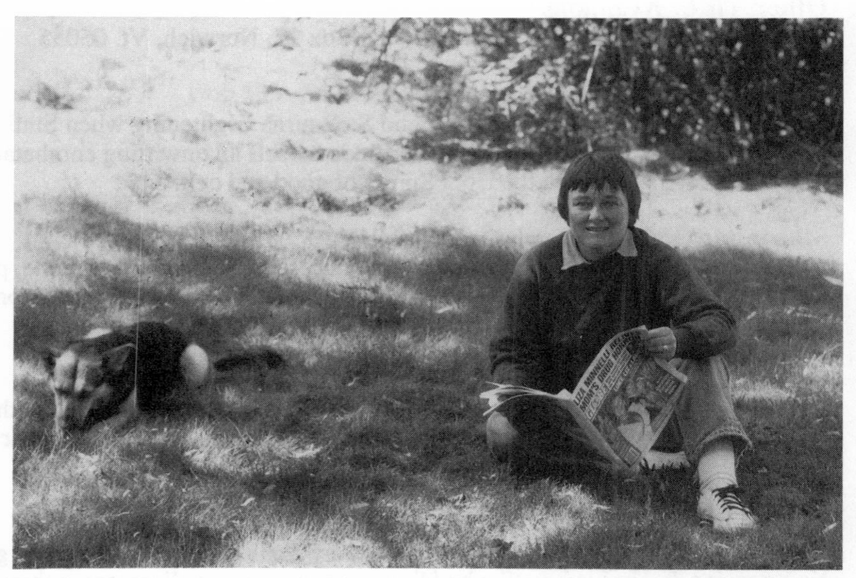

photo by Helena Negrette

In addition to writing the Stoner McTavish novels, Sarah Dreher is a practicing clinical psychologist and playwright. Her play—*8 x 10 Glossy* was recognized by the Alliance for Gay and Lesbian Artists in the Entertainment industry for "The responsible portrayal of lesbian characters and issues in the entertainment media."

She lives in Amherst Massachusettes with her life partner, two dogs, and associated wildlife.

Other Titles Available
Order from New Victoria

Gray Magic by Sarah D
A peaceful vacation with
ill with a mysterious disea
the great struggle between

Stoner McTavish by Sa
The original Stoner McTa
tical partner Marylou, and
rescue dream lover Gwen.

Something Shady by Sa
Travel Agent/Detective St
lover Gwen and risks beco
missing nurse.

All Out by Judith Alguire
Winning a gold medal at
Kay remains determined, u
her ability to go all out for

Look Under the Hawth
A stonedyke from the mou
her long lost daughter and,
anist looking for her birth

Runway at Eland Sprin
Anna, a pilot carrying sup
conflict when she agrees to scout and fly supplies for a big game hunter. Sh
turns to Jilu, the woman who runs a safari camp at Eland Springs, for love an
support.

Promise of the Rose Stone by Claudia McKay ($7.95)
Mountain warrior Isa goes to the Federation to confront its rulers for her peopl
She is banished to the women's compound in the living satellite, Olyeve, whe
she and her lover, Cleothe, plan an escape.

Morgan Calabresé; The Movie by N. Leigh Dunlap ($5.95)
Some of the funniest comic strips to come out of the Lesbian/Feminist pres
Politics, relationships, life's changes, and softball as seen through the eyes o
Morgan Calabresé.

Radical Feminists of Heterodoxy by Judith Schwarz ($8.95)
Revised edition of the history of Heterodoxy, the club for unorthodox wome
that flourished in Greenwich Village from 1914 until the 1940s. Many origin
photos and cartoons.